Alan Brinkley

Alan Brinkley

A Life in History

Edited by David Greenberg, Moshik Temkin,
and Mason B. Williams

Columbia University Press   New York

Columbia University Press
Publishers Since 1893
New York Chichester, West Sussex
cup.columbia.edu
Copyright © 2019 Columbia University Press

Library of Congress Cataloging-in-Publication Data
Names: Greenberg, David, 1968– editor of compilation. | Temkin, Moshik, 1971–editor
    of compilation. | Williams, Mason B., 1983– editor of compilation.
Title: Alan Brinkley : a life in history / edited by David Greenberg, Moshik Temkin,
    and Mason Williams.
Description: New York : Columbia University Press, [2018] | Includes bibliographical
    references and index.
Identifiers: LCCN 2018025043 (print) | LCCN 2018029554 (e-book) |
    ISBN 9780231547161 (e-book) | ISBN 9780231187244 (hardback : alk. paper)
Subjects: LCSH: Brinkley, Alan. | Historians—United States—Biography. |
    College teachers—United States—Biography. | Harvard University—Faculty—
    Biography. | Columbia University—Faculty—Biography.
Classification: LCC E175.5.B79 (e-book) | LCC E175.5.B79 A43 2018 (print) |
    DDC 973.07202 [B] —dc23
LC record available at https://lccn.loc.gov/2018025043

Columbia University Press books are printed on permanent
    and durable acid-free paper.
Printed in the United States of America

Cover design: Julia Kushnirsky
Cover image: David Levine © Matthew and Eve Levine

For Alan Brinkley

Contents

PART II. Reminiscences

Acknowledgments

All three of us had the privilege of studying with Alan Brinkley in Columbia University's history department. Among the lessons we learned from him is that although the writing of history may seem to be a solitary act, it is, in fact, highly collaborative. Accordingly, we wish to thank the many people whose work made this book possible. Evangeline Morphos, Alan Brinkley's wife, contributed to this undertaking from the outset. She gave generously of her time, offered thoughts and insights, put us in touch with many of Alan's friends and colleagues, helped to coordinate innumerable details, and lent her unstinting support. Elly Brinkley, Alan's daughter, not only contributed a splendid essay of her own but also consulted on the general shape of the book. Other contributors to the volume, especially Eric Foner, Scott Berg, and Frank Rich, also helped us think of ways to make the book both a tribute to Alan and a work of scholarship in its own right.

The book grew out of a conference at Columbia University in Alan Brinkley's honor held on April 15–16, 2016. For their invaluable help organizing that event, which took place at the beautiful Maison Française, we thank the staff of the Department of History, including Patrick McMorrow, Patricia Morel, Sharee Nash, Najila Naderi, and Natalie Hernandez. Columbia Provost John Coatsworth, Professor Kenneth Jackson of the

Lehman Center, and Professor Rashid Khalidi, then the history department chair, helped us to secure crucial funds and support. So did Mark Zuckerman of the Century Foundation, on whose board Alan Brinkley served for many years. Columbia University colleagues Betsy Blackmar, Matt Connelly, Eric Foner, Ira Katznelson, Alice Kessler-Harris, Mae Ngai, and Anders Stephanson took part in the conference or lent key assistance. So did valued colleagues and former Alan Brinkley students who made the trip to Morningside Heights to participate in a truly memorable weekend: we are grateful to Brian Balogh, Chris Capozzola, Ellen Fitzpatrick, Beverly Gage, Rob Genter, Gary Gerstle, Michael Kazin, Bob Lifset, John McMillian, Craig Steven Wilder, and Neil Young for their participation in the conference and to the many others who traveled from far and wide for the occasion. We also thank Columbia University President Lee Bollinger, who opened the conference with a tribute and welcome, and Conan O'Brien, Brinkley's Harvard undergraduate student in the 1980s, who graciously (and hilariously) appeared by video.

We could not imagine a more appropriate home for this book than Columbia University Press, where Bridget Flannery-McCoy was enthusiastic about the project from the outset, expertly editing the manuscript and guiding it through the publication process. Christian Winting assisted in the editorial process throughout. Two external reviewers provided helpful (and helpfully modest) critiques that strengthened the essays. Sherry Goldbecker copyedited the manuscript, and Ben Kolstad coordinated the production. Lisa Hamm designed the excellent cover. We thank the estate of the late illustrator David Levine for the use of his classic line drawing of Alan that originally appeared in the *New York Review of Books*. We extend our appreciation as well to the folks at C-SPAN for letting us use the transcript of Brian Lamb's interview with Alan on *Booknotes*.

Personally, we would like to thank our families for their love and support: Suzanne Nossel and Leo and Liza Greenberg; Muriel Rouyer and Noam and Oren Temkin; and Alexis Schaitkin and Emerson Williams.

Our biggest thanks go to Alan Brinkley. For the three of us, as for the other contributors to the volume, and indeed for scholars and students across the profession, he has been not only an exemplary scholar and teacher but also a kind and generous mentor and friend. This book is a tribute to him.

Foreword

A CAREER IN FULL

ERIC FONER

It is quite an honor to write this foreword to a volume celebrating the life and career of Alan Brinkley. I will not use this occasion to discuss in any detail his scholarship—its influence will be apparent in the pages of this book, both implicit in the work of his outstanding students and addressed directly in many of the chapters that follow. Let me simply say that Alan's writings have transformed our understanding of twentieth-century American politics. His books, notably *Voices of Protest, The End of Reform, Liberalism and Its Discontents*, and *The Publisher*, are models of historical scholarship—and, of course, they are written in a wonderfully accessible style.

And, to employ a much abused word, they are remarkably relevant. Over a century ago, in his presidential address to the American Historical Association, Charles Francis Adams noted that the level of our political discourse was not "so elevated" that it could not be improved by the addition of a historical perspective. This is even more true today than in 1901, when Adams spoke.

The central themes of Alan Brinkley's scholarship—the strengths, limits, and vulnerabilities of the twentieth-century American liberal tradition; the challenges to it, both internal and external; the connections between popular movements and partisan politics; and the enduring legacies of the New Deal—are, in a sense, still topics of debate in our current politics. Interestingly, though, perhaps his most influential article in a scholarly journal is not directly about liberalism at all. It is "The Problem of American Conservatism," published in 1994 in the *American Historical Review*; it launched a small cottage industry on the subject, to which a good number of Alan's students, some of whom are included in this book, have contributed.

Of course, no discussion of Alan's scholarly contribution would be complete without mentioning his American history textbooks, which in various versions have brought Alan's historical perspective to hundreds of thousands of high school and college students throughout the country. As all his colleagues and students well know, Alan is extremely congenial. He testified before the Texas School Book Commission and somehow managed to persuade them that his textbook would not destroy the loyalty of the state's students to the United States of America—despite his inclusion of Thomas Jefferson and the separation of church and state. Of course, I am his competitor in this corner of the publishing world, but it is typical of Alan that when I started out writing my own textbook, he offered sage advice on all aspects of the project. And now, when I speak with sales representatives of my publisher, W. W. Norton, and ask what textbooks institutions are using if they are not using mine, the answer is, invariably, "Brinkley." (I should add that one little-known aspect of this world is that teachers who assign textbooks are known to the publishers as "users"—so there are "Brinkley users" and "Foner users," which sounds vaguely illegal.) In any event, Alan and I long ago decided that the textbook market is big enough for both of us.

Aside from his remarkable achievements as a scholar, Alan's qualities as a teacher are legendary. Wherever he has taught, he has filled large lecture halls. I have not had the pleasure of hearing him lecture in a classroom. But as a colleague, I have seen how he mentors students individually and what the ensuing results have been. The very high quality of the dissertations he has supervised is a testament both to the brilliance of the students he has attracted to the Columbia history department and to the critical attention he lavishes on their work. Our offices were across from each other in Fayerweather Hall for twenty-five years, and I well remember seeing the long lines of students, undergraduate and graduate, waiting to see him, noting how much time he spent with each one and how inspired they seemed when they emerged. After they all departed, Alan and I would frequently sit in his office or my office and chat about history or politics or the Yankees and other weighty subjects. (This was the reason I regretted his decision, in 2003, to accept President Lee Bollinger's invitation to become provost of the university. It was typical of Alan that he put service to the university above his own teaching and writing career. But it meant, so long as he remained provost, the end of our long conversations on the sixth floor of Fayerweather Hall.)

Many of Alan's graduate students are now important historians in their own right. Their overall quality is a tribute to them—and to Alan's instruction and mentoring. They also reveal the wide range of historical issues whose study he inspired. But the students and their writings do not share a single point of view. They differ with each other and, not infrequently, with some of Alan's own work. My point is that Alan has not tried to create a school of followers or force his students into a single mold. What unites his work with theirs is not any predetermined conclusions but rather a set of questions, or preoccupations, that guide their concern with the history of political culture, political ideas, and the intersections of politics and society. It is appropriate that most of Alan's teaching career has been at Columbia, for these are the characteristic questions of what might be called the traditional Columbia approach to history and are most closely associated with the historian Alan most closely resembles in his approach, literary style, and public impact: Richard Hofstadter.

Like Hofstadter, Alan is a public intellectual par excellence. Alan has long been the go-to person for journalists seeking historical insight into our contemporary politics, and he has appeared many times on television and has been frequently quoted in the press. In his own writings in the *New York Times*, *New Republic*, *New York Review of Books*, and a host of other venues, he has brought up-to-date history to a large reading public. In this, he is fully in the tradition of Hofstadter as well as other Columbia luminaries of an earlier generation such as Allan Nevins, Henry Steele Commager, and, if one wishes to go back that far, Charles Beard.

But, of course, Alan lives in a different era, with different modes of communication than they had, and he is equally comfortable using the internet to comment on some of the less exalted expressions of American culture—for example, in his blogs, in conjunction with his wife, Evangeline Morphos, and his daughter, Elly Brinkley, about *Mad Men* and *Girls*. Lest one think that Alan's tastes in culture are purely lowbrow, however, I should add that he is also an opera lover. Indeed, my wife and I really came to know him and Evangeline through the serendipity of having the same subscriptions to the Metropolitan Opera. So for many years we have met up for dinner before performances or for a drink during the intermissions, where Alan has proved himself a very discerning critic of productions and performances. (Some of this insight into theatrical production, to be sure, he has probably obtained by osmosis from living with Evangeline, a theater, film, and television producer.)

I am not sure when I first met Alan. I do vividly recall my first extended contact with him, in 1990, when Columbia was wooing him from CUNY. (Alan had been there since 1987, after Harvard, in a notorious decision, denied him tenure.) This contact was not easy to arrange. That spring my wife, my daughter, and I were living in Moscow, where I was teaching as Fulbright Professor of American History. John A. Garraty, the chair of Columbia's history department at the time, somehow managed to reach me in Russia and asked me to phone Alan to lure him to our department—to tell him how wonderful teaching at Columbia is, etc. etc. This was easier said than done. International calls from Moscow had to be booked two or three days in advance, and one never knew if the call would actually go through. But the Soviet gods were on our side; I did reach him, and we had a long conversation not only about Columbia but also about his favorite subject: liberalism. This conversation was enlightening, but as the minutes ticked by, I became more and more nervous because international calls from Moscow were dauntingly expensive (and Professor Garraty, well known for his frugality, later informed me that there was no line in the departmental budget for reimbursing recruiting calls from Russia). But perhaps getting a call from the USSR showed Alan how excited we were at the prospect of his joining the department and helped persuade him to come here.

Since then, I have come to know Alan extremely well, and I want to mention just a few of his qualities. Alan is a very modest person. Self-importance is not a quality absent from the academic world, but as with Richard Hofstadter, there is no trace of it in Alan. His modesty is also reflected in his writing, which is stylish and clear but often understated. He does not make sweeping claims about all of American history or trumpet the originality of his arguments. Sometimes, in fact, this quality may lead readers to underestimate the analytical power of his work.

Over the years, I have also come to be impressed by Alan's good judgment and, for want of a better word, integrity. His even-handedness should not suggest that he does not care deeply about crucial questions within and outside the university. As history department chair from 2000 to 2003 and then provost from 2003 to 2009, he helped to lead first the department and then the university through some turbulent, difficult times. He somehow managed to combine impartiality with a firm commitment to what he believed was right. More than fifteen years ago, when the graduate teaching assistants first attempted to organize a union here, the dean of the graduate school asked each department chair to schedule a meeting with graduate students in order to dissuade them from signing up. Many chairs did so. But Alan, the history chair, promptly responded that he had total confidence in the ability of our graduate students to assess evidence and come to their own conclusions—that is what they are being trained to do—and that he would not arrange any such meeting. Subsequently, as provost, Alan added a powerful voice to the defense of academic freedom. Later, when certain Columbia faculty members came under political attack from outside groups dissatisfied with their teaching, Alan insisted that it would violate academic freedom to monitor faculty statements in the classroom at the behest of partisan critics. But as anyone who has had a conversation about politics with him knows, he is not only an astute observer of the political scene but also someone who cares deeply about current politics. When Alan has criticisms to offer of recent presidents—I won't mention any names—he can express his viewpoint with sometimes surprising passion.

Alan is an ideal family man, devoted to Evangeline and Elly. He is also a dog lover who spent an inordinate amount of time dealing with the needs of the original pampered pet, Jessie, who recently departed this mortal coil at an advanced age. Jessie's amazing longevity no doubt owed a great deal to the attention showered on her by Alan, Evangeline, and Elly.

In summary, Alan Brinkley is brilliant, insightful, generous, open-minded, loyal—all the things you want in a colleague, friend, teacher, and scholar. This book is a fitting tribute to him and his long, outstanding career. Let me add my personal thanks to the administrative staff of the Columbia Department of History and to David Greenberg, Moshik Temkin, and Mason B. Williams for doing their sterling work editing this book and organizing the conference in Alan's honor that preceded it.

And, now, on with the show.

PART I
A Historian's Work

1

A Personal History

ELLY BRINKLEY

Like many American families in the 1950s and 1960s, the three Brinkley brothers would gather around the television set each night at 6 p.m., waiting for a clipped voice to tell them what was happening in the world—whether it was the Cuban missile crisis, the civil rights movement, or some other weighty matter of the day. In postwar America, the price of material comfort was an underlying anxiety about the fate of the world. But the Brinkley brothers watched with an extra measure of attentiveness. Should the anchor misdeliver a line or make a mistake, he would have to retape the nightly news for the West Coast feed. And that meant that dinner would be late.

Such began my father's eager interest in politics. Illustrious careers often originate with such prosaic beginnings.

My grandfather was David Brinkley, a prominent television newsman. He made his name as coanchor of NBC's flagship evening news program, *The Huntley-Brinkley Report*, from 1956 to 1970 and then became coanchor of *NBC Nightly News*. In 1981, he began hosting *This Week with David Brinkley*, a show that revolutionized the Sunday morning news program format.

History was a living thing to my father, not least because he grew up in Washington, DC, immersed in the politics of the day. My grandmother loved to entertain, and guests to the Brinkley home ranged from Jack and Jackie Kennedy to Ella Fitzgerald. During high school, my father had a summer job as an intern in the Johnson White House and shuttled memos back and forth between offices in the West Wing.

My father's personal history—the history of his family—was more remote. My grandfather's life remains a bit of a mystery even to those who were closest to him. My father often commented that David Brinkley's memoirs were—as, I suspect, many celebrity memoirs are—partly apocryphal. My grandfather was torn between a celebration of the folksy charm of his North Carolina upbringing and a sense of shame about the poverty in which he grew up. He was the youngest of his siblings by quite a few years. His own father died when he was young, and he had a strained relationship with his cold and difficult mother. My father's sense of him was that as a lonely young boy, he spent a lot of time doing work around the house and the rest of his time in the library.

My grandparents met at NBC, where my grandmother was a dictationist, officially tasked with answering the phone and transcribing stories from reporters out in the field. These dictationists, almost all young women, not only had to transcribe but also often had to edit the stories and in some cases rewrite them entirely. My father described it as "a pretty common way in which women with great talents were quietly contributing to things that men took the credit for."

My father's Aunt Mary—my great-aunt—found a job in Washington as a private secretary to Senator Joe McCarthy. Her husband, Ed Driscoll, was a government investigator and one of the most beloved people in the family. Though he divorced my great-aunt when my father was young, he remained part of the extended family until he died. I remember hearing stories about the brash and charming Ed Driscoll. My father said that his aunt's fierce devotion to McCarthy might have stemmed from the same attachment she had to Ed—who my father says had the same kind of rough, alcoholic charm that McCarthy did.

Perhaps because of this family connection, it was extremely important to my father that I understood just how much his mother, unlike Aunt Mary, hated Joe McCarthy. My grandmother was a fierce liberal, and McCarthy embodied a specific form of evil that made him an object of her obsession. I later learned that there was a personal undercurrent to the hatred: my grandmother would occasionally visit Mary in the Senate Office Building, and McCarthy would make passes at her.

This fact was one of many I learned while reading my father's journals recently. Almost ten years ago, several years after my grandfather died, my father began keeping a journal. He was inspired, in part, by the publication of Arthur M. Schlesinger Jr.'s *Journals: 1952–2000* in 2007. Arthur had been part of my grandfather's circle and a figure of my father's youth who came to be one of the biggest professional influences of his life. My father found Schlesinger's journals fascinating and wanted to keep a similar sort of record. His own project began as little more than a catalog of what he was reading, what theater and opera he saw, and whom he met for lunch or dinner. Even these more dispassionate earlier entries were elegantly written with a keen eye for detail, especially when he talked about literature and art. (My father's cultural acuity owed much to my mother, a theater producer with a PhD in eighteenth-century English literature, who expanded his cultural vocabulary, giving him more sociohistorical texts to interpret and cherish.) Over time, though, more and more of his past started to creep in until the "journals" became something very different. "Odd that this journal, which started as a record of what I was doing, has become a kind of memoir of my father and my childhood," he wrote.

The timing of this personal shift maps onto the progression of the illness that would soon come to eat away at his remarkable mind. Perhaps this was a coincidence, but it seems to me that he was trying to hold onto something of his childhood and his father that he felt was beginning to slip away— or, perhaps more accurately, to make sense of something that had always eluded him, before it was too late.

Childhood memories and family history also started making their way into his diaries as he embarked on a new book about the postwar period. It was the biggest project he had undertaken about a time that he had lived through—and a time that his family had shaped, however modestly. The memoir-*cum*-journal seems to be a natural extension of his work, particularly given the subtle and perceptive historical details and analyses that accompanied his personal anecdotes. These analyses were not out of place, particularly when the events he described were historically significant as well as personally significant.

Some of the most vivid memories he wrote about involved accompanying his father to political conventions, experiences that were as formative personally as they were professionally. He was fifteen at his first convention, the 1964 Republican gathering in San Francisco where Barry Goldwater became the nominee. "I loved the city and the convention and everything around it," my father wrote. "The Goldwater people crowding the lobby and jeering my father while handing out 'Stamp Out Huntley-Brinkley' buttons and at times scaring me with their seeming hatred; the furious shouting up at the booth when Eisenhower denounced sensational journalists."

Four years later his experience at the Democratic convention in Chicago in 1968 was, unsurprisingly, particularly memorable. The convention became a symbolic battleground of the generational war that was waging in America. He had what he described as a "token job" with NBC. Most of his time was spent in the convention hall. Although he didn't see the famous battle in Grant Park between the Vietnam protesters and Mayor Richard Daley's police department, he drove by the scene late at night on the way back to the hotel. Debris was everywhere, and the stench of tear gas hung in the air. He described the convention hall the next day as "filled with loathing." Mayor Daley and Abe Ribicoff, the Connecticut senator, traded invectives and obscenities, and my father recalls my grandfather betraying his own contempt for Daley into a hot mike: "Pretty gutsy, Abe."

On the last night of the convention, Daley supporters with silk-screened posters that read "We Love Mayor Daley" filled the galleries ahead of the paying ticketholders. My father picked a ripped poster stamped with a dirty footprint up off the convention floor and, as he describes it, "for perhaps the only time in my life, I became a journalist." He asked the Daley supporters where the posters came from, and they revealed that the local Democratic Party had organized the group, provided them with the posters, and bused them in from all over the city. He told his father about his investigation, and his father put the story on the air that evening. "You might think that this would be a transformative moment in which I fell in love with journalism," my father wrote. "But just asking a stranger about a poster was almost terrifying, and perhaps it was then that I began to realize that I was not made for journalism."

My father described being at conventions with my grandfather as both "thrilling and somewhat degrading." He thought of himself as a kid getting in everyone's way, even though, as a political junkie even then, he was eager to watch the events unfold. It was at conventions that he felt closest to his father, which was ironic given how busy and almost unapproachable my grandfather must have been during those weeks. But as someone whose intellectual connections with people were often deeply emotional, my father must have felt that conventions offered him a rare opportunity to participate in my grandfather's life and to see the world as he saw it—mixed up in history-making events, both observing them and shaping them. He charted a course for himself that did not include journalism but that was nonetheless inspired by the world in which he grew up.

It was at Princeton that my father was first able to try to understand the world—from outside the Washington bubble in which he had been ensconced and to understand himself outside the context of his father. It proved more challenging than he had perhaps anticipated to escape his father's fame. He told me that the day he moved into his freshman-year dorm, swarms of students gathered in a half moon around his father's car— some of them affectionately chanting "Goodnight, Chet," the sign-off that ended every broadcast of *The Huntley-Brinkley Report*. My dad had already chosen to room with Nick Hammond, his best friend from high school, who was a child actor and a star of *The Sound of Music*—at the time the highest-grossing film ever. Together with my grandfather's arrival on campus, this decision made my father's wish for privacy and relative anonymity seem like a fantasy.

Soon enough, though, my father became known for other reasons on campus. He developed a reputation as one of the brightest minds at Princeton. My father would never have shared a fact like this with me, modest as he was, but it was something that his college classmates had told me, and it was something that was relayed to me over and over again when I joined my father at his forty-fifth reunion.

One of the first major exercises of the new independence that college had afforded my father was a trip to Europe with his best friends from

Princeton, Nick and Scott Berg. The trip was technically a research assignment given to them by a wealthy Princeton alumnus, but in reality, it was a boondoggle European road trip. It was the summer of 1969, and like most people around the world, they waited to see the first moon landing. Apollo 11 was circling for hours, and there was no way of knowing when it was going to land. They couldn't stay up any longer and went to bed. A few hours later the woman renting them the room where they were staying started banging on their door with her cane. When they answered, she pointed to the sky and said, "*Luna*." She ushered them upstairs to her apartment where the four of them watched the moon landing on her snowy black-and-white television.

The next day they were at a gas station in the middle of nowhere. A German man and his son were in the car next to theirs. They heard my father and his friends speaking with American accents. The man got out of his car and, one by one, shook each of their hands. This was the first time my father experienced a major historic event that was not moderated by his father.

At Princeton, he found a new outlet to understand the history-making events that were part of the fabric of his childhood. He discovered his love of history under the tutelage of Nancy Weiss Malkiel, then an assistant professor and one of the first female faculty members. His senior thesis, "The Gospel of Discontent: Huey Long in National Politics, 1932–1935," became the basis for his graduate dissertation, which, in turn, developed into his first book, *Voices of Protest*.

He did not expect, though, to go into academia. Perhaps this is evident from his choice of major: he did not major in history but rather in the Woodrow Wilson School's undergraduate interdisciplinary public policy major. After my father graduated, he applied to law school. He was unsure whether or not becoming an attorney was really what he wanted to do, but as was the case for many smart and ambitious college graduates feeling lost, law school seemed like an appealing place to turn. He was accepted at Harvard Law School, was all set to go, and had even found an apartment in Cambridge for the fall. The final step was to tell my grandfather about his decision.

David Brinkley had a lifelong distrust of lawyers. His hatred of attorneys was an important piece of trivia in the image that I had of him: he loved red pistachios and perfectly ripe peaches, and he hated lawyers. My father invited Nick Hammond to the dinner at which he intended to let my grandfather know that the damning title "Esquire" would be appended to the legacy of his name. During dinner and before my father could make his confession, Nick made a joke about lawyers, and my grandfather responded with such virulence that my father abandoned not only the announcement but also the entire idea of a law career.

Instead, my father applied to graduate school in history at Harvard. In later years, he expressed dismay at the number of his most brilliant students who chose to go to law school. He understood, of course, all the reasons that people choose not to enter academia. The financial and professional instability that today accompanies obtaining a doctoral degree in the humanities was not as severe when my father entered grad school—though good jobs were still hard to come by, and he knew that. I wonder if he felt it was a shame that the law in particular was getting so many great minds or that the law simply attracted the kinds of minds he wished to recruit to history.

Despite the distance from my grandfather's work that history afforded him, my father's academic work sometimes had a personal resonance. My father was once asked to review a book on the Kennedy assassination. He got the galleys and was surprised to find an anecdote about his mother in there. My grandmother, as the author told it, was at dinner at the White House shortly before the Kennedys left for Dallas. She had a bad feeling about the trip and warned Jack not to go. "There's no way that happened," my father said. He knew that if it had been true, his mother would have been talking about it for the next thirty years.

My father is by no means a purist about his discipline. He does not think that the only valid way to view the world is through a historical lens. But he does believe, I think, that history can encapsulate all the valid ways to think about the world. To him, the world is about people and about ideas, and what is history if not a way to understand people and ideas?

The closest and most intimate dimension of my relationship with my father has always been the intellectual one. I always felt that he took my ideas seriously and never felt that he condescended to me, even when perhaps he should have. When he read a book he thought I would like, he would give it to me to read. I'm sure there are books he withheld because he thought they might be too advanced, but he actually thought to consider whether *I* would like it, not just whether a ten-year-old might like it. He also would read the young adult books that I was enjoying. He was genuinely interested in my thoughts and ideas. When I would write a research paper for school, he would take me to Butler Library to look for resources.

Many children believe that their parents know everything. Parents contain the world epistemologically in many ways that, to a child, are very real. For me, the omniscience of my father was less mythical than it might be to most children, or perhaps it is a misconception I have yet to grow out of—and have no desire to do so.

My dad used to indulge me when I would sing songs down the street as long as they were things he liked. He was delighted when I got into a Gershwin phase at the age of nine. I remember walking down a side street on the Upper West Side, swinging hands with my father and singing "Let's Call the Whole Thing Off." When we got to the line "You sarsaparilla and I sarsaparella," I paused to ask my dad what sarsaparilla was. "You know," he said, "I can't tell you." So inconceivable was it to me that he might not know something that, for years, I was convinced that sarsaparilla was something illicit. My parents, who in addition to letting me read anything I wanted would let me sit in their room while they watched HBO, never refrained from sharing information with me because they thought it was inappropriate; *sarsaparilla* thus became the mother of all dirty words to me.

He was a fierce advocate of my curiosity, yet he was never pedantic or imperious in the ways in which he encouraged my intellectual development. When I was little, maybe six or seven, I developed an obsession with *I Love Lucy*. I don't remember how I first stumbled on it, but I was hooked. I had read classic children's literature and had felt transported to other time periods before, but there was something visceral and immersive about the way I saw the fifties in the show. The 1950s of *I Love Lucy* were not the 1950s of my father's childhood—or of anyone's, really. But my father, watching the show through my eyes, seemed to see anew the cultural relevance and unique sensibility of the show. He decided to put a little sidebar in his textbook about the show and even asked me to read it before he submitted the draft.

For as long as I can remember, my father was working on *The Publisher*. He was a notoriously fastidious person, organized to a fault. His desk, though, during the Luce period, was littered with correspondence and old issues of *Life* magazine. I loved poring over the old magazines as a young child, and though I'm sure I destroyed my dad's careful cataloging of them, he never seemed to mind.

My father's work has always contained strong biographical elements, and he was fascinated by the individuals who populated the histories he wrote, bringing to life a wide cast of American characters through his writing. In his later work, he moved from writing biographically informed history to writing biography itself. His last three books— *Franklin Delano Roosevelt*, *The Publisher*, and *John F. Kennedy*—were all biographies. But as he made this transition, he remained more interested in the broader historical questions than in the personal details. In his research for *The Publisher*, my father interviewed Henry Luce's mistress, Jeanne Campbell, for whom he had nearly left Clare Boothe Luce. When my mother asked if he had discovered any salacious tidbits about Luce, my father's answer to her was "Nothing that really helps us understand his view of 'The American Century.'"

This lack of interest in personal details was a hindrance to his understanding of his own family history—or perhaps a result of it. Over the past few years, my father, according to his journals, was struggling to understand his father as a father rather than a public figure. He had always attempted to understand his father from his historical perspective—the lens through which he viewed everything in his world. He expressed continual bewilderment at his renewed interest in his father ten years after his death, something that did not surprise my mother or me in the slightest, largely because looking at personal history in this way was very new to him.

My mother abounded with anecdotes of her youth—she told stories not only of her family but also of a rich cast of characters in her world. The world of my father's youth was much less clear to me, and much of what I learned came from reading the notes and journals he had started keeping. I felt as if these journals were a gift he has left me, answering questions I hadn't had the chance to ask him.

Even as I am trying to understand my father's relationship to his father, and mine to my father, another area of family history has come into the picture. My grandmother was diagnosed in the 1980s with ALS, then still commonly known as Lou Gehrig's disease. By the time I started forming memories of my grandmother, she had almost entirely succumbed to the disease. She was completely paralyzed except for her eyes. I remember talking to her on the phone and hearing only the hum of her ventilator in reply.

Watching my grandmother die was one of the hardest things my father ever did. I didn't realize the effect it had on him until he became sick himself. During a phase of his illness, he would fixate on certain elements of his past, and what he fixated on most was his mother's death. "It was horrible" became his refrain. Loving someone with this disease is, in essence, an act of grief in slow motion. In some ways, the illness affects loved ones as profoundly as it does the patient.

Only in late 2016 did we discover that my father is affected by a mutation of the C9orf72 gene that, depending on where it manifests, causes either ALS or frontotemporal dementia. Children of those who test positive for the gene mutation have a 50 percent chance of inheriting it. This mutation is incredibly rare, accounting for only 6 percent of cases of ALS, already a rare disease affecting only 20,000 Americans per year. Accepting the decline of my father, the person I love and admire most in the world, has been devastating.

In many ways, the current political moment is primed for an Alan Brinkley analysis. A Huey Long–like figure is riding a populist wave, redefining contemporary American conservatism in response to a crisis in both liberalism and conservatism. The historical legacy of Barack Obama might have interested my father intellectually and historically in much the same way that Franklin Roosevelt's did, and Donald Trump's ascendancy in the wake of the Obama presidency certainly would have too. It was frustrating to my father that he couldn't engage professionally in the political situation, but it was more frustrating to me that the nation was deprived of what would have been a voice of reason. Thankfully, my father's profound impact on the field and on his students means that echoes of his voice will still be heard for generations to come.

2

The "Dissident Ideology" Revisited

POPULISM AND PRESCIENCE IN
VOICES OF PROTEST

MOSHIK TEMKIN

Voices of Protest was an unlikely project for Alan Brinkley. In the 1970s, when he was working on the dissertation that would become his first book, the Harvard history department was not known for his field of interest, twentieth-century U.S. political history. (Arthur M. Schlesinger Jr. had left years earlier—first for the circles of presidential power, then for the lights of New York.) Its strengths in American history were decidedly in colonial America (Bernard Bailyn), immigration (Oscar Handlin), and urban history (Stephan Thernstrom). Brinkley's dissertation adviser was the somewhat lesser-known Frank Freidel, author of a multivolume biography of Franklin D. Roosevelt.[1] Nor was there anything in particular about Brinkley's personal or family background to suggest that he might, as a young scholar with liberal proclivities, be drawn to the history of populism, protest, or radicalism and that of marginal or dubious figures.

And yet Brinkley received his PhD after turning in a remarkable study of two such political figures—as he later called it, a "comparative biography as political history."[2] One of his subjects was Huey Long of Louisiana, the small-town lawyer who rose in the 1920s to become the "Kingfish," the state's all-powerful governor, then its senator, and finally a national political figure; before being murdered in 1935, he was gearing up for a possible presidential challenge to Roosevelt. The other was Father Charles Coughlin, a Canadian-American Catholic priest who rose from an obscure start as a parish priest in a suburb of Detroit, Michigan, to command a radio audience of tens of millions of Americans and wield an inordinate degree of political influence before being sidelined. Brinkley saw both men, and their followings, as perhaps the most significant domestic political challenge to Roosevelt at the height of the Depression, a time of deep and unprecedented crisis for American politics and society. Recounting the stories of the political movements that these two men created—Long's Share Our Wealth and Coughlin's National Union for Social Justice—enabled Brinkley to analyze the impact of the Depression on American political culture at large and to examine Long's and Coughlin's critiques of the New Deal and the Roosevelt administration as part of a longer history of American dissent and resistance to centralized power, economic inequality, financial elites, and perhaps even capitalism itself.

The book was a huge critical and commercial success, especially for a debut. It won the National Book Award, was widely and effusively praised in both scholarly journals and major national newspapers and magazines, and made Brinkley the new young star of American political history. Thirty-five years after its publication, it is still widely assigned in both undergraduate and graduate American history courses. And in the past few years, it has made an unexpected return to the public sphere as the rage and resentments that propelled a dubious New York real estate mogul and reality TV star to the White House sent journalists and observers desperately searching for historical explanations and precedents. *Voices of Protest* has been included in various lists of books considered essential to understanding the current American state of affairs, although its inclusion in such lists is based on an implicit and questionable premise that Brinkley might not accept: that Donald Trump is a genuine populist heir to the political legacies of Coughlin and especially Long.[3] Still, it is a sign not only that *Voices of Protest* is good history but also that it is evergreen, dealing with themes in American history that have remained with us and are perhaps stronger today than at any time since the Depression. Brinkley's analysis of Long,

Coughlin, and their movements is as convincing and resonant as it was when he first wrote it.

Although Harvard was Brinkley's training ground (and later his academic employer), he found his primary inspiration and models for history writing elsewhere in the Ivy League. The two scholars whose work he engaged with most meaningfully, Richard Hofstadter and C. Vann Woodward, had been at Columbia and Yale, respectively. The books of theirs that most influenced him were Hofstadter's *The Age of Reform* and Woodward's *Origins of the New South*.[4] Indeed, *Voices of Protest* can be seen as picking up where these two seminal books left off. The connection was not direct, as both those works were published in the 1950s and *Voices of Protest* appeared in 1982, but Brinkley's project was intended, in a sense, to examine the worlds, and especially the political cultures, that were created by the processes and legacies Hofstadter and Woodward each brilliantly discussed.[5]

But whereas Brinkley was deeply influenced by these two historians, *Voices of Protest* also represented a sort of rebellion against them. Hofstadter had taken a dim view of the late nineteenth-century populists, acknowledging their grievances against capital, elites, and banks but linking populism to isolationism, xenophobia, anti-Semitism, and even the paranoid frenzy of the McCarthy years (the backdrop to Hofstadter's writing of *Age of Reform*). Although historians of the New Left and their heirs would reject and even belittle Hofstadter's view of populism, instead seeing the movement as a precursor to the social and political activism of the twentieth century, Brinkley never belonged to the New Left and was not a 1960s radical or a Marxist. His "rebellion," as such, was not a radical challenge to mainstream liberalism but rather one from within the liberal tradition. As Anders Stephanson recently put it, "Brinkley is a radical amongst liberals," perhaps because, unlike Marxists who "slide into" liberalism, Brinkley "has always been a liberal."[6]

Woodward's book had depicted the New South (circa the 1910s) as a sort of "colonial economy," in which a reeling South, post–Civil War and post-Reconstruction, entrenches itself in racial segregation and hostility to the conquering North at the same time that its political economy becomes subordinated to northern (really eastern) capital, primarily to the benefit of a few local business interests and distant financial elites and to the detriment of small farmers, former slaves, social and public services, and the environment. This social and political world—the so-called Solid South—was mired in poverty and underdevelopment even as it became integrated into a new national industrialized economy, pitting poor whites against even poorer African Americans, turning Jim Crow into a way of life, and perpetuating social and economic inequality. It was the perfect setting for the rise in the late 1920s of Long, who inherited and benefited from the southern populist impulse in important ways but who also broke with other southern political-populist traditions, especially in his general eschewing of race-baiting and xenophobia.[7]

Brinkley's ambivalent intellectual relationship with Hofstadter and Woodward—inspired by them at the same time that he implicitly challenged them—connects to one important background element of *Voices of Protest*, which Brinkley raised straigh a tway in his preface: the debate over mass politics and mass movements. This was (and is), of course, a debate that transcends 1930s America or even American history. Although already in the 1920s Walter Lippmann had expressed his suspicion, echoed by others subsequently, of the "public," the scholarly fascination with (and fear of) "the masses" took off in the wake of World War II, when it became a central feature of intellectual life and academic production.[8]

Brinkley well described the two sides of this debate: on one side were those hostile to mass politics, which to them "represents the most frightening tendencies of modern society . . . the victory of the dark forces that have in this century produced fascism, Stalinism, and other terrors." To such critics, Brinkley noted, "the Long and Coughlin phenomena have appeared as menacing examples of irrational mass behavior, a challenge to American traditions of tolerance and individual freedom."[9] On the other side of the debate were those who were sympathetic to, or even celebratory of, mass politics. As an example, Brinkley invoked Long biographer T. Harry Williams, of Louisiana State University, who he said had described the Louisiana politician "as a 'good mass leader,' a crusading force for progressive change who challenged powerful, reactionary elites." He also noted that Williams quoted the French Catholic thinker Jacques Maritain in proposing that "Long's mission ... was 'to *awaken* the people ... to something better than everyone's daily business, to the sense of a supra-national task to be performed' "—in other words, to be part of something larger than themselves.[10]

After explaining how both Long and Coughlin could be interpreted in either of these two ways (Hofstadter was in the camp hostile to mass politics; in *Age of Reform*, he mentioned Long once, lumping him with various right-wing extremists and southern racists, along with the Nazi-sympathizing aviator Charles Lindbergh and the yellow journalism magnate William Randolph Hearst, as an example in American life of "the demand for reforms . . . combined with strong moral convictions and with the choice of hatred as a kind of creed"[11]), Brinkley stated that he does not adopt either approach. Instead, he argued, "Long and Coughlin were not the leaders of irrational, anti-democratic uprisings. Neither, however, were they the vanguards of a great, progressive social transformation. Instead, they were manifestations of one of the most powerful impulses of the Great Depression, and of many decades of American life before it: the urge to defend the autonomy of the individual and the independence of the community against encroachments from the modern industrial state."[12]

Brinkley developed this thesis in one of the book's middle chapters, "The Dissident Ideology," where he made the foundational case for coupling Long and Coughlin. Without this chapter, the book might read as two interesting studies that never quite connect. Long and Coughlin had different backgrounds, trajectories, vocations, and ambitions. Not only was one a politician and the other a priest, but also, as Brinkley pointed out, the two men did not know each other very well, regarded one another with some suspicion, and probably did not think that they had much in common. When Long was shot and killed in 1935, he had Coughlin's support (for what that was worth) for his political ambitions. But that hardly seems like a good enough reason to treat the two men as a connected phenomenon. What they *did* have in common, Brinkley argued, was a core set of notions about American life, expressed in a simple but powerful message: "an affirmation of threatened values and institutions,"

as Brinkley put it, "and a vision of a properly structured society in which
these values and institutions could thrive." And, he continued, Long and
Coughlin shared a common view of the "obstacles to this vision, a set of
villains and scapegoats upon whom it was possible to blame contemporary
problems." Lastly, per Brinkley, "they offered . . . a prescription for reform,
resting upon a carefully restricted expansion of the role of government."
Ultimately, what they shared most was the fight to overturn decades or more
of national consolidation and economic development along capitalist
lines—a fight that, as Brinkley viewed it (perhaps following Hofstadter),
was a hopelessly lost cause.[13]

In retrospect, the "Dissident Ideology" thesis is not entirely convincing,
but it *is* bold. It might be argued that what Long and Coughlin had most
in common was not any ideological affinity or shared political heritage but
rather their personalized, almost obsessively egomaniacal relationships
with President Roosevelt that followed a similar path: initial admiration
and cautious alliance, followed by growing critique and then by out-and-
out attack. (In some ways, *Voices of Protest* is really about Roosevelt and
his political skill in blunting or coopting Long's and Coughlin's attacks on
"the system.")

But Brinkley did not dismiss Long and Coughlin as merely oppor-
tunistic rabble-rousers exploiting the misery of Americans hit hard by
the Depression in order to further their own power or simply enrich
themselves. Rather, he placed the two men in a longer arc of American
history, connecting them to the populists of the 1880s and 1890s, the
broader history of American federalism and the long-standing impulse
to fight centralization and the consolidation of power in the hands of
unaccountable, unseen, distant elites. The catastrophe of the Depression
served to drive home, for many millions of Americans, a sentiment that
predated that event: that the individual's autonomy was under threat from
the modern state, maybe even from modernity itself, and that entire communities and a way of life were being destroyed, sacrificed for the benefit
of a few undeserving rich and powerful.

For Long, the primary villains were the wealthiest families in America (Rockefeller, Carnegie, Mellon, etc.), whom he railed against (often humorously), using them as gluttonous props in his flamboyant speeches. In his Share Our Wealth program, he proposed, among other things, a cap on wealth, ensuring that every American would have a home "and the comforts of a home, including a radio, and an automobile," so that "none shall be too rich, and none shall be too poor."[14] For Coughlin, the culprits that caused the sufferings of God-fearing Americans were the New York financiers and bankers he held responsible for the international monetary system. (And given this emphasis on international bankers, it should come as no great surprise that Coughlin descended into base anti-Semitism in later years.) Brinkley gave Long and Coughlin credit for meaning what they said, even if what they said could be incoherent or illogical. Indeed, one of his great breakthroughs in the book was to do something that was far from commonplace in 1982: to take Long and Coughlin seriously, not view them as cranks.

Those who know Huey Long from the satirical portrayal of the power-thirsty Willie Stark and his evil naked cynical ambition in Robert Penn Warren's 1946 novel *All the Kings Men* (later a fine 1949 film directed by Robert Rossen) will not recognize him in Brinkley's book.[15] Although in the aftermath of World War II Long was typically seen through the harsh prism of fascism or communism, even more than he had been when he was alive, Brinkley set that facile notion aside and acknowledged the reality of what these figures complained about and the plausible reasons that many people in the United States during the Depression had for supporting them. Brinkley took pains never to dismiss either the substantive claims that Long made (amid all the bluster) or the sufferings of ordinary people that made Long's message compelling to so many.

Nor will all those who, since 2016, have had to suffer through countless articles in which Long has been invoked as a precedent to Donald Trump recognize that Long in *Voices of Protest*. Long was no corrupt, rich conman glibly asserting, as candidate Trump did on the campaign trail in 2016, that he loves the "poorly educated." (Long highly valued education both rhetorically and in practice.) His intentions, at least for his constituents, were noble, at least initially, and his empathy with their predicament genuine. And in the end, the main source of his power was that what he was saying was far from fantastical. As Brinkley rightly explained, "one reason for the appeal of the messages of Long and Coughlin was that they described an objective reality. The concentration of wealth and power they decried was real, part of a larger process of national consolidation that was affecting all of American life. . . . Americans were for the most part responding entirely rationally to a real economic problem."[16]

In this passage, there is something not only incisive but also prophetic; Brinkley, the young historian, was capturing a basic truth about American life that was little more than a blip in 1982, lay nearly dormant for more than a generation, and then reexploded in American politics in just the past few years. Yet at the same time that he explained the strength of Long's and Coughlin's messages and the organic basis for their support, Brinkley also pointed out all their internal contradictions and lacunae, without pulling punches. When Long or Coughlin lied or embellished, which was often, Brinkley called them out. If he ultimately found them to be flawed and lacking, both as public figures and as individuals, it was not a snap judgment on his part but a conclusion reached after a fair, thorough consideration.

What he did *not* do was settle for the easy put-down—that is, refer to Long or Coughlin as a demagogue as a way of disparaging their radical politics. This, too, set him apart from a mainstream liberal view. It is telling, for example, that Woodward began his (favorable) review of Brinkley's book in the *New York Review of Books* with "It is not often that we get a book as good as this one about demagogic public figures like Huey Long and Father Coughlin," whereas Brinkley himself does not apply the word *demagogic* or variations thereof to his subjects anywhere in the book itself.[17] (Brinkley used it only when quoting others and neutrally.) "American Demagogues," by the way, was also the headline given to the (favorable) review of the book in the *New York Times*.[18] But, of course, as Brinkley implicitly recognized, the problem with Long was not his "demagoguery" or the fact that many voters, especially poor ones, liked him—it was that he behaved like a dictator in Louisiana, first as governor and then as U.S. senator, and seemed poised, before he was killed, to replicate that political comportment on the national stage. A much bigger problem than Long and Coughlin, however, was the social, racial, and economic conditions that enabled the rise of figures like them in the first place.

In spite of the conceptually sophisticated way Brinkley treated Long and Coughlin as parts of the same historical phenomenon, they never quite sit together comfortably in the book. Ultimately, dissident ideology aside, the two men headed two separate movements and, arguably championed different causes. Their plan to join forces in challenging Roosevelt never came to fruition.

One major difference between them was that Long was far more interesting, and sympathetic, and this comes across clearly in the book. One way we can tell is that Brinkley often used just the first name "Huey" for Long, whereas Coughlin was always "Coughlin." But I suspect that this unspoken preference for Long probably also reflects Brinkley's deep engagement, especially at this early stage of his career, with southern history, especially Louisiana history (early in his career, Brinkley was considered as much a southern historian as a political historian),[19] as well as his deep and abiding, even loving, interest in politics: the day-to-day work of politics, the ideas behind political movements, political charisma or lack thereof, and unlikely successes or failures.

Long, unlike Coughlin, didn't primarily talk on the radio, though he did that also—and quite well. He accomplished things. He built things. As Williams pointed out to the Southern Historical Association, when Long became governor in 1928, Louisiana had only 296 miles of concrete roads, 35 miles of asphalt, 5,728 miles of gravel, and 3 major bridges, none of which crossed the Mississippi River (trains had to be separated into cars and ferried across). By 1935, the state had 2,446 miles of concrete roads, 1,308 miles of asphalt, 9,629 miles of gravel, and more than 40 major bridges.[20] Long also invested in public education, higher education, and public health. Louisiana remained desperately poor when Long died (and remains poor today), but it had more modern hospitals, better-equipped schools, and a real research university in Louisiana State University.

Long did those things not as a talker but as a politician and elected official—albeit eventually a ruthless and autocratic one. That probably made him more of a real political and public force than Coughlin ever was or could be and a more complex figure. Among other things, Long's authoritarianism makes *Voices of Protest* a valuable tool for teaching that extends beyond the history of the 1930s or populist politics. Many of my own students have come from poor, developing countries that have fragile democracies; for them, a figure like Long is quite recognizable. This can generate an animated discussion: How does one judge a trade-off between loss of liberty and development? How much of one's political or democratic freedom is one willing to sacrifice in order to combat poverty, illiteracy, and disease? Is that sacrifice actually necessary? In writing about 1930s Louisiana, Brinkley captured questions that are relevant in many parts of the world. Reactions to Long among my students suggest that he may be as divisive today as he was in the 1930s. Perhaps not surprisingly, there is still a correlation between social position and attitude toward Long. Elites don't like him; those from less elite backgrounds tend to have a friendlier view.

There is more that the political historian can get from Long than from Coughlin for several reasons. One gets the sense that Coughlin hit his peak as a public force in 1935, whereas Long was only really getting started when he was assassinated that year. And Long was a distinctly *southern* politician. Some of the richest and most suggestive parts of *Voices of Protest* are the ones concerned with southern political culture, and Brinkley could be quite vivid, colorful, and humorous, and even full of pathos, when he dealt not just with Long himself but also with the gallery of eccentric characters that seemed to populate southern politics at the time. Brinkley, it is clear, has always loved a good character. These parts of the book have the most palpable sense of time and place—like a well-done period film that gets the atmosphere and the details exactly right. Indeed, some of Brinkley's most memorable writing in *Voices of Protest* consists of physical descriptions, which he somehow manages to connect to issues of substance. Consider the following quote about Long just before he became governor in Louisiana in 1928: "He had an appearance of perpetual agitation, head, arms, or body always moving, with untamable hair falling constantly across his forehead. To some, he looked almost comical, but most who saw him carried away a different, if somewhat diffuse impression—of a man of power, a man driven, a man with a sense of mission."[21]

Regarding this last part—"a man of power, a man driven, a man with a sense of mission"—a lot of the discussion of Long (as well as of Coughlin) has revolved around what exactly that mission was. The elephant in the room is fascism. Of course, Long was accused in his own time of being an American Mussolini or Hitler, especially by his many rivals and enemies, and those accusations only increased after he was killed. The very fact that he was murdered, at age forty-two, can seem to be a natural and direct result, an almost inevitable outcome, of his politics (a problematic assumption). In *All the King's Men*, Long—in the thinly disguised form of Willie Stark—was portrayed as fascist, corrupt, and authoritarian—a reflection of a popular culture that had just experienced a bloody war against fascism and was immersed in a frightening Cold War against communism. But there were important reasons for viewing Long (along with Coughlin, whose ideas would veer toward explicit Nazi sympathy) as a kind of fascist, and Brinkley addressed the issue directly in a short and brilliant appendix entitled "The Question of Anti-Semitism and the Problem of Fascism," which asks whether we should view the Long and Coughlin movements in their prime as American strains of fascism.[22]

One thing that Brinkley astutely pointed out is the common origins of both European fascism and the Long and Coughlin movements in nineteenth-century agrarian-based populism; thus, not only were there similarities between, say, the Long movement and European fascist parties in the 1930s, but also they were drawing on some similar political traditions. But Brinkley was also right to point out the major differences: namely, the issue of wealth concentration, which was at the center of Long's program but not really the point for the European fascists, and the intense nationalism—and religious, ethnic, and racial jingoism—at the center of the fascist program in Europe, with differences, of course, between, for example, the German Nazis and the Italian fascists. The appendix ends with the nuanced and convincing conclusion that even though European fascism and the Long and Coughlin movements have several things in common, their similarities are ultimately outweighed by their differences.

In this same context, one of the most overlooked aspects of *Voices of Protest* is its ahead-of-its-time framing of American history in a global context. By studying Depression-era American political movements in relation to developments in Europe at the same time, Brinkley was offering not only a cosmopolitan approach to American political history but also, indirectly, one of the few serious analyses of American far-right politics of the era (though Long, as Brinkley would surely concede, hardly belongs in that category).[23] Nevertheless, the appendix shows its age. Brinkley's discussion of whether or not Huey Long was a fascist revolves principally around ideology, which is typical of the time Brinkley was writing the book. A look at the issue of fascism from a more up-to-date perspective, such as that found in the work of Brinkley's Columbia colleague Robert O. Paxton, which focuses on the forms and actions of fascists and the dynamics of their rise to power rather than on their words or ideology, would have been revealing—and perhaps would have made Long look more like a fascist.[24]

A second criticism is that the appendix (and the book generally) would have been well served by a deeper discussion of the relationship between Long's rhetoric and proposals and the socialist and communist movements—and not only in the United States. There is some of that in the book, mostly included to show how much the socialists and the communists in the United States despised Long and Coughlin. (This should emphatically answer the question of how much of a socialist or a communist Long really was.) The socialists' and communists' contempt for Long does not, however, shine enough light on the actual political differences between Share Our Wealth and the radical left because the latter's hatred of Long was rooted as much in jealousy of his popularity among poor Americans and his much greater appeal to the masses (which, as Brinkley pointed out, was a source of great frustration to such people as Norman Thomas, the Socialist Party leader) as in differences in doctrine. Brinkley could have made an excellent book even better by drawing on the literature on the interwar period in European history that dwelled on the commonalities (and differences) between communism and fascism—which, in a way, could be seen even in the personal trajectory of Mussolini himself (originally a radical left-wing syndicalist) as well as in the strong anti-bourgeois and antiliberal ideology that both of these movements shared in the wake of World War I.[25]

Three-plus decades after its publication, *Voices of Protest* reads as a sur-prisingly pessimistic book. Even if one knows that Brinkley is a progres-sive liberal and that his sympathies lie mostly with the New Deal and its policy makers, there is a melancholy feel to his account of the ways the Long and Coughlin movements crashed up against the existing order. On this point, we should remain wary of exaggerating the significance of Long and Coughlin in terms of presidential politics. It is understandable that Roosevelt looms so large in the narrative given that both Long and Coughlin were so obsessed with him and that he so thoroughly dominated the political scene of the day. But as Brinkley showed, neither Long nor Coughlin really represented a threat to Roosevelt's electoral prospects, despite their bombast and popularity among ordinary Americans. There were so many protest and dissident movements in the mid-1930s—which Brinkley described—that it is hard to imagine the sort of unity necessary to change the system to the extent of actually voting a president as popular as Roosevelt out of office. Yet it remains hard to envision what might have happened had Long survived past 1935.

The importance of the Long and Coughlin movements, then, was really as *protest* movements—distinctly American experiments with extraparty mass politics. And these movements ended in failure. Thus, *Voices of Protest* is also ultimately about the limitations of protest politics in the United States versus the so-called system, the establishment. Writing this book led Brinkley to turn his gaze more fully toward that system, that establishment—the liberal New Deal establishment that had so calmly and impressively withstood the Long and Coughlin insurgencies. Intellectually, then, Brinkley's next project—which culminated in *The End of Reform*, published thirteen years after *Voices of Protest*—was an examination of the Roosevelt presidency, the federal government, and the liberal order as the vehicles of change—for better or for worse—in American public and political life.

3

The End of Reform

A RECONSIDERATION

MASON B. WILLIAMS

Alan Brinkley once observed that no one growing up in the 1950s in Washington, DC, could escape the lingering presence of Franklin Roosevelt. Alan's father, David Brinkley, had attended some of Roosevelt's press conferences during World War II and counted them (as Alan wrote) "among the most memorable events of his very eventful life"; Alan's mother had "devour[ed]" the volumes of Arthur M. Schlesinger Jr.'s *The Age of Roosevelt* trilogy as they were published in the late 1950s.[1] As his own career unfolded, Alan Brinkley would return time and again to Roosevelt and the New Deal—its nature, its challengers, and its enduring legacy. His first book, *Voices of Protest*, examined both the populist challenges posed to the New Deal by Louisiana Senator Huey Long and the "radio priest" Father Coughlin and Roosevelt's efforts to blunt and coopt those challenges. In his second scholarly book, Brinkley turned his attention from the dissident critics of the New Deal to the New Dealers themselves, from the critics of the New Deal state to the people who built it. His labors would yield *The End of Reform*, one of the most important interpretations of the New Deal published in the last half century.[2]

Though *The End of Reform* marked a departure from Brinkley's previous work, it also shares some of the core concerns that animated *Voices of Protest*.

As Moshik Temkin has explained in chapter 2 of this volume, Brinkley's first book told the story of unsuccessful (perhaps quixotic) political opposition to the growth of centralized, distant, seemingly unaccountable power. *The End of Reform*, too, examined the eclipse of older ways of envisioning American society in the face of modernization. It documented the passing of a reform *mentalité* colored by the "reverence [of populists, midwestern progressives, and Debsian socialists] for the democratic potential of small producers" and of the Progressive generation's desire to reshape the institutional structure of modern capitalism. And it charted the rise of a new liberal approach, committed not to restructuring American industry but to helping it grow and to compensating for its inevitable flaws.[3] Brinkley continued to treat the interwar period as the site of a struggle between those committed to a vanishing older order and those who would make their peace with a new one. With *The End of Reform*, he shifted his attention from the rearguard actions of the defenders of the old order to the often turbulent intellectual course of a cohort of liberal policy thinkers who accepted economic centralization and expanded state power as inevitable by-products of modernization. In doing so, he engaged with a new set of questions about the promises and limitations of liberal economic thought and the liberal state.

The early to mid-1980s, when Brinkley started work on *The End of Reform*, were an especially fruitful time for scholarship on the New Deal. One reason was obvious: the rise of Ronald Reagan and the New Right (and, by the time Brinkley published the book, Newt Gingrich's congressional revolution). The simple fact that it was no longer possible to see liberalism as the dominant force in American politics led historians to reassess both how the New Deal coalition came together and why it collapsed; in the Age of Reagan, the New Deal seemed both more remarkable and more frail.

The End of Reform thus belongs to a generation of scholarship on the New Deal that was written against the backdrop of the eclipse of the Great Society and the New Left on one hand and the ascent of the New Right on the other. The liberal historians of the 1950s had lauded the New Deal for fulfilling the promise of the American reform tradition (in Schlesinger's *The Age of Roosevelt* trilogy) or transcending the limitations of that tradition (in Richard Hofstadter's *The Age of Reform*). In contrast, scholars of Brinkley's generation and outlook were acutely sensitive to the fragilities of the New Deal project.[4] Yet unlike the New Left historians of the late 1960s and early 1970s, who took the New Deal's limitations as their primary subject,[5] they believed that something unusual *had* occurred in the mid-1930s. For that reason, theirs was a search for, as Steve Fraser and Gary Gerstle put it in their seminal volume *The Rise and Fall of the New Deal Order* (in which the first version of Brinkley's argument appeared), the "missed opportunities, unintended consequences, and dangerous but inescapable compromises" that circumscribed and ultimately undermined the liberal promise of Franklin Roosevelt's first term—leading, finally, to the collapse of the New Deal order.[6] *The End of Reform*, Brinkley noted forthrightly, was among other things an effort to understand "why modern American liberalism had proved to be a so much weaker and more vulnerable force than almost anyone would have imagined a generation ago."[7] Tellingly, the last clause of *The End of Reform*'s final sentence is "the sources of American liberalism's present travails."[8]

Another influence, perhaps less obvious, was the economic turmoil of the 1970s, which cast the history of the New Deal's economic policies in a new light.[9] Schlesinger's *Age of Roosevelt* trilogy had established the basic contours of postwar scholarship on the New Deal, and its third volume had popularized the idea of a "first" and a "second" New Deal. In 1933–34, the story went, the New Dealers attempted to remake the American economy, replacing cutthroat competition with the mechanisms of cooperative planning—an impulse best represented by the National Recovery Administration and the Agricultural Adjustment Administration. Then, beginning in 1935, the New Dealers turned away from the planning idea and instead tried to reform the existing capitalist economy through a mix of regulation, countervailing economic powers, a more generous social safety net, and compensatory fiscal and monetary policy. Schlesinger had seen strengths and weaknesses in both efforts. He believed that, in making the turn toward the second New Deal, liberals had engaged in a "certain lowering of ideals, waning of hopes, narrowing of possibilities."[10] But he also thought they had become more "skeptical" and "tough-minded." He believed that whatever the limits of its ambitions, the liberalism that took shape in 1935–36 had saved democracy and prepared the United States to lead the postwar world.

As liberal political thinkers struggled to contend with stagflation and the apparent failure of Keynesian economics, Schlesinger had second thoughts. During delivered remarks at a 1975 memorial service at the Franklin D. Roosevelt Presidential Museum and Library in Hyde Park, New York, Schlesinger noted: "New social advances may create new social contradictions." The economic crisis of the 1970s, he suggested, should lead liberals to search for a different usable past in the New Deal. "I don't know what the answer is, but I wonder whether some elements of the answer may not be found in the experience of what historians have called the First New Deal." The idealistic planners who had been elbowed aside in 1935, he argued, may have possessed a "more realistic conception" of the modern market economy than the tough-minded lawyers who had sought reform in the second New Deal.[11] The torturous economic history of the 1970s, in short, had led historians to ask whether something valuable had been lost in the evolution of New Deal economic thought. By the time Brinkley's argument took shape in the mid-1980s, it was apparent that the New Deal had left the American state poorly equipped to address not only stagflation but also the decline of older industries, the stagnation of working-class incomes, and rapidly growing inequalities of wealth and income.

If *The End of Reform* was marked by the historical context in which it was written, it also reflected changes in how historians of twentieth-century America were approaching their subject—indeed, it is perhaps the book of Brinkley's that most obviously reflects the scholarly moment in which it was produced. One important influence, which Matthew Dallek discusses in chapter 7 of this volume, was the resurgence of interest in the state as a category of analysis. As Brinkley was beginning work on *The End of Reform*, a group of young social scientists (including Brinkley's colleagues Theda Skocpol and Ira Katznelson) were challenging their fellow scholars to think more deeply about the role of state institutions and actors in shaping political struggles. Much of the scholarship on the New Deal, Brinkley explained in the introduction to *The End of Reform*, had been written on the assumption that policy was "a response to popular movements, interest groups, political coalitions, party structures, and corporate elites."[12] This view helped to explain some key features of the New Deal, he noted. "And yet there remain public questions which exist within a more contained and exclusive political sphere"[13]—including the questions of political economy that he was to trace in *The End of Reform*. The essay that first presented the argument at the heart of *The End of Reform* wore this influence on its sleeve: "The New Deal and the Idea of the State."[14]

Perhaps more than most works of historical-institutionalist analysis that emerged from the call to "bring the state back in," underlying social and cultural developments exercise a powerful and at times even decisive influence on the political and intellectual history that unfolds in *The End of Reform*. Brinkley's state is relatively autonomous, but its actions are profoundly shaped by social forces external to it. The most important of those forces in *The End of Reform* is the emergence of a mass-consumption economy—a concept that had become an important subject and organizing framework in the 1980s among historians working on many different periods of American history.[15] The literature on mass consumption functions in *The End of Reform* much as the organizational synthesis had in *Voices of Protest*. If the displacement of "island communities" (in Robert Wiebe's term) by national forces of state and economic power had provided the deep social context within which Huey Long's and Father Coughlin's movements had unfolded in *Voices of Protest*,[16] the work of the liberal intellectuals and policy makers who populate *The End of Reform* was shaped by the transition from an economy of scarcity, organized around production, to one of abundance, focused on consumption.

These emerging literatures on the state and consumption offered Brinkley conceptual tools with which to answer the big questions raised by the events of the 1970s and 1980s: What were the sources of liberalism's travails? Why had New Deal liberalism proven incapable of meeting the great economic challenges of the late twentieth century? These questions led Brinkley, along with a number of his contemporaries, to the decade following Franklin Roosevelt's triumphant reelection in 1936—the years in which the range of possibilities present in the early New Deal narrowed and alternatives were lost.[17]

Brinkley's primary move in *The End of Reform* is to treat the New Deal not as a "bright moment in which reform energies briefly prevailed" but rather as "part of a long process of ideological adaptation."[18] Through that process, Brinkley writes, American liberals gradually shed their long-standing doubts about "the institutional structure of modern capitalism," slowly reaching an accommodation with modern capitalism and, in the process, reorienting their strategies toward compensating for capitalism's "inevitable flaws and omissions without interfering very much in its internal workings."[19] The corporatist vision of the National Recovery Administration; the planning aspirations of the National Resources Planning Board; the antimonopoly tradition; the vision of an independent, syndicalist labor movement—all gradually fell away, replaced by a commitment to compensatory spending to ensure growth and maximal employment on one hand and an adequate social safety net on the other.

This redefinition of liberal thought occurred, Brinkley writes, "slowly and at times almost imperceptibly," coming not as "the result of a blinding revelation or sudden decision" but rather "from innumerable small adaptations" to changing circumstances "that gradually but decisively accumulated."[20] Running through all these adaptations and tying them all together, Brinkley identifies a "basic change in the way many Americans had come to look at modern economic life": they came to believe that "protecting consumers and encouraging mass consumption, more than protecting producers and promoting savings, were the principal responsibilities of the liberal state."[21]

All of this would have been difficult to foresee on the frigid, rainy morning in January 1937 when Franklin Roosevelt was sworn in for the second time. Fresh off one of the greatest electoral triumphs in American history, he began his second term with a rousing call to extend the New Deal, promising the "one-third of a nation ill-housed, ill-clad, ill-nourished" that his government would "make every American citizen the subject of his country's interest and concern."[22] In the heat of the presidential campaign, he had boasted that the "forces of selfishness and lust for power" had met their match in his first administration and would "meet their master" in his second.[23] Now he made a more tempered, but no less ambitious, pledge to "erect on the old foundations a more enduring structure for the better use of future generations . . . and in so doing, [to fashion] an instrument of unimagined power for the establishment of a morally better world."[24] Who, in light of the last four years, would have doubted Roosevelt's ability to meet his aims? Roosevelt seemed (as one columnist wrote) a "colossus bestriding the American world."[25]

But events quickly overran FDR's ambitions. The legal challenges hanging over some of the New Deal's signature accomplishments all but forced Roosevelt to confront the Supreme Court; the scheme he devised for doing so not only cost him political capital but also brought into the open deep divisions between traditional Democrats and the newer elements of the New Deal coalition. Then, in the fall of 1937, the American economy collapsed. Roosevelt's greatest political asset, Brinkley notes, was that he had presided over four years of steady economic expansion—growing wages, profits, and output, which by the spring of 1937 had regained their pre-Depression levels (though unemployment remained stubbornly high). The "Roosevelt recession" thus plunged the administration into a panic. "It looks to me as if all the courage has oozed out of the President," Secretary of the Interior Harold Ickes wrote in his diary. "He has left things drift. There is no fight and no leadership." Secretary of Agriculture Henry Wallace voiced privately the administration's greatest fear: that Roosevelt's presidency might "end like Hoover's."[26]

The first part of *The End of Reform* charts the administration's search for a response to this perplexing turn of events. Brinkley shows how several distinct groups within the New Deal's orbit fought to capitalize on the crisis to push their own vision of economic policy to the center of the New Deal reform program. One group, centered in the Treasury Department and represented by Treasury Secretary Henry Morgenthau Jr., echoed the business community's claim that the recession was a direct result of antibusiness policies—runaway spending, support for labor unions, and progressive taxation. Its members proposed cutting federal expenditures and balancing the budget to restore "business confidence."

A second group encompassed both the "brain trusters" of the early New Deal and the champions of business-government coordination like those in the Business Advisory Council. They argued that the inherent wastefulness and irrationality of an unplanned economy had driven the nation into yet another of the bust cycles that were an intrinsic feature of a competitive, uncoordinated capitalist system. Further, they proposed business-labor-state cooperation in the interest of creating a more ordered economy capable of functioning as a single rationalized machine. A third group, consisting of a network of young lawyers and economists who took on the moniker "the New Dealers," blamed the Roosevelt recession on monopolistic business practices: the economy had collapsed, they argued, because businesses had kept prices artificially high, dealing a blow to mass purchasing power and thus derailing the New Deal recovery. Unlike traditional antimonopolists, they did not envision a return to a small-scale, independent economy but rather proposed to meet big business with big administration, calling for a technically capable state regulatory apparatus that could force business to keep prices low and consumption high.

But it was a fourth group that emerged triumphant: a motley group of economists and government officials led by "relief czar" Harry Hopkins, the conservative Utah banker turned Keynesian Federal Reserve Board governor Marriner Eccles, and a "deceptively meek young economist" named Lauchlin Currie, who envisioned government spending as an engine for economic recovery. Espousing a set of ideas consistent with John Maynard Keynes's theories (though Brinkley sees Keynes himself as a relatively minor influence), they viewed the recession as a product of underconsumption, caused by a deficiency of mass purchasing power. The American economy had recovered in the mid-1930s, they argued, because the New Deal's emergency spending programs had inadvertently filled the demand gap. In the winter of 1937–38, they convinced Franklin Roosevelt to make compensatory spending an explicit government policy—which Congress did in the spring of 1938. In Brinkley's account, the spenders won out not because they won a decisive intellectual victory but because their approach had few obvious drawbacks and enjoyed support both from the other intellectual camps and from important pressure groups—governors and mayors, unions, local businessmen, and unemployed workers. Thus did American liberals back into a commitment to Keynesianism—and to the idea that maximizing mass consumption represented the key to economic health.

The transformation of liberal economic thought was thus well under way when the United States entered World War II. But it was the experience of the war years above all, Brinkley argues, that made the decisive difference. Many liberals entered the war believing that the struggle for democracy on the global stage might lead to a renewed reform spirit at home. But instead the war placed major obstacles in their way. The Republican Party continued to make gains in Congress, and Roosevelt himself devoted less attention to domestic issues. The war also "encouraged liberals . . . to reconsider their positions, to adjust to the sobering political realities of the 1940s and the new ideological world the conflict created."[27] By the end of the war, the diverse, jumbled collection of political ideas that had coexisted in the early New Deal had developed into "something resembling a consensus," a new liberal economic creed.[28]

The experiences of war forced liberals to reconcile themselves to a number of new realities. Rising fears of totalitarianism compelled them to confront the charge that an assertive brand of statist reform represented a step on the road to "collectivism" and "regimentation"; the act of addressing these arguments, Brinkley suggests, put New Deal liberalism on the defensive, pushing it toward a posture of the "vital center." The return of economic growth (and, for the first time under Roosevelt, full employment) undercut the rationale for a planned economy; economic growth itself now seemed capable of providing the kinds of social benefits that had been at the heart of the New Deal vision. At the same time, liberals lost their battles with military officials and corporate dollar-a-year men to turn the war agencies into machinery for a planning state. And collaboration with the wartime state (and the political failure of ambitious plans for industrial democracy) led the labor movement to forsake "the struggle to win a significant redistribution to wealth and power within the industrial economy"; it emerged from the war committed to economic growth and to the steady improvement of living standards among its members, but it was no longer a force for the radical transformation of the American economy.[29]

Brinkley concludes *The End of Reform* on a tragic note. The assumptions and ideas of postwar liberalism, he writes, helped to underpin the most dramatic period of economic growth in American history. Yet the redefinition of liberalism charted in *The End of Reform* left liberals, and the American state, unprepared to deal with some of the key problems of the last third of the twentieth century: sluggish growth, concentrated poverty, and increasing inequality. The result was "confusion and at times paralysis among liberals themselves, and the growth of a powerful conservative opposition casting doubt on the ability of government to play any useful role in resolving America's dilemmas."[30]

Upon its publication, *The End of Reform* stirred relatively little controversy among historians—a testament perhaps to how persuasively Brinkley had answered the historical questions at the heart of the book.[31] Reflecting its deep engagement with the history and nature of the American state, *The End of Reform* received its most searching and sustained review attention from political scientists. In a special symposium devoted to the book in the journal *Studies on American Political Development*, several scholars asked whether Brinkley had paid too much attention to ideas and not enough to institutions.[32] The substance of economic governance had changed after 1938, after all, not primarily because liberal ideas were changing but because liberals had lost control of Congress—not to regain it, reliably, until the mid-1960s.[33] Brinkley replied, rightly, that his was a history of ideas, a "description of the changing ways in which liberals conceptualized their task,"[34] rather than an analysis of policy formation; as he had noted in his essay "The New Deal and the Idea of the State," ideas were not "the only, or even the most important, factor in determining the form American government would assume."[35] Yet subsequent work on political institutions (above all, Ira Katznelson's work on Congress[36]) has added a crucial dimension to our understanding of *why* American governance assumed the form that it did in the 1940s.

Among historians, the aspect of *The End of Reform* that has least stood the test of time is the conceptual framing offered in the book's introduction—where Brinkley draws a distinction between "reform liberalism," characterized by "the need to ensure the citizenry a basic level of subsistence and dignity, usually through some form of state intervention,"

and "rights-based liberalism," focused on "increasing the rights and freedoms of individuals and social groups" without making "broad efforts to
reshape the capitalist economy."[37] As useful as this distinction might be in
concept, in twentieth-century American history, economic and "group"
or "identity" claims have long been intertwined to the point where the
distinction lacks much historical use (and risks abuse in hands less able
than Brinkley's).[38] An important body of research interested in the social
and cultural history of politics in the New Deal era has demonstrated
that key New Deal constituencies supported economic reform precisely
because it promised to increase the rights and freedoms of individuals and
social groups. Conversely, after World War II, those groups and movements most commonly associated with rights-based liberalism were often
the strongest proponents of economic reform.[39] Finally, a large body of
scholarship on the New Deal era has shown how deeply economic reform
itself was racialized, which further complicates the distinction between
reform and rights-based liberalism.[40]

The historical argument at the heart of *The End of Reform* has held up
much better: subsequent historical scholarship has complicated Brinkley's
account without fundamentally undermining it. Of particular note is the
way that historians have pushed back (often obliquely) against Brinkley's
claim that a focus on consumption gradually displaced a focus on production over the course of Roosevelt's presidency. Meg Jacobs, in her
2005 book *Pocketbook Politics*, documented the importance of consumer
politics and ideas about consumption in the heyday of the New Deal; she
also suggests that consumption-oriented policy approaches could be just
as interventionist as production-oriented ones, showing how the Office
of Price Administration gave rise to a highly statist brand of consumer
politics.[41] A number of scholars have shown that the production-focused,
investment-minded state embodied in the New Deal works and regional
development agencies survived well into the postwar era: even as the
liberal lawyers and economists at the heart of *The End of Reform* turned
their attention to consumption and full employment, other members
of the New Deal coalition worked to sustain, and to justify, the federal-
regional growth coalitions forged in the mid-1930s.[42] (In reading the
last chapters of *The End of Reform*, one is struck by the degree to which

the macroeconomic proposals of figures like Lauchlin Currie and Alvin Hansen depended on developmentalist infrastructure spending.)

A quarter century after its publication, *The End of Reform* continues to inspire innovative scholarship. The recent flourishing of research on the history of American capitalism, in particular, has highlighted aspects of the book that were not widely appreciated a decade ago. Though he did not present it quite this way, Brinkley documents the rise of a group of national state-builders who conceived of something called "the American economy" (as distinct from American industry) as an object of policy intervention and state management. He also suggests some of the implications of this redefinition of the object of governance. In *The End of Reform*'s final chapter, for instance, Brinkley draws a distinction between the New Deal effort to provide work for the unemployed and wartime liberals' commitment to "full employment." We should note that this shift in the way liberals thought to treat the American economy implies a revolution in the techniques of government and in the institutions and knowledge communities involved in governance. This shift from WPA-style works programs jointly administered by social workers/engineers and local governments to macroeconomic management by economists was institutionalized in the passage of the Full Employment Act of 1946, the "last great legislative battle of the Roosevelt presidency" and the closing scene of Brinkley's book.[43]

For these reasons, as Brinkley's former student Timothy Shenk has argued, the late New Deal was more than a watershed in the history of liberal ideas. It was also a crucial passage in which a particular knowledge community—economists—and a particular policy objective—the health of "the economy," as measured by quantitative abstractions such as GDP[44]—gained a privileged position in American governance and discourse.[45] Future research on this crucial shift in governance may uncover important transitional moments within post-World War II economic liberalism. Though Brinkley suggests in *The End of Reform* that liberal thinkers shifted their attention away from redistribution in the 1940s, he also shows that these thinkers were highly concerned with the problem of how to realize a broad distribution of purchasing power. It may be that liberals turned away from questions of (re)distribution only later, once a decade of income compression had appeared to justify it. Moreover, historians searching for the mainsprings of the unruly populist revolts of the late 20th and early 21st centuries will surely return to the odd collision of democratic aspirations and technocratic governance that emerged from the late New Deal.

Twenty-first-century readers of *The End of Reform* are left to ponder one final irony: the very decade in which liberals supposedly surrendered their interest in redistribution, the 1940s, happens to be the decade in which the most striking downward redistribution of wealth in modern American history occurred.[46] As Brinkley's contemporary Nelson Lichtenstein has written, reviewing his own seminal work on the labor movement in the 1940s, the bargains of the World War II era look better today than they once did.[47] The contemporary crisis of inequality and the publication of books such as Thomas Piketty's *Capital in the Twenty-First Century* have moved inequality of wealth and income to the center of scholarly attention, challenging scholars of American politics and capitalism to take a fresh look at the political and intellectual underpinnings of shared midcentury growth as well as the reasons that singular period came to an end.[48]

Some books open conversations, and others provide the last word. In its own time, *The End of Reform* did primarily the latter. The comparatively spiritless conversation that followed its publication suggests the extent to which Brinkley answered conclusively the questions he had posed. And, in fact, it still seems unlikely that anyone will surpass Brinkley's treatment of the redefinition of New Deal thought. But now there are new questions to ask. As scholars set out in search of answers to those questions, they will find that Alan Brinkley has prepared the way.

4

After Reform

THE ODYSSEY OF AMERICAN LIBERALISM IN
LIBERALISM AND ITS DISCONTENTS

DAVID GREENBERG

It is a pleasing irony that in *Liberalism and Its Discontents*, Alan Brinkley's 1998 collection of reviews, lectures, and essays,[1] the single most influential piece has been "The Problem of American Conservatism." Originally published in the *American Historical Review*, the wide-angled historiographic essay helped spark a blaze of research on the American right. As Brinkley noted in that article, his own generation of political historians, informed by midcentury works like Louis Hartz's *Liberal Tradition in America*, had taken the study of liberalism as the central question of American history. But for the next generation, who grew up in the Reagan-Bush era, Brinkley's essay helped to clarify that explaining conservatism's rise was, for that moment at least, the more urgent task. That, in turn, gave rise to a second irony: the outpouring of new work about the political right prompted by Brinkley's call to scholarly action has left a paucity of new scholarship on postwar liberalism—and within the small literature that does exist, *Liberalism and Its Discontents* has become an indispensable volume.[2]

As with any collection of essays, the unifying theme of *Liberalism and Its Discontents* had to be discovered and articulated after the fact. The essays were written between 1982 and 1997 and encompassed a variety of genres: long review-essays for Robert Silvers's much-admired *New York Review of Books* and Leon Wieseltier's storied book pages in the *New Republic*, invited lectures given at Southern Methodist University and Oxford University, peer-reviewed journal articles, magazine pieces for the *New Yorker* and the *New York Times Magazine*, and chapters in academic collections. Yet somehow, though reworked only modestly for publication in this book, these essays exhibit a remarkable evenness of tone and sensibility. As to their unifying argument, Brinkley's efforts to express one recall Richard Hofstadter's comment, in one of the later editions of *The American Political Tradition*, that he had coughed up a preface to those collected pen portraits only to satisfy his editor. Disavowing grand designs, Hofstadter had written that he balked at imposing a contrived frame on what he insisted were discrete essays—but he conceded that "all the sketches had been the conception of a single mind" and that there probably did exist "some single and distinctive angle of vision . . . which might . . . be generalized in a brief introductory passage."[3]

Like Hofstadter, Brinkley blanches at tying his diverse writings together too tightly. In the book's introduction, he modestly proposes—and modesty is Alan Brinkley's signature mode of argument—that his volume might "help illuminate the ways in which liberalism has changed in the years since the beginning of the New Deal, how different it has become from the set of ideas that sustained Franklin Roosevelt and his followers in the early and mid-1930s." Fused to this historical inquiry, moreover, is a more baldly political concern about the fortunes of liberalism in the 1980s and 1990s, when these pieces were written. "What is liberalism?" Brinkley asks. "What has happened to it?" How did the full-bodied political philosophy that dominated the America of Brinkley's youth become a beleaguered creed—attacked from left and right, disavowed by leading Democratic politicians, and accused of being at once too paternalistic and too wedded to promoting rights at the expense of responsibilities?[4]

Brinkley has no single-bullet theory. But the book contains clues to a general explanation. Implicit in *Liberalism and Its Discontents* is the argument that after World War II, liberalism was undone not just by external threats from the New Left and the New Right but also by its own internal contradictions and weaknesses. The book, after all, isn't called *Liberalism and Its Challengers* or *Liberalism and Its Critics*; those were the names of books by other scholars concerned with similar questions.[5] Rather, Brinkley's Freudian title evokes a psychological struggle within the liberal mind, gesturing at something inherent in liberalism that has kept it from being fully at peace with itself. Though the book's chapters were written at different moments, they collectively trace this discontented liberalism through many decades and guises.

In a volume containing pieces about both the New Deal's idea of the state and Hofstadter's *Age of Reform*, about both the televangelist Oral Roberts and the history of national political conventions, a common theme can be hard to discern. But a close reading shows that a unifying thread is indeed present in most, if not all, of these pieces: the idea that liberalism's thinness in the post–New Deal years proved inadequate to sustain mass support. It's a theme that echoes other contemporaneous works, such as Michael Sandel's similarly titled *Democracy's Discontent: America in Search of a Public Philosophy* (also published in 1998), Robert D. Putnam's *Bowling Alone: The Collapse and Revival of American Community*, and Robert Wiebe's *Self-Rule: A Cultural History of American Democracy*.[6] It also happens to be an argument that Brinkley would make in more deliberate, systematic fashion a decade later, in a 2007 essay called "Liberalism and Belief." In that piece, Brinkley explicitly identifies the main problem facing late twentieth-century liberalism as "the absence of an animating faith or passion" at its core.[7] It is not a stretch to discern a similar refrain in the earlier book.

If *Liberalism and Its Discontents* doesn't expressly aim to account for liberalism's late twentieth-century travails as programmatically as the 2007 essay does, the book's agreeable ramble through so many of liberalism's key moments and figures gives it a richness and variety that the shorter piece cannot afford. And the book does return, time and again, to Brinkley's abiding worry that liberalism's pragmatism and proceduralism, its consumerist orientation and its "rights talk," came to provide contemporary Americans an insufficient basis for passionate belief in what had once been a hardy creed. By the 1980s, he notes, it was conservatives who had taken up the stirring language of insurgency and radical change, whereas liberals were plodding along with the sensible reformism that had led them to success in the postwar decades but was now yielding fewer gains in the realm of public policy and generating little excitement among voters.

The difference between conservatism and liberalism was easy to see. From the 1980s onward, conservatism furnished its adherents with a clear, potent, and inspirational public philosophy: limited government, low taxes, strong defense, family values. As observers have noted ad nauseam, it was an eight-word bumper-sticker encapsulation of their public philosophy. Liberal leaders, in contrast, have struggled for years now to articulate what they stand for in a pithy, attractive form; their efforts tended to be long-winded or mundane. Worse still, ever since the 1980s political leaders have shunned the liberal label altogether, allowing it to become, most infamously in the 1988 presidential campaign, an epithet.[8] Or they have followed Bill Clinton—the single figure who did the most to revitalize liberalism in the last forty years—and have masked their liberalism by eschewing the toxic term, substituting the unctuous euphemism *progressive*.[9] Or they have resorted to evasive locutions like that of Vermont governor Howard Dean in 2004: "If being a liberal means a balanced budget, I'm a liberal. If being a liberal means adding jobs instead of subtracting them, then, please, call me a liberal."[10] (Dean was hardly the only one to talk like this.) Liberalism in our times has too often been defensive, apologetic, and uncertain about what it had to say.

To those who are intimately familiar with the nuances and historical vicissitudes of liberalism, the difficulty that Democratic politicians exhibit in defining their philosophy may be puzzling or frustrating, since the core principles of contemporary liberalism are not hard to identify. Individual theorists, if asked to articulate a positive definition of contemporary American liberalism, will differ in their emphases. Yet most would endorse something close to the 2012 formulation of the sociologist Paul Starr: "Liberalism stands for a belief in an equal right to freedom and dignity, advanced by a government of constitutionally restrained powers." Starr added that "in different historical contexts, liberals have varied in their understanding of that ideal and the policies needed to achieve a free and prosperous society and a secure world" but that liberal policies and rhetoric have been rooted in a strong conception of rights, expanding definitions of equality, an activist role for government, and, in economics, "providing all citizens minimum protection against risks beyond their control and equal opportunity in the making of their lives."[11]

However coherent and well formulated this definition, though, it rarely mobilizes anyone in the world of workaday politics and public discourse. For one thing, it's far from an eight-word bumper-sticker slogan. For another, it's a statement about means as much as ends, about procedures as much as outcomes—and means and procedures seldom provide the office-holder or office seeker (or voter) with a compelling raison d'être.

During the New Deal era, where the loose narrative of *Liberalism and Its Discontents* begins, liberalism didn't suffer from this debility, at least not to the same degree. There was much less hand-wringing about its failure to excite the masses. Ending the Depression and, later, winning World War II were causes that were easy to rally around. In his account of the Roosevelt years, the journalist Michael Janeway quoted from the economist Rex Tugwell, a charter member of FDR's brains trust:

I am strong,
I am big and well-made,
I am muscled and lean and nervous,
I am frank and sure and incisive . . .
My plans are fashioned and practical;
I shall roll up my sleeves—make America over![12]

Or, as Arthur M. Schlesinger Jr. wrote in *The Vital Center*, under Roosevelt, "American liberalism has had a positive and confident ring. It has stood for responsibility and for achievement, . . . it has been the instrument of social change."[13]

Into the postwar years, the vision that Franklin Roosevelt had articulated continued to furnish Americans with pride and purpose. In fact, by the 1950s, it seemed to many observers that liberalism had no credible alternatives as a public philosophy except at the margins. Famously, or infamously, Lionel Trilling wrote in *The Liberal Imagination*, "Liberalism is not only the dominant but even the sole intellectual tradition. For it is the plain fact that nowadays there are no conservative or reactionary ideas in general circulation . . . [only] irritable mental gestures which seek to resemble ideas."[14] Innumerable historians of conservatism have used that quotation to highlight the hubris, insularity, or myopia of liberals like Trilling.

But although the great critic was clearly too contemptuous of conservative political thought, he wasn't wrong to note its marginality in the public discourse of the postwar years.

In fact, the conservatism that emerged in opposition to the liberal domination that Trilling perceived was one that implicitly accepted the foundational liberal ideas at the core of the American project. As Brinkley astutely notes in his conservatism essay, "American conservatism in the twentieth century has rested on a philosophical tradition not readily distinguishable from the liberal tradition to which it is, in theory, opposed." He quotes Hartz: "To be an American conservative, it is necessary to reassert liberalism."[15] Into the early 1950s, all manner of conservatives—not only Friedrich Hayek and Herbert Hoover but even Robert Taft and Joe McCarthy—described themselves as liberals.[16] Even today, most post–World War II conservatives, unlike their nineteenth-century predecessors, endorse the basic liberal tenets of liberty, equality, and justice, even if they disagree with self-identified liberals on the policies to achieve these ends. Conservatism's quiet, unacknowledged acceptance of these principles speaks to a durable liberalism at the hidden foundations of the postwar American polity.[17] In short, twentieth-century liberalism won the big battles: the achievement of a mixed economy and a welfare state; the rejection of political and social advantages based on race, religion, or gender; the relaxation of traditional social norms over sex, the family, lifestyle, manners, and mores; and the recognition of the value of international order based on law and human rights, with the United States in the forefront of promoting that order.

But Brinkley's book raises the intriguing possibility that postwar liberalism may have been in some ways a victim of its own success. For all its grand triumphs, liberalism in political practice fared less well in the ensuing fights that were waged *within* the boundaries that it had previously established: fights over the size and scope of activist government, over how aggressively the state should promote certain forms of equality, over how much traditionalists should be expected to tolerate nontraditional cultural behaviors, and over the balance of diplomacy and force in the exercise of American global leadership. On many of these questions, Americans accepted the basic premises of liberalism (strong rights protections, a mixed economy, pluralism, internationalism) but came to prefer those policy solutions prescribed by self-identified conservatives. Over time, too, liberals came to disagree quite a bit among themselves on the best responses to these questions. Thus, in the aftermath of the 1960s, amid the conservative back-lash to the Great Society and the upheaval in cultural values, liberals were hard-pressed to voice a strong and clear set of shared principles for winning fights over particular policies, whether taxes, social policies, or America's role abroad.

The structure of *Liberalism and Its Discontents* implies that to understand the aimlessness of liberalism of the 1990s, we should start with the pur-poseful New Deal liberalism of the 1930s. The most intellectually intricate arguments in the book derive from Brinkley's extensive research on the reshaping of liberalism under Franklin Roosevelt—research that found its fullest expression in *The End of Reform*. During Roosevelt's presi-dency, Brinkley argues, liberal policy makers turned away from sweeping plans to fundamentally restructure the American economy (or what he calls, perhaps with too much understatement, "reform") and instead embraced Keynesian fiscal policy to spur growth and satisfy consumers.[18] "Consumption," says the New Deal economist Alvin Hansen in one Brin-kley essay, "is the frontier of the future." In Brinkley's reading, Hansen turned out to be right.[19]

Several of the early chapters of *Liberalism and Its Discontents* deal with the variegated character of liberalism under Franklin Roosevelt. On two occasions, Brinkley approvingly cites Hofstadter's description of Roosevelt's program as a "chaos of experimentation." Rejecting the view of the New Deal as a coherent blueprint for the economy, Brinkley sketches an improvisational, ever-changing, and even incoherent set of policies—which even the president himself is at pains to explain.

One reason for this chaos was the unprecedented nature of the Great Depression and the uncertainty about what policies would bring it to an end. But another reason for the New Deal's protean character, Brinkley argues, was Roosevelt himself—the closest thing that this book has to a protagonist. Brinkley has always insisted on the important role of individuals in history, and FDR is a classic example of the individual who mattered.[20]

He put his personal imprint on the New Deal. Notably, though, while he came to define modern liberalism, FDR wasn't himself theoretically inclined. He once described his ideology by saying "I am a Christian and a Democrat—that's all." Brinkley calls him "a man for all seasons, all parties, and all ideologies."[21]

This is a bit incomplete. Roosevelt did define himself as a liberal and explicitly rejected terms like *socialist* or *radical*.[22] But his liberalism was obviously pragmatic in nature—its pragmatism constituting its chief difference from the moralistic liberalism of the previous generation's progressives. Characteristically, Brinkley sees both pros and cons in FDR's hardheaded pragmatism. "Roosevelt's fundamentally political nature—his rejection of all but a few fixed principles and his inclination to measure each decision against its likely popular reaction—may have been a significant weakness, as some of his critics claimed, or his greatest strength, as others insist," he writes. "His challenge was to mediate among their diverse and often conflicting views." In a subsequent chapter, Brinkley argues that doubt about whether the New Deal possessed an internal coherence extended well beyond the president. "I really do not know what the basic principle of the New Deal is," says Alvin Hansen. "I know from my experience in the government that there are as many conflicting opinions among the people in Washington under this administration as we have in the country at large." Brinkley directs our attention to the inconsistencies and disagreements that Hansen observed.[23]

For a while, these inconsistencies troubled policy makers. But eventually, in Brinkley's telling, the New Dealers—perhaps not fully consciously—made a virtue of what had been a liability. They came to regard the absence of an overarching vision as a kind of vision unto itself, a gift of flexibility. Instead of eradicating problems, government would manage them.

This shift happened for two reasons. First, Brinkley writes, "The war . . . pushed a fear of totalitarianism (and hence a generalized wariness about excessive state power) to the center of American political thought." He notes, "Liberals who had once admired the collective character of some European governments looked with horror at the totalitarian states America was now fighting and saw in them a warning about what an excessively powerful state could become." Liberals felt with new urgency the need to protect the rights of free speech and political dissent and human rights more generally as well as the principles of equality under the law for racial and religious minorities—all of which totalitarian regimes denied. Although *Liberalism and Its Discontents* includes few essays about foreign policy, Brinkley recognizes that the fight against Nazism and communism presented liberals with a stark choice about the future of not just the country but also the world. In articulating the case against these brutal regimes, liberals rediscovered their core principles of civil rights and civil liberties, freedom of speech and freedom of conscience, which the Nazis and communists sought to crush.[24]

Much of this is implicit in *Liberalism and Its Discontents*. Much more central to Brinkley's story of liberalism's transformation were the failures of state planning at home. Within a few years, he notes, the "sorry history" of the National Recovery Administration, which was struck down by the Supreme Court in 1935, and the inefficacy of other statist solutions that Roosevelt attempted gave New Dealers "a sobering lesson in what *not* to do again." Thurman Arnold, Henry Wallace, and many others soured on such blunt approaches aimed at restructuring "the corporate world." They came instead to devise more supple and less coercive methods—one might say more liberal methods—to "raise purchasing power and stimulate aggregate demand."[25]

Brinkley doesn't moralize in his writing, but he writes of the pivot from ambitious state planning to flexible economic management with a tinge of ruefulness. Why this shift should be seen as a cause for sadness instead of celebration isn't clear. It is true that communists, socialists, and other left-wingers in the 1930s scorned FDR as insufficiently radical (as did New Left historians in the 1960s and 1970s), but that has never been Brinkley's worldview. And, in fact, the liberalism that emerged from Roosevelt's presidency underwrote an era of stunning achievements in public policy and social progress. It witnessed shared prosperity, growing opportunity, expanding rights, historic strides toward racial and religious equality, a heyday for labor, and broad support for government aid to education, science, medicine, and research—"a Periclean age," in the words of John McCloy.[26] Yet Brinkley intimates that despite these extraordinary results, the transformation in liberalism led somehow to a retreat from something nobler, even a hollowing out. He never explicitly posits a causal link between "the end of reform" and liberalism's later discontents, but he strongly implies one.

When we get to Brinkley's essays on the 1960s, we begin to understand the link better. These essays, many of them book reviews, don't fit snugly into the narrative begun by the chapters on the New Deal. But they're similar in character in that they probe the debilitating tensions within twentieth-century American liberalism: tensions between its mandate to promote social progress and its attachment to social order, between its idealism and its pragmatism, and between its desire to uphold a universalist vision and its need to accommodate emerging assertions of racial, sexual, religious, and ethnic differences. The rights-based individualism that emerged from the New Deal, in Brinkley's account, lacked the depth, emotional content, or perhaps the nimbleness to resolve these tensions, which in the end were finessed rather than tackled. They remain with us today.

In "Icons of Establishment," an amalgam of a book review and a magazine profile, Brinkley assesses the unelected policy makers Henry Stimson and John McCloy—classic American statesmen who shuttled among law and finance and government, holding high posts in administrations led by presidents of both parties. Should we think of these wise men, who served over many decades, as admirable practitioners of a responsible, non-ideological foreign policy that brought America stability and security? Or were they paragons of a privileged elite, insufficiently attuned to democratic currents, whose anticommunism and grandiose sense of destiny stifled the aspirations of Third World peoples? Brinkley, typically, sees both sides and steers a middle course. Ultimately, he finds more significance once again in these men's personal qualities—the "certitude, elitism, and self-conscious integrity" as well as the "smugness, insularity, and moral myopia"—than in any vision they advanced for America's role in the world. He thus shows us, with neither rancor nor reverence, the dual-sided nature of one variety of postwar liberalism.[27]

Brinkley exhibits a similar ambivalence toward John F. Kennedy, using him to grapple with the strains between liberalism's idealistic and realistic sides. "The historical John Kennedy, as opposed to the Kennedy of legend, was a cautious, practical, skillful politician, driven by political realism much more than by lofty ideals," Brinkley writes in a 1993 essay. He maintains that Kennedy's popular image as an idealist didn't correspond to his real (and realist) self. In this case, Brinkley perhaps draws the contrast too sharply. The prevailing public images of political leaders may often be partial or distorted, but they usually express actual qualities. However romanticized our memories of JFK, he did promote a dynamic, positive view of government—a decidedly liberal vision. "Kennedy's image of mission and purpose and idealism," Brinkley notes, marked "a time when it was possible to believe that politics could be harnessed to their highest aspirations for themselves and for their country . . . a time when the nation's capacities seemed limitless, when its future seemed unbounded, when it was possible to believe that the United States could solve social problems and accomplish great deeds without great conflict and without great cost." Returning his readers to the present, Brinkley continues: "He is a reminder, too, of how much more difficult it has proved to confront those problems than the promise of the 1960s suggested."[28]

In the Kennedy essay, Brinkley was asking whether JFK's inspirational summonses had unrealistically raised hopes for dramatic progress. And after debunking the Camelot image, he goes on to conclude that Kennedy boosters such as Arthur M. Schlesinger Jr. were correct: that "Kennedy did set in motion . . . powerful forces of change. He did evoke a sense of energy and ambition that inspired a generation (and inspires many still). He did come to symbolize . . . a new sense of mission in American life, tied to an expansive vision of committed and active government."[29] This was a liberalism reminiscent of FDR's—frank and sure and incisive.

Interestingly, in *Liberalism and Its Discontent*, the figure Brinkley seems to admire most is not Kennedy but Allard Lowenstein, whose life and politics Brinkley explored in a review of William Chafe's biography, *Never Stop Running*. A student activist and anti–Vietnam War congressman who led the "Dump Johnson" campaign of 1967–68, Lowenstein straddled the worlds of New Left radicalism and institutional liberalism. He serves here as a lens to examine the tensions between those two political tendencies. Lowenstein, says Brinkley, "had much of the passion and idealism and energy of the New Left, but he was himself always firmly committed to, even if at times skeptical of, the liberalism of his youth—convinced that within it could be found a way both of creating profound social change and of preserving the essential institutions of American life." In particular, Lowenstein held that liberalism's leaders hadn't sufficiently prioritized racial equality in the past. Yet at the same time he contended that the defiant racial and ethnic particularism that began to flourish in the 1960s and 1970s threatened liberalism's appeal as a unifying philosophy. His ability to criticize both the complacency of the Democratic establishment and the shortsightedness of New Left radicalism represented the kind of unsparing clarity of vision that liberals needed. "It seems unlikely," Brinkley adds, again returning to the present moment, "that Lowenstein would ever have found the political world of the 1980s and the 1990s a comfortable place" because liberalism had by then "self-consciously shed the crusading idealism that, to Lowenstein, was its most important and redeeming quality."[30]

Although the main thread of *Liberalism and Its Discontents* traces the history of the problems bedeviling late twentieth-century American liberalism, the book also includes edifying treatments of other political traditions and ideologies that were advanced in opposition to the dominant liberalism—populism, radicalism, and conservatism. Their successes and failures also shed light on liberalism's fortunes.

Brinkley deals with populism not just in his book *Voices of Protest* but also in an essay in *Liberalism and Its Discontents* about Huey Long, the Louisiana demagogue who galvanized opposition to FDR in the early 1930s. The essay can be seen as a companion piece to *Voices of Protest*. It is an extended reckoning and critique of the portraits of Long limned by two writers who did the most to frame understandings of the Kingfish before *Voices of Protest* was written: biographer T. Harry Williams and novelist Robert Penn Warren. Although Brinkley rejects Williams's overly sympathetic take on Long, he sees some validity in Williams's "emphasis on Long's achievements and . . . tolerance for (and at times even celebration of) Long's unorthodox methods."[31] The essay has implications for liberalism too: Brinkley suggests that when liberalism fails or falters, as it did in the early New Deal years, it invites others from outside the liberal tradition to step in—others whose popular appeal liberals should not lightly dismiss. Long's ability to stir the masses not only contained the obvious warnings about the public's susceptibility to demagoguery but also offered lessons about populism's attractive qualities—passion, emotion, clarity, simplicity—that liberalism itself often seemed to be lacking.

If Brinkley is surprisingly charitable toward his populists, in "The Therapeutic Radicalism of the New Left," he is strikingly harsh in evaluating 1960s radicalism. A review of two seminal books about the New Left by Maurice Isserman and James Miller, the essay puts forward a counterintuitive but compelling argument for the New Left's failure: that the movement "did not so much betray its commitments to 'participatory democracy' and 'personal authenticity' as succumb to them."[32] Like the liberalism of the post–New Deal era (and indeed like all ideologies put into political practice), New Left radicalism contained clashing tendencies. It began with a strain of collectivism or communitarianism but included as well a call to individual self-realization. The former tendency held some promise in Brinkley's view, and he is most sympathetic to early New Left undertakings like the Economic Research and Action Project of SDS, which helped poor people in urban communities. But he faults the New Left for descending into a narcissistic politics of the self. Radicals successfully prodded the Democratic Party, and many other leading liberal institutions and individuals, to move leftward on various issues, most notably on the Vietnam War. But they never overthrew the Hartzian individualism—the foundational importance of individual rights and equality under the law—that set the boundaries of American political discourse. The dream of collectivism did not get very far.

The final and strongest of liberalism's rivals has been the conservatism of the post-1960s era. Brinkley's essay on the postwar right, "The Problem of American Conservatism," conceives of postwar conservatism as fundamentally a reaction and correction to liberalism. Where post–New Deal liberalism came to be seen as too statist and bureaucratic, conservatism defended the free market; where the liberalism of the Warren Court and the civil rights movement fostered a rights-based individualism, conservatism held up the norms of the family and the community; where liberalism championed cosmopolitan, universal values, conservatism reasserted tradition and order. Brinkley doesn't pinpoint when and why conservatism began to rival liberalism as a public philosophy for the nation. But—in a notable contrast with the argument of *The End of Reform*—"The Problem of American Conservatism" points to events of the 1960s, and not the New Deal, as the main cause of this shift. The civil rights movement and subsequent movements for equality, the Great Society and its expansion of government's role, the Vietnam War and the subsequent liberal retreat from internationalism, the revolution in manners and morals, the across-the-board revolt against established authority—these developments called liberalism's wisdom and efficacy into question with broad swaths of the public, including many of its longtime adherents, and made rival ideologies more attractive. In trying to explain why liberals found it so hard to rally voters in the 1970s and 1980s, Brinkley points not to the abandonment of "reform" in the 1930s and 1940s but to the increasing discomfort of liberal politicians and spokesmen, starting in the 1960s, with the language of patriotism, family, propriety, and responsibility. "The politics of the 1980s and 1990s suggest," he writes, that "the effort to make the values and assumptions of liberal, secular Americans the value of all Americans . . . has failed."[33]

So how did we get from the 1960s to the present? Apart from a few hints, *Liberalism and Its Discontents* doesn't seek to answer that big question. Indeed, it includes few essays that deal at all with America since the 1960s. But its clues and leads and suggestions are, to use Hofstadter's phrase, "the conception of a single mind"—a mind that, perhaps more than that of any historian of his era, has thought deeply about liberalism's vicissitudes and fortunes. If *Liberalism and Its Discontents* as a book is to leave a legacy as powerful and tangible as the reams of scholarship prompted by Brinkley's seminal essay on conservatism, it can do so by inspiring the next generation of political historians to explore what happened to liberalism after the 1960s. The next frontier in contemporary political history may well be to explain why liberalism fell on such hard times—and also why it has continued, despite the headwinds, to achieve some startling victories.

5

Objectivity and Its Discontents

REFLECTIONS ON *THE PUBLISHER*

NICOLE HEMMER

Political historians give little attention to the news media as a political institution—a force that substantively shapes how laws are developed, presidencies constrained, elections decided, and public opinion shaped. Although works of political history are rife with accounts of individual journalists, publications, and broadcasters, the media as a whole are regularly treated as atmospheric rather than structural. They constitute a powerful institutional and political force that too often escapes historians' direct analytical gaze.

Media historians—some, at least—try to credit the importance of the media as an entity in the course of historical events. And Alan Brinkley—although seldom classified as a media historian in the way that Susan Douglas or Michael Schudson is—has long been attuned to the interplay of media and politics, particularly as forces in the making and unmaking of American liberalism. Consider the two volumes that currently bookend his impressive body of work. Both *Voices of Protest* and *The Publisher* tell the story of activists seeking to bring about political change largely through the use of media. In *Voices of Protest*, radio was the preferred medium; in *The Publisher*, it was the weekly newsmagazine. And even though Henry Luce, the founder and longtime editor in chief of *Time* magazine, may seem a world apart from the radio preacher Charles Coughlin and the Louisiana politician Huey Long, the three men shared two things: an antipathy toward FDR and a belief that they could best achieve their political goals through media work.[1]

Brinkley's analysis of these figures' media activism reveals that media played a constitutive role in the making and unmaking of the New Deal order. In the powerful and consolidated media environment of midcentury America, ideas of consensus and objectivity could be questioned but not dethroned—at least not until they began collapsing under their own weight in the 1960s. *Voices of Protest* showed how Long and Coughlin, as critics of the New Deal, turned to the airwaves to build a political base from which to challenge Roosevelt's agenda. Mirroring Roosevelt's own efforts to use radio to persuade Americans through his fireside chats, Coughlin and Long battled for hearts and minds—and, for a brief time, votes—in the same way, seeing the new broadcast medium as an essential component of modern political activism. Radio helped Roosevelt build and maintain a powerful coalition, but it also helped his opponents knit together national opposition movements even at the height of the New Deal's popularity.

There were limits, though, to this type of media activism, ones that Luce would run into as well. Brinkley notes that the time and energy poured into radio programs distanced both men from their organizational efforts, which petered out after a few years. It was one thing for a president, who relied on the party to organize voters, to spend his time on radio. The two populist leaders had a rougher go of it. For Luce, on the other hand, running a media empire absorbed all his time and energy. Yes, he would dabble in politics, throwing his energies and influence behind candidates, but the organizational work of politics never held his attention.

Whereas *Voices of Protest* recovered the ideas and actions of people outside the emerging New Deal order, *The Publisher* focuses on someone working at the heart of it. Luce did not work as a Roosevelt supporter— he was a Republican and a Roosevelt critic—but in an era of a rough bipartisan consensus on foreign and domestic policy, he was nonetheless an architect of the era's soft liberal accord. In assessing Luce's career as one of the leading publishers of the twentieth century, Brinkley shows how

Luce wielded his media empire to try, with varying degrees of success, to shape American politics. Luce made a series of business and editorial decisions designed to promote the policies, candidates, and ideas that he believed in, particularly through his magazines *Time* and *Life*. He advocated the American century (his view that America should, starting with World War II, assume the helm of a new global order), he plumped internationalist candidates like Wendell Willkie and Dwight Eisenhower, and he advanced definite opinions about World War II and the Cold War—going so far as to fire writers such as Theodore White who contradicted his positions. In doing these things, Luce believed he was using Time, Inc., to save not only America but also the world.

Throughout *The Publisher*, Brinkley plays with the ideas of objectivity and consensus—ideas at the heart of midcentury journalism and politics—to create a new line of analysis about the development of American liberalism, one that has media activists at its heart. Even though he began his career writing about media activists, *The Publisher* is the sort of book he would not have been able to write in the early 1980s. Where *Voices of Protest* sought to understand how radio activists used their medium to challenge the New Deal, *The Publisher* went into the belly of the beast, tackling all the contradictions and challenges of midcentury liberalism, broadly understood, from the inside. The view of liberalism in this book builds on the complex, capacious, incomplete liberalism that Brinkley mapped in *Liberalism and Its Discontents*, a liberalism that might not have had space for, say, Charles Coughlin but certainly made room for Huey Long.

In bringing media activists into the heart of the liberal project and in showing how they both reflected and reinscribed its messy contradictions, Brinkley displays the power of media figures as political actors. They are as central to the process of defining and redefining liberalism as the elected officials and political theorists more commonly credited for that work.

It should come as no surprise that Brinkley would be sensitive to the power of media. Through his father's career, which began at the height of the television networks' power and ended as cable news and the internet challenged their dominance, he saw up close how news media operated and what influence their creators could have. But writing about television may have hit a little too close to home. Brinkley instead focused on radio and the national newsmagazines. Luce's power, in particular, is not to be underestimated. Another biographer noted that Luce has been called "the most influential private citizen in the America of his day."[2] His empire was vast—*Time, Fortune, Life, House & Home, Sports Illustrated*, and the radio and newsreel production *March of Time*. And it wasn't just the variety of products. By the late 1930s, some seventeen million Americans were reading each issue of *Life* magazine; an estimated twenty million consumed *March of Time*. And he published not only some of the best writers of the age, including Calvin Trillin, Hugh Sidey, Ernest Hemingway, and James Agee, but also top photographers like Dorothea Lange and Robert Capa.

Luce's career effectively began in 1922, when he joined Brit Hadden, a longtime friend and collaborator, to form Time, Inc. They were both twenty-three years old.[3] Young and brash, and with little to lose, Luce and Hadden believed they could build an influential new magazine. They sallied forth against the emerging dogma in the journalism of their day: objectivity.

Objectivity was not a product of New Deal liberalism, but it was arguably a force that aided its emergence. The origin of the practice of objectivity in journalism is found in the late nineteenth century, when Adolph Ochs bought the *New York Times*. To distinguish the second-rate newspaper from its more popular counterparts, particularly those pioneering new forms of sensationalistic yellow journalism, he dedicated the *Times* to objective reporting. The word *objectivity* wouldn't become a common descriptor of news reporting until the 1920s, but thanks to Ochs, the hallmarks of the practice were part of the paper's reporting from the start of his tenure.[4]

American journalists who practiced objectivity were making a set of claims about truth: that the veracity of their stories could best be evaluated by how well they adhered to standards of disinterestedness, accuracy, factuality, and fairness—and less overtly but no less importantly by their deference to official information and institutional authority. (That last quality would be part of the unmaking of the era of what has been called "high objectivity" in journalism.) During the first half of the twentieth century, as journalism school became a rite of passage for many aspiring reporters and a professional code began to emerge, objectivity became increasingly central to a shared definition of "good reporting."[5]

As a professional standard, objectivity was more of an ideal to strive for than a reality to be achieved. But as an ideal, it shaped journalistic practices and norms for much of the twentieth century. Objectivity had become an expectation for mainstream reporting by the 1930s, reaching the height of its influence in the 1950s and 1960s.

Objectivity had a politics, and it was the politics of liberal consensus. The triumph of objectivity in the postwar era coincided with the rise of Harvard sociologist Daniel Bell's famous idea of the "end of ideology," articulated in his 1960 book of that title. Just as impassioned political stances, in Bell's account, had been pushed aside in favor of the technocratic policies of the postwar era, so, too, had emotion and advocacy in journalism taken a backseat to what philosopher Thomas Nagel later called the "view from nowhere." The politics of technocracy over ideology dovetailed nicely with a journalistic profession that valued objective reporting over emotional appeals, ideologically infused argument, or partisan cheerleading.[6]

It would probably be a step too far to suggest *The Publisher* could be subtitled *Objectivity and Its Discontents*—but the idea of journalistic objectivity stalks its pages. It squats in the corner as Luce and Hadden lay the framework for *Time* as a publication distinct from that bastion of objectivity, the *New York Times*; it lurks in the room as they land on the magazine's house style.

In pushing back against the *Times* and its influence on journalism, Luce and Hadden focused on both the paper's values and its style, two connected concepts. Hadden trashed the Grey Lady as "unreadable." He saw it as prim and corseted. And it was—but for a reason. Its uniform columns, gray monoliths stretching the length of the page, and airless prose were purposeful: the lack of personality and showiness reflected the paper's goal of neutrality.[7]

Not so *Time* magazine. "Timese," the slangy, clangy language of the publication, was a direct rebuttal to the *New York Times*'s voicelessness. Brash and blustery, Timese was beholden to no convention, not sentence structure or usage or coinage. It was all voice—actually voice *and* virility:

the Grey Lady slam was as much about gender as color, the sense that failure to take a stand betrayed softness, even weakness.

Yet for all this, the power of objectivity was irresistible. Brinkley notes that from the start, Luce and Hadden presented *Time* as "objective" and "unbiased." In an era when objectivity was king, they still felt pressured to kneel before the throne. Such assertions showed that the founders of *Time*, unorthodox as they wanted to be, understood the cultural and political power of objectivity and were unwilling to relinquish all claims to it.

But even though *Time* did not yet fully reflect Luce's political opinions in the 1920s and 1930s, it was nonetheless already a deeply opinionated magazine. As Brinkley writes, "Its insistence on expressing its own views on almost everything it reported . . . was a fundamental part of its character." For the founders of *Time*, it was more important to declare objectivity than to practice it, a sign of both the idea's power and its deeply contested nature.[8]

As Luce built his empire, even the ritual genuflections toward objectivity ceased. With world war and the 1940 election approaching, Luce insisted that analysis must give way to political advocacy. Building a bridge between objectivity and advocacy, he argued that his magazines should create a "journalism of information *with a purpose*." That description was a better fit for the muckraking magazines of the early twentieth century than the objective reporting that ruled over at the *Times*. But Luce had big political goals, and he wasn't about to abandon the powerful media corporation he controlled in order to achieve them.[9]

Nor was Luce shy about his political aims. Luce was invested in strengthening the Republican Party—although he was far less conservative than the newspaper barons who wanted the party to tilt hard right. By the time of the 1940 campaign, Luce had his reporters advocate for his favored candidate, Wendell Willkie, who in May was polling at only 3 percent in his bid for the Republican nomination. So heavy was the pressure to promote Willkie that one *Time* correspondent cabled from the campaign train: "Take me off this train. All I can do is sit at the typewriter and write, 'Wendell Willkie is a wonderful man. Wendell Willkie is a wonderful man.'"[10]

In promoting Republican candidates, Luce was joining a robust tradition, one that had been bedeviling Franklin Roosevelt since he entered office. Tensions ran high between Roosevelt and the men he dubbed the "press lords," newspaper publishers who made no secret of their anti–New Deal sympathies. Typical of these press lords was Frank Gannett, founder of the Gannett Corporation and owner of several New York newspapers, who helped found the National Committee to Uphold Constitutional Government in 1937. A short-lived organization meant to counter Roosevelt's court-packing plan, the committee sought to convince "leaders of thought" that Roosevelt was a dictator in the making whose plans for a managed economy would send the United States down the totalitarian path paved by Italy and Germany. In addition to his work for the committee, Gannett sought to organize the anti–New Deal vote in the 1938 midterms and made his own quixotic presidential bid in 1940.[11]

Although Gannett was unusually involved in electoral politics and political organizing, he was not the only press lord arrayed against the New Deal. Roy Howard of the Scripps-Howard newspaper chain, William Hearst of the Hearst conglomerate, and Robert McCormick of the *Chicago Tribune* were all outspoken supporters of the Republican Party. McCormick shaped the editorial pages of his *Chicago Tribune* into one of the central sites of protest against the growing federal state.[12]

Because of the prominence of publishers like Luce and the press lords, the main complaint about the news media in this era was directed not against liberals but against conservatives. Liberal commentator George Hamilton Combs, debating press bias with conservatives Fulton Lewis Jr. and William Buckley in 1955, complained that the main barrier to effective Democratic governance was "a preponderantly, in fact almost exclusively, Republican press." His was a common charge, not just in the New Deal era but for much of the twentieth century, until conservatives unseated it in the Nixon era with their countercharge of "liberal media bias."[13]

As Brinkley shows, again and again Luce claimed that blending advocacy and news was not only legitimate but also morally right. Others at the magazine did the same. A telling incident is Luce's long battle with Theodore White, who regularly sent *Time* editors unfavorable reports on the Chiang regime in China. Luce, a booster for both China and Chiang, felt White was blinded by his dislike of the regime and his sympathy for the communists. As Brinkley notes, it was a battle born not

of difference but of similarity: "They saw journalism as a form of advocacy; and as their opinions diverged, their relationship inevitably frayed
and ultimately collapsed precisely because they both had passionate views
that they believed needed to be expressed."[14]

The conflict between Luce and White reminds us that objectivity was
not the sole value governing twentieth-century journalism. At the same
time that Ochs was remaking the *New York Times* into a vehicle of voicelessness, another set of journalists was offering a competing vision. Writing
for newspapers and magazines, muckrakers viewed journalism as a site of
activism, a venue for political and social change. Far from exiling emotion,
they wrote empathy into every line; far from repudiating politics, they wove
it into every phrase. They had demonstrable impact, leading the charge for
a number of progressive reforms that, in many ways, laid the groundwork
for the New Deal.

In setting out the ways that Luce negotiated and navigated the objectivity ideal, Brinkley shows that the advocacy press never really went away,
never really receded into the background—instead, it absorbed objectivity's
authority. As such, he shows that objectivity was both a powerful and an
embattled idea in midcentury America, much like liberalism itself.

If objectivity was the center of gravity for media at midcentury, liberal
consensus was the center of gravity for politics. In the introduction to
The Publisher, Brinkley argues that Luce's magazines reflected "a set of
values and assumptions in which Luce believed and that he assumed were
(or at least should be) universal. Part of his considerable achievement was
his ability to provide an image of American life that helped a generation of
readers believe in an alluring, consensual image of the nation's culture."[15]

As Brinkley's other work has shown, this was a remarkably contentious
consensus. Indeed, consensus, like objectivity, was more an argument about
how American politics and culture *should* work than a description of how
they did.

Yet consensus was a powerful force shaping politics during the era of
New Deal liberalism. This was an era when institutional neutrality was
considered the special genius of the American system. In a world roiling

with the terrors of totalitarianism—fascism and communism—American politicians and intellectuals celebrated the technocratic state and its institutions as spaces free from the passions and pitfalls of ideology. The connection between the anti-ideology ethos and American politics was a direct one. Two years after the publication of Bell's *End of Ideology*, President John F. Kennedy declared that the major domestic challenges of the era "do not relate to the basic clashes of philosophy and ideology, but to the ways and means of reaching common goals." This was a statement of faith: with the black freedom struggle in full swing, conservatism on the rise, and a left-wing student movement beginning to challenge the core ideas of liberalism, ideology was far from banished. Still, Kennedy's belief in a national consensus pursued through dispassionate management rather than ideological clashes was a broadly shared faith.[16]

That is, it was a faith shared by those who saw themselves as part of what historian Arthur M. Schlesinger Jr. called "the vital center" in his 1949 book of that title. Schlesinger (who wrote Kennedy's 1962 speech quoted above) chided those on both the left and the right who did not hew to this agreed-on middle, which viewed New Deal domestic policies and liberal anticommunism as the only viable Cold War position. Luce had many political convictions that were quite different from Schlesinger's—Luce was a free-market conservative, Schlesinger a New Deal liberal. But Luce could nonetheless join with Schlesinger as part of the vital center because of their shared commitment to liberal anticommunism, as opposed to the anti-democratic creeds of the ideological left and right. Thus, Luce as a moderate, establishment conservative could shape the consensus from within, whereas those on the far left and the far right had to challenge it from without.[17]

This consensus was, paradoxically, understood as both liberal and non-ideological, relying on an understanding of liberalism as a sort of technocratic, rather than passion-driven, project. Although the mainstream establishment may have been quite comfortable with the assumptions undergirding that understanding, neither the socialistic left nor the right of what would later be called the conservative movement agreed. Where defenders of consensus saw neutrality, its opponents saw a slick bit of propaganda, a mask slid over an overtly ideological project. Indeed, claims to neutrality heightened their opposition because these claims were used to relegate them to the fringes—to suggest that, as the real ideologues, they were illegitimate in an era that had put to rest such nonsensical, dangerous politics. Both the left and the right thus sought to expose the ideological agendas of these ostensibly neutral institutions, attacking the press's claims of objectivity, the universities' claims of neutrality, and the government's claims of technocracy.

In time, their view—their politics—would win.

Consensus was itself an ideology, eventually cracked apart by the very political groups it had attempted to consign to the fringes. But for a few decades, it was successfully sustained by bipartisan consensus in politics and a narrowly proscribed sense of objectivity in media. Luce was a major contributor to that project.

An opponent of the New Deal, Luce may not seem a likely champion of consensus. Yet throughout *The Publisher*, Brinkley shows how the *Time* empire contributed to the ideas of broad cultural unity, prosperity, American exceptionalism, and anticommunism that underwrote the liberal consensus. This was self-evidently true in Luce's famous essay, "The American Century," which appeared as an editorial in the February 17, 1941, issue of *Life* magazine. In it, Luce made the case for U.S. intervention in World War II in sweeping, world-historic terms: America had an opportunity to pick up the reins of world leadership, to shape the future and the world in its image, to ensure that the twentieth century would indeed be the American century.[18] It was a bold, influential essay, and following the war, Luce's vision did indeed become the backbone of America's foreign-policy consensus.

But Luce made the case for consensus far more visibly, and arguably far more powerfully, in his picture magazine, *Life*. When it launched in the 1930s, *Life* had as its core philosophy likability. That made it an Eisenhower magazine in a Roosevelt age. But Brinkley notes that likability was itself a political stance. It "rejected the critical view of social reality" that documentary photographers in the Farm Security Administration brought to their work during the Depression. The politics of the photographs in *Life* and the photographs of someone like Dorothea Lange were worlds apart.[19]

Life presented its politics as a sort of antipolitics, much the same way that objectivity and consensus did. In the postwar era, *Life* magazine served as the photo album of the liberal consensus. Brinkley lays out the democratic idea behind *Life*, "a magazine for everyone." "Just as *Life* in the 1940s had been the great chronicler of the war," Brinkley writes, "it became in the 1950s the great chronicler of prosperity and consensus." The magazine celebrated business and labor, science and suburbia, and, above all, the middle class.[20]

It also had what was, for its time, a radical empathy, finding the humanity in all its subjects, wealthy or poor, white or black, native-born or immigrant. Its text even pointed to the humanity of Klansmen, a detail that suggests the moral complications of finding the good in everything. There was a politics to that as well—and a moral complexity not unique to *Life* and Luce. It was of a piece with a New Deal coalition that included white southern Democrats, some of them members of the Klan, as well as African Americans lobbying for recognition of their civil rights. That coalition relied on a politics of moral compromise: accepting and empowering the parts of the coalition that refused to recognize the rights and humanity of the other.

The overriding message: This was not a country that required a revolution. It was a country where the Good Life already reigned—until it didn't. *Life* begin slipping into irrelevance as the liberal consensus cracked apart. (The magazine folded in 1972, though it would return in various incarnations; Luce himself died in 1967.) As Brinkley argues, a magazine dedicated to the Good Life didn't have a place in a country whose loose consensus had been shattered by political assassination, declining prosperity, rising civil rights movements, angry white backlash, a failing war abroad, and a frail consensus. Government had been at the heart of the consensus; faith in government was lost.

As consensus crumbled, so, too, did the objectivity ideal that helped sustain it. Under pressure from activists on both the left and the right, from critics of the war and critics of the government, from journalists hungering to be both advocates and adversaries, the objectivity ideal did not disappear, but it lost its gravitational pull. Objectivity had to share space with alternative media values and, in the process, underwent its own redefinition.

Unable to retain deference to government sources as a defining characteristic of objectivity and unable to maintain that ideology had actually lost its influence in American life, journalists adapted: they offered instead objectivity by way of balance, serving up the views of the left and the right and tasking their audiences with sorting out who was right. American politics, and American media, had passed into a new era.

This radical transformation of media values did not simply mirror the changes happening in politics. Rather, their mutual collapse reveals the constitutive role that media played in the making, and unmaking, of American liberalism. Brinkley never fully theorized this relationship—it emerges in his work less as an explicit argument than an implicit one. Still, the combination of his first and final works with his broad corpus of analysis on the rise and fall of American liberalism offers a powerful, if subtle, argument: we cannot understand the flows of American politics without understanding the impact of American media.

What this suggests for other eras is that we attend more closely to, say, how partisan newspapers helped create the American party system, against the wishes of late eighteenth-century statesmen, or to the way fractured and decentralized media are shaping our current political moment. Whatever the subject of study, political historians would do well to follow in Brinkley's footsteps, bringing media to the center of their analysis as he so regularly and masterfully has done in his own.

6

The Liberal's Imagination

"THE PROBLEM OF AMERICAN CONSERVATISM" THEN AND NOW

JEFFERSON DECKER

If you were to measure a work of scholarship by the number of dissertations, journal articles, and books it inspired other historians to write, "The Problem of American Conservatism" may be Alan Brinkley's most influential publication. That is not because the essay, originally published in the *American Historical Review* in 1994, was his most extensively researched or complex article. As he confessed up front, his observations on American conservatism were "not the product of any personal scholarly research on conservatism (or any personal engagement with or sympathy for conservative politics)."[1] Perhaps for that reason, the essay lacked some of the nuances and ironies for which his works on the Great Depression and the New Deal are appreciated. Yet "The Problem of American Conservatism" directly or indirectly inspired all sorts of new scholarship on the American right— including a number of influential books by Brinkley's former students at Columbia University.[2] American conservatism has matured into a vibrant subfield of American political history since the mid-1990s, in part because so many historians took up the intellectual and historiographical challenges that Brinkley laid out more than two decades ago.[3]

This was possible because the "problem" that Brinkley identified was, in part, sociological. Historians of the United States, he wrote, had "displayed impressive powers of imagination in creating sympathetic accounts of many once obscure areas the past." But a "basic lack of sympathy for the right"—most professional historians are liberal or left-wing in their personal politics—made them less inclined to perform the same duties for those with conservative or right-wing perspectives.[4] Moreover, he might have added, would-be historians of the right may have wondered whether such imaginative feats might be viewed with suspicion by the committees of scholars (again, mostly left-wing and liberal) who hire junior faculty or evaluate them for tenure. So by recasting American conservatism as a problem that desperately needed to be solved (or, in another passage, as an "orphan" that needed to be adopted), Brinkley helped to make new work on American conservatism seem not only legitimate but also urgent.[5] It is disappointing that it sometimes takes a "certification narrative" from a well-known scholar to encourage graduate students and junior scholars to pursue a certain line of research.[6] And some excellent research on the American right no doubt was under way before "The Problem of American Conservatism" saw print or would have happened even in its absence. But Brinkley pushed open a door, and a number of us eventually rushed through it.

Of course, there is a potential peril—another "problem"—when any essay proves this influential—and particularly so when its author is not himself a specialist in every aspect of the subject matter. Some of Brinkley's readers may have become too attached to his framework for describing the American right, to the point that related stories or different analytical approaches have been ignored. Others may have accepted Brinkley's injunction that "conservatives were people whose ideas or grievances should be taken seriously"[7] without thinking critically about what it means to take people "seriously" or what the potential pitfalls are of letting political actors or social movements speak for themselves. It is possible for historians to be too polite to their sources—to perform acts of imagination so sympathetic that they lose any sense of critical distance or independent judgment. This can be particularly problematic if the sources in question are being less than completely honest—with the public or with themselves. Perhaps historians need to consider different ways of approaching conservative ideas and actions— and how conservatives have helped to shape American political history.

Recent events in American politics make that sort of critical reappraisal more important than ever. In the 2016 presidential election, Republican voters embraced the candidacy of a vulgar, louche businessman, even though almost all of the leading voices and institutions of the conservative "movement" initially lined up in opposition. Donald Trump's personal exploits mock the preferences for moral order professed by most of the conservatives mentioned in Brinkley's essay. Perhaps more important, Trump broke (at least during his campaign) with conservative orthodoxy on a large number of issues, from trade and the welfare state to the Iraq War and Russia, while appealing to cultural grievances in ways that even some of his GOP allies denounced as offensive or racist. In 2016, the issues that once seemed to be central to the appeal of American conservatism failed to motivate large numbers of Republican primary voters, and the institutions of the conservative movement were unable to prevent a hostile takeover of the Republican Party. This is as good a moment as ever to reconsider what we thought we knew about the American right—and how we should study it in the future.

For Brinkley, the problem of American conservatism began with definitions. There was no clear consensus—or even much of a historiographical literature—on what constituted "the right" in an American context. Alexis de Tocqueville was at least partially correct back in the nineteenth century when he pointed out that the United States lacked the formal aristocracy based on inherited rank and privilege that formed the social foundation for the kind of conservative politics that existed in most of Europe. Louis Hartz was likewise at least partially correct in the mid-twentieth century when he noted that many U.S. "conservatives" drew philosophical inspiration from many of the same eighteenth-century thinkers and principles that U.S. liberals did. That meant that American conservatism had neither a consistent basis in class politics nor a distinctive philosophical pedigree. Moreover, spokesmen for American conservatism rarely offered a coherent set of principles or ideas that could be easily characterized with consistency. "Conservatism," Brinkley explained "encompasses a broad range of ideas, impulses, and constituencies, and many conservatives feel no obligation to choose among the conflicting, even incompatible, impulses that fuel their politics."[8] Historians of the right, in other words, face a bewildering variety of conservatisms, each of which can seem as if it has a history all its own.

Partly for these reasons, several major schools of twentieth-century American historical writing ignored or discounted conservatism rather than tackling it head-on. For example, many of the consensus historians of the mid-twentieth century dismissed conservatism as a political outlier and second-rate intellectual tradition. They believed that liberalism, at least as a philosophical tradition, had dominated the American political imagination from the founding of the republic to the present. That meant that even those Americans who called themselves conservatives shared a philosophically liberal understanding of state and society, based on a shared commitment to representative government and moderately regulated capitalism. Conservatism was widely considered a cause bereft of real ideas—and thus was easy to ignore.

The consensus scholars eventually faced a challenge by various New Left historians of 1960s and 1970s, who brought conflict over fundamental principles back into the story of the American past. But the New Left historians, with a few exceptions, wanted to uncover the history of radical, populist, or left-leaning critiques of liberalism—to show how people on the margins had challenged the vital center. Indeed, some New Left historians treated the centrist, technocratic "corporate liberalism" that emerged in the first half of the twentieth century as the dominant political force to which the outsiders and radicals objected—and thus the only "American conservatism" necessary to explain.[9] To be sure, important works on American conservatism got written and read; for example, Brinkley mentioned (and drew on) George Nash's influential 1976 study of conservative writers, philosophers, and public intellectuals.[10] But the body of research remained small, especially compared to the real-world achievements of conservatives in electoral politics, and much of what did get produced failed to register in the larger historiographical debates among academic historians or shape their larger narratives about U.S. politics.

As a corrective, Brinkley sketched out a few of the major "ideas, impulses, and constituencies" of the twentieth-century right that were distinct from— and directly opposed to—corporate or vital-center liberalism. He began with a tradition of antistatism that had challenged New Deal–era expansions of federal power in the name of free markets or local autonomy. In the 1940s, the Austrian economist Friedrich von Hayek became an American sensation when *Reader's Digest* condensed his book *The Road to Serfdom* and helped make it a best seller. And antistatist conservatism had natural regional constituencies in American politics. In the South, racial conservatives feared (with good reason) that the federal government would use state power to undermine local institutions and customs in order to secure civil rights for African Americans. In the West, where the federal government is an enormous (if distant) regional landlord, the state has often seemed like an impediment to economic growth and development. "The belief that unfettered economic freedom has been responsible for Western economic growth . . . may be a myth," Brinkley pointed out. But it is nevertheless "a durable one."[11] It meant that libertarian political ideas found a base of support in the political culture of a vast region whose population grew rapidly throughout the twentieth century.

Second, Brinkley discussed a series of "normative concerns" about family, morality, and religion among Americans who valued social stability and civic virtue and who worried about the "cult of liberty" on the left.[12] He offered a number of different examples of these concerns among intellectuals and authors: Russell Kirk's *The Conservative Mind*, which attempted to adapt ideas about order and tradition originally associated with Edmund Burke to an American context; Catholic intellectuals like William F. Buckley, who worried about the "relativism and excessive individualism" of modern liberalism; and writers like T. S. Eliot and Willa Cather, who rebelled against the "acquisitive, materialistic values of modern industrial society."[13] Brinkley also examined the intellectual shadow cast by Leo Strauss, the German-Jewish émigré philosopher who believed that modern political thought had "eroded the moral and intellectual foundations of civilization" and whose students developed a thriving subfield within political theory.[14] Traditionalists, Catholics, and Straussians were not simply critical of the "anything goes" attitude that sometimes characterized the liberal cult of liberty; they were also skeptical about the advance and cultural influence of science and technology. Some Straussians developed complicated traditions of hermeneutical textual analysis as an alternative to the empirical modes of thought that they perceived as failing.[15] But normative conservatives did not need to go nearly that far to believe that certain orthodoxies, bits of received wisdom, or hidden truths may be there for a reason or to fear that efforts to rethink or tinker with them might ultimately prove lethal to society.

Finally, and for Brinkley most importantly, was the strand of conservatism marked by religious fundamentalism—especially the resurgence of evangelical Protestantism since the 1970s. Many liberals did not foresee the ferocity of the political battles over abortion, gay rights, or the Equal Rights Amendment that emerged in the later decades of the twentieth century. At a more fundamental level, they struggled to understand how a rebirth of religious fundamentalism could be possible in the first place. "The resurgence of right-wing fundamentalism in the United States has unsettled many liberal and left-oriented scholars because it had seemed to contradict some of their most basic assumptions about modern society," Brinkley argued. "A rational, economically developed society, progressive intellectuals have tended to believe, does not spurn modernity. It does not reject progress."[16] Yet the late twentieth century demonstrated that millions of Americans could live and work in a society driven by advanced science and high technology—and still believe in biblical inerrancy at home, at church, and in the voting booth. It was difficult, at least for some scholars, to imagine how that was possible—how "rational, stable, intelligent people" could have a "world view radically different from their own."[17]

Even the best efforts of publicists and politicians to reconcile or paper over the contradictions of these three impulses did not produce a single, coherent ideology. Unlike Nash, who emphasized how Buckley and his magazine *National Review* brought libertarians and traditionalists together under a single banner, Brinkley saw these three impulses as distinct and often in tension. Indeed, Brinkley argued, conservatives were better characterized by what they were not than by what they were. They were not a series of hesitant or resistant forces trying to constrain or limit the growth of the federal welfare or regulatory state—to ensure that America got corporate liberalism instead of European-style social democracy. Nor were they know-nothing, parochial types who slowed down the ultimate triumph of science and technology in especially "backward"

parts of the country. Rather, conservatives offered genuine—and genuinely powerful—challenges to the liberal state, cosmopolitan values, and
empirically driven, rationalist modes of thinking. And they generated
popular enthusiasm—often far more enthusiasm than the liberalism they
tried to combat. If historians hoped to understand American politics
in the twentieth century, they needed to have something to say about
conservatives.

In the two decades since "The Problem of American Conservatism" was
published, historians have found a great deal to say about the right—from
its politicians to its institutions to its movement culture and electoral base.
Multiple historians have examined the intellectual histories of free-market
ideas and the challenge to Keynesian economic models. Others have traced
the origins and evolution of the Christian right as a potent force in the
Republican Party and American politics—and still others have documented
the transformations of the Republican Party, southern politics, or the U.S.
Congress.[18] Historians filtered Brinkley's marching orders through their
own interests, intellectual frameworks, and archival constraints, which
meant that some of the subjects raised in "The Problem of American
Conservatism" have gotten much more attention than others. The Christian
right, which now mobilizes millions of voters in every election cycle, has
understandably received more attention from academic historians than
Leo Strauss and his small clique of admirers in academia—though the latter
would still be a fantastic topic for an intellectual historian looking for a new
project.[19] I am not sure the profession is any closer to defining American
conservatism as a coherent ideology than Brinkley was in 1994. But we have
become much more aware of the history and diversity of the American
conservative tradition and better at the acts of "sympathetic imagination"
necessary to reconstruct the lives and worldviews of people with whom
many of us have significant moral and political disagreements.

That research is not uncontroversial. Historians who study the right have
sometimes been accused of being *too* sympathetic in their imagination—
to the point of being naïve about their subject matter. Take one subject
to which Brinkley devoted relatively little attention in "The Problem of

American Conservatism": the conflicts over race, ethnicity, and civil rights that roiled American politics and helped realign the demographic and regional bases of both political parties over the half century following World War II. It would not be crazy to think that a primary impulse—perhaps *the* primary impulse—powering American conservatism in that period was never anxiety over the liberal state or concerns about normative morality so much as the organized defense of advantages based on race and class. To be sure, many self-proclaimed conservatives took courageous stands against bigotry, expended time and political capital trying to make racial integration work, or demonstrated a serious commitment to the well-being of economically disadvantaged communities. But, on balance, the public policies and judicial philosophies promoted by conservatives have favored the interests of white Americans over the interests of racial or religious minorities and the interests of the well-to-do over the interests of the less affluent. Perhaps those interests—as much as opposition to the liberal state or concerns about normative morality—should be front and center in any study of the American right.[20]

This framing mechanism might solve some puzzles that "The Problem of American Conservatism" left unsolved, such as conservativism's rather inconsistent record of antistatism in practice. Race might explain why Republicans have often seemed relatively content with expansive welfare states when the beneficiaries are primarily white people but have focused their fire on programs that seem to benefit African Americans or recent immigrant groups.[21] It might explain why conservatives have supported highly statist wars on drugs and crime so long as blacks and Latinos—and not the children of affluent white people—face the highest rates of incarceration.[22] But it poses a problem for the historian trying to offer sympathetic reconstructions based on archival sources. If defending race- or class-derived social advantages was the point of conservative politics, some conservatives were not always particularly forthcoming about it, even in private correspondence. For that reason, a historian who earnestly reconstructs the world from archival materials runs the risk of passing off the more palatable rationalization as the real motivation. Would that historian be better off approaching the right from a position of skepticism instead of sympathetic imagination? If so, the primary intellectual work might be revelatory: decoding dog-whistle appeals to voters, unearthing hidden agendas, and exposing dishonesty (including forms of self-delusion).[23]

Another, perhaps related, approach would be to examine whether conservatism as a social movement—like all social movements—was ever chiefly about ideas or traditions or simply a way to justify visceral likes and dislikes with the trappings of coherent argument. What if the things that have bound the right together were not commitments to free markets or natural law or biblical literalism (as important as those might have been to certain individuals) but rather a collection of resentments and frustrations directed at a series of perceived domestic enemies (uppity racial minorities, know-it-all college professors, clever lawyers, busybody bureaucrats, smug nonconformists, and the various bad actors all of them were assumed to coddle)? Perhaps American conservatism has always been animated less by the rejection of the liberal state than by deep cultural rifts over the sources of social authority, membership in the American community, and who gets to wield power. This story may, once again, be about race and ethnicity—who counts as a "real American" with a strong claim to cultural citizenship. But it may also be about education, occupation, or regional identity. Do people achieve political and cultural authority because they have succeeded in business, earned an advanced degree, stood at the head of the classroom, led a congregation, had access to a mass-media microphone, or managed to get elected? What happens when one source of cultural authority seems to displace others?[24]

Implicit in both of these alternatives is the notion that scholars should not approach the history of conservatism the same way we approach most other social and political movements. Sure, liberals also have had allied interest groups that need to be placated (even, on many occasions, at the expense of some platonic ideal of the common good); liberals also have had their symbolic politics and appeals to cultural authority, especially the authority conferred by education. But unlike modern conservatives, liberals never had to square defenses of existing, often hereditary, inequalities with an official national commitment to democratic pluralism. Since World War II, it could be argued, U.S. conservatives did—and they could not really square that circle without some degree of obfuscation or denial. If that is true, using the same methodological approach and sympathetic imagination we use to study liberals might lead us astray; it might project a symmetry between social and ideological movements that did not really exist. Better perhaps to take the approach of Nancy MacLean, who, in her recent controversial book on the libertarian right, approaches her subjects as a "fifth column" mounting an inside assault on American democracy—because their ideas and objectives could not otherwise withstand "public scrutiny and rise or fall on their merits."[25]

To be clear, I do not mean to endorse these alternatives as a better way forward. As a matter of temperament and training, I much prefer Brinkley's approach. I am skeptical about historical approaches that reduce compli-cated ideologies to one or two defensive impulses; I worry about prejudging (and thus misreading) historical source material.[26] My book on conserva-tive lawyers and legal activists takes seriously conservative concerns that an expansive regulatory state responding to a nascent environmentalist move-ment placed unfair burdens on property owners and undermined funda-mental institutions of a market-based economy; it would have been beyond presumptuous for me to have read the lives and careers of the people mak-ing those arguments as some roundabout effort to reinforce white privilege. If I had done so, I would have missed a chance to explore what the various conflicts and controversies were within the conservative movement—and how the resolution of those conflicts helped shape the conservative policy agenda.[27] But historians ought to think carefully about how they approach the right and be honest with readers about why they make the choices that they do. Too often historians simply sprinkle a few pejoratives through-out the text, establishing their partisan bona fides without really making a case for a particular historical or methodological approach.[28]

All that said, it is striking to reread "The Problem of American Conservatism" today and find that conflict over civil rights or the racialized realignments of the major U.S. political parties received so little atten-tion from Brinkley in the 1990s. That absence, which was also reflected in some of the early institutional histories of the U.S. right, is itself a problem. It means that Brinkley never really establishes one of the key puzzles that histories of American conservatism need to solve: Why, at many differ-ent points in time and in many different contexts, has the appeal of con-servatism been so disproportionately concentrated among white people?

There are always exceptions, of course, but as a general matter, conservatives have done an exceedingly poor job of attracting black, Latino, and Asian American supporters—even those who share many of their views on normative moral issues or who have made enough money to appreciate upper-income tax cuts. There is presumably some reason for that. If we fail to investigate that impulse, we will do a disservice to history. We will also have a hard time explaining what happened in 2016.

The unexpected presidency of a playboy real estate mogul and reality-television host has magnified some of the intellectual fault lines noted above. For many of those in the conservative "movement"—especially those wedded to the traditions embodied by Buckley and *National Review*— Donald Trump marks a dramatic break from a conservatism founded on a mixture of free-market economics and normative morality.[29] Trump has endorsed protectionist trade barriers and brings a zero-sum approach to deal making that seems to resist even the most basic insights of Adam Smith.[30] He makes a virtue of selfishness, living lavishly while stiffing contractors and creditors.[31] His rise to the presidency calls into question histories of the right that emphasize the consequences of conservative institution building—as most official institutions and media of the American right opposed his campaign, some of them even after he secured the GOP nomination. It also calls into question histories that emphasize the politics of conservative respectability—for example, the marginalization of perceived extremists and explicit racists. From this perspective, Trump's ascendancy seems like a jarring break from the varieties of conservatism that historians influenced by Brinkley have tended to study—or perhaps a revival of an anticosmopolitan, isolationist "old right" many assumed was marginalized decades ago.[32]

At the same time, certain aspects of the Trump phenomenon probably feel distressingly normal to many Americans—especially members of racial, ethnic, or religious minorities. Many Latinos, for example, have probably wondered from time to time how many white people consider them fully "American." They did not need Donald Trump questioning the objectivity of Gonzalo Curiel—an American-born judge with Mexican immigrant parents who handled the mass fraud lawsuit against Trump University—to consider this possibility; Trump's statements on the matter simply confirmed what many already suspected.[33] In comments about African American communities, Trump repeated stereotypes about black criminality and social breakdown that are unfortunately quite common in white America. Democratic pluralism may have triumphed in elite discourse and in the bipartisan boilerplate of mainstream U.S. politics, thanks to national revulsion at the genocidal racism of Nazi Germany and to the heroic efforts of the civil rights movement. But the everyday reality for people of color has never matched the official story or bipartisan slogans. On this view, Trump's break from tradition was his willingness to blurt out what many of his supporters already believed.

For that reason, some scholars have seen Trump more as a figure of continuity than one of change. During the 2016 campaign, for example, historians N. D. B. Connolly and Keisha N. Blain published a mock syllabus for a master course on "Trumpism" that was fascinating for what it excluded as much as for what it included. This document treated Trump not as an aberration or a break from the recent American past but as a representative "product of the American lineage of racism, sexism, nativism, and imperialism." In particular, its authors saw Trump as the fruition of various visible and invisible social transformations over the past quarter century: the gentrification of Manhattan and other select urban areas into a sort of playground for a globe-trotting financial elite, law-and-order policing and prosecutions that fill prisons with young black men, and levels of income inequality not seen since the Roaring Twenties, if we even saw them back then. Works primarily about conservative ideas, institutions, and social movements, especially those written after and influenced by "The Problem of American Conservatism," were not included.[34]

Connolly and Blain did assign reading by Alan Brinkley in the first week of their "course," but that work was not "The Problem of American Conservatism." Rather, it was *Voices of Protest*, Brinkley's book about the New Deal dissidents Huey Long and Father Coughlin. *Voices of Protest* is, of course, also highly relevant to the present as a study of how economic crisis and inequality can push politics toward extremes and of how the lines between populist rabble-rousing and demagoguery are sometimes fuzzy.[35] But the omission of nearly any recent scholarship influenced by "The Problem of American Conservatism" on a historiographical or methodological level in a reading list about a right-wing presidential candidate is a disconcerting statement about the current relevance, at least to some scholars, of that particular scholarly intervention—and the state of the field of historical research that it helped to inspire. Is it possible for Brinkley's essay to have inspired an avalanche of new scholarship—and for little of that scholarship to actually help us comprehend the right-wing regime in power today?[36] Or, as historian Leo Ribuffo recently put it, "Why is there so much scholarship on 'conservatism,' and why has it left the historical profession so obtuse about Trumpism?"[37] Is it time perhaps for historians to move on?

Yet "The Problem of American Conservatism" was never just about conservatism and the "problems" that it caused historians; it was also about the forces shaping American political history more generally. One of Brinkley's central points was the wide gulf between conservatism and corporate liberalism—a distinction that too many historians seemed too eager for too long to elide. Indeed, this was an issue to which Brinkley returned in his response to a symposium about his essay that was convened by the *American Historical Review*. When discussing American conservatism, Brinkley asserted, one cannot consider only the forces that limited liberalism or gave U.S. government its distinctive size and shape; rather, we need to consider root-and-branch challenges to activist government, empirical reasoning, and cosmopolitan values.[38] Today perhaps we might apply a similar skepticism to historical approaches that assume we live in an era of hegemonic "neoliberalism" and consider that state of affairs to be the new "triumph of conservatism." This means understanding the recent success of an antiglobalist, explicitly nationalist right in the United States (and much of Europe) that challenges cosmopolitan values and even, at times, certain forms of free-market orthodoxy. But it might also require the sort of investigation of the successes, failures, and ironies of the contemporary center-left that Brinkley offered in his studies of American liberalism in the 1930s and 1940s.[39] Those investigations might help us contextualize the achievements as well as the limitations of more-recent Democratic administrations—to see how they pushed to expand certain elements of the welfare and regulatory states even as they held their fire or pared back benefits elsewhere. Such research might also help us understand the intense partisan conflicts that raged during those administrations over the legitimacy of interventionist government or the morality of redistributive taxation and spending—even though Bill Clinton and Barack Obama were routinely derided as centrist, pro-corporate sellouts by their critics to the left.

"The Problem of American Conservatism" also reminds us of the fundamental difficulty of confronting "stable, intelligent people" with a worldview that is incompatible with our own. Contemporary liberals sometimes wonder how so many Republicans could doubt that global warming is real at a time when temperatures are rising year after year and it appears possible to watch the polar ice caps melt away in real time. They also wonder why the president of the United States seems to take offhand speculation on *Fox and Friends* with the sort of literalism that some people bring to the Book of Genesis or the Koran. Brinkley did not discuss evolution of right-wing news media directly in "The Problem of American Conservatism," and those media were far less extensive in 1994 than they are today.[40] (The Fox News channel debuted in 1996.) In his reflections on religious fundamentalism, though, Brinkley discussed the challenge of writing the history of people who seem to live in a universe of alternative facts, many of them incompatible with the world that the historian inhabits personally or can reconstruct from the available data. We sometimes assume that our country's various epistemological bubbles are a recent phenomenon, the product of cable news, the internet, or social media. But maybe they are a new manifestation of a deeper American tradition: our frequent embrace of belief systems that simplify our messy reality and purport to explain our place in this world. And if it is too hard for empirically minded college professors to get their heads around that possibility—well, then we might again have a problem.

7

Alan Brinkley and the Revival of Political History

MATTHEW DALLEK

In the modern era, public events are not ephemera; they are often among the central realities of everyday life. No individual, no community in modern America, can live an isolated, unbroken life, insulated from the behavior of the state or national economic institutions.
—Alan Brinkley, "Writing the History of Contemporary America," 1984

In the late 1970s and early 1980s, as Alan Brinkley was emerging as a major scholar of twentieth-century American history, traditional political history was widely perceived to be in decline, if not in crisis. In 1979, the year Brinkley completed his PhD at Harvard, the historian Tony Judt provocatively charged "the new social history" of the 1970s with producing "history with the politics left out."[1] Two years later the historian Peter H. Smith captured a popular view in the profession when he wrote that "the new concern . . . with the daily lives of ordinary people" meant that "there will not be much" political history any more.[2] If the field of political history was not totally dead, it lay, prostrate and abandoned, at the bottom of the heap, at least in the eyes of some contemporary historians. Between the 1970s and the 1990s, as Princeton historian Julian Zelizer has written, the study of political history was "in the professional dumps."[3]

Of Alan Brinkley's many contributions to the field of twentieth-century American history, his leadership in the revival of political history surely ranks among the most important. Over the course of Brinkley's career, political history has enjoyed a remarkable renaissance within the field of U.S. history—thanks in no small measure to the role he played in keeping it alive, charting its future course, and training the next generation of scholars.

As other essayists in this volume have remarked, growing up as the son of a famous newsman in postwar Washington, DC, meant that Brinkley was immersed in national politics practically from the cradle. He came of age intellectually in the milieu of postwar liberalism but also amid the emergence of the New Left. In high school and college, he encountered the writings of consensus scholars who, he has written, "had few doubts about the centrality of liberalism both to their own time, and to the whole of the American experience."[4] But he also encountered the New Left's critiques of liberalism's failures and vulnerabilities. An appreciation of both liberalism's strengths and its limitations was to mark Brinkley's scholarship; so was a healthy appreciation of alternative, antiliberal American political traditions. In one of several interviews with Brinkley's students and colleagues conducted for this essay, Michael Flamm, a professor of history at Ohio Wesleyan University, suggests that his former adviser's career served "as a bridge between the radicalism of the New Left and the liberalism of the vital center." He says that "the New Left raised powerful and profound questions about liberalism" and that Brinkley absorbed these questions in lasting ways and began to search for the internal defects that had drained some of liberalism's power and undercut its seemingly unassailable position in American politics. Equally so, Brinkley's ability to straddle these clashing worlds further enabled him to take "the challenges and critiques from the right" and from populist dissidents seriously.[5]

At the time Brinkley emerged from Harvard's PhD program, political history was not quite as dead as the jeremiads might have suggested. If the "traditional" political history of events and elites was démodé, a rising generation of historians was beginning to lay the groundwork for a new kind of political history. Young scholars such as Lizabeth Cohen, Alan Dawley, Gary Gerstle, Michael Kazin, Roy Rosenzweig, and Sean Wilentz, though predominantly regarded as "new labor" historians, were writing histories of popular political mobilization. Cohen, for instance, demonstrated how working people in Chicago, in her words "joined together to undertake new kinds of political action" and shaped the trajectory of the New Deal through their social and political organizing.[6] Work of this kind was clearly of a piece with Brinkley's first book, *Voices of Protest*, which charted the social and ideological underpinnings of Depression-era dissident politics.[7]

Together, these scholars bridged the study of political elites, ideas, and institutions with social processes in a way that would appeal to subsequent generations of scholars, and they absorbed it into their own work. The 1980s concluded with the publication of *The Rise and Fall of the New Deal Order, 1930–1980*, a landmark in the revival of political history, in which Brinkley's essay "The New Deal and the Idea of the State" played a starring role.[8]

By this time, Brinkley's work exhibited another key influence, which, like the sociocultural analysis of the new labor history, would shape political history for the next several decades. In the mid-1980s, a cohort of social scientists called on their disciplines to "bring the state back in."[9] Brinkley became one of the first historians of American politics to answer their call, and analysis of the state became integral to the development of his second major work: *The End of Reform*. Though he remained interested above all in the transmission of political ideas within American society, he shifted his focus from the ideas of dissidents in the populist tradition to those of liberals working to define the role of the national state. "I began my work on the character of liberalism and the state convinced that the state-centered approach to policy was inadequate to explain the New Deal," he wrote in the book's introduction. He noted that he still believed this; "yet there remain public questions which exist within a more contained and exclusive political sphere."[10] His essay for Fraser and Gerstle's *The Rise and Fall of the New Deal Order*, which analyzed the activities of administrators, policy makers, and intellectuals in shaping the American state during Franklin Roosevelt's second and third terms, helped put analysis of the state and its institutions at the center of political history.

As he was helping to revive the *practice* of political history, Brinkley was also working to rehabilitate the *idea* of political history. Although younger scholars were producing innovative research on political topics in the 1980s, political history as a field of study had been largely eclipsed and left for dead. Brinkley entered this debate as one of the earliest historians to call for more synthetic interpretations of twentieth-century America that included attention to political developments. In 1984, Brinkley published an essay in the general-interest academic journal *Daedalus* that urged twentieth-century American historians to push politics, broadly conceived, to the middle of their scholarship. He acknowledged that political history in the 1980s primarily consisted of "biographies, political narratives, and policy studies" and that these studies had failed to "produce questions or controversies capable of connecting [the field of political history] with the larger world of historical scholarship."[11] At the same time, he argued that the scholarship of social historians, having "opened vast new areas of human experience for historical study," had mostly ignored the impact of the American state, electoral politics, and policy making. Twentieth-century American society was defined by its "interconnectedness," and Americanists seeking to find "larger patterns that give the era meaning" ultimately should recognize

> the increased importance of public, political events in realms of human existence previously isolated from those events. However appropriate it might be to study earlier centuries by isolating social structures from political developments, by looking at communities in isolation from the larger, public world, it is virtually impossible to do so in the twentieth century. In the modern era, public events are not ephemera; they are often among the central realities of everyday life. No individual, no community in modern America, can live an isolated, unbroken life, insulated from the behavior of the state or national economic institutions.

So historians should "broaden their focus and diversify their approaches, to connect the political narrative . . . to the social, cultural, and economic forces that form the context of politics."[12] Brinkley was not issuing his call all by himself. Political scientists including Theda Skocpol were pioneering American political development as a field that studied how institutions and policies shaped political behavior. Eric Foner around this time pointed out how "the failure to consider politics . . . often left social history bereft of the larger context which alone could have imparted a broader meaning to its findings."[13]

Still, Brinkley was among the early advocates for bringing the political narrative back in the literature on the United States in the twentieth century. Two years after Brinkley published his essay, William Leuchtenburg delivered a lecture, "The Pertinence of Political History," to the Organization of American Historians, in which he picked up on some of the themes in Brinkley's *Daedalus* essay. Leuchtenburg declared, "I do not see how we can conceivably write a credible history of this country and ignore the state. . . . The force of the state has been especially manifest in our own century." He added, "The upheaval of World War I, the Bolshevik revolution, the rise of Hitler, the earth tremors loosed by World War II, and, above all, the Holocaust are evidence enough of what has been wrought in other lands. If in this country developments have not been so traumatic, here, too, especially since the Great Depression, the role of the state has bulked large."[14]

While he was at work on *The End of Reform*, Brinkley's professional circumstances abruptly changed. In 1986, Harvard University made an "inexplicable . . . and tragic mistake," in the words of historian David Donald, when Harvard's Faculty of Arts and Sciences dean, A. Michael Spence, declined to grant Brinkley tenure. The news was stunning enough to rate a story in the *New York Times*.[15] But what Donald termed "tragic" was tragic only in a myopic sense: Harvard had deprived itself of a brilliant young historian. Yet, with the benefit of hindsight, it is fair to say that Brinkley's departure from Harvard paved the way for the career he ultimately had. In 1991, when Brinkley arrived at Columbia, he was in a position that would enable him to help bring political history back as a field of study.

Upon setting foot in the history department's Fayerweather Hall, Brinkley was tenured, enjoyed the strong backing of his department and university, and seemed secure in his belief that Columbia's history program could again become an energetic center for aspiring historians whose main interests were in twentieth-century American political history. In the field of political history, Columbia had the most distinguished history department in the United States through much of the twentieth century, a tradition forged by historians such as Charles Beard, Allan Nevins, Henry Commager, and Richard Hofstadter. Their work featured certain intellectual hallmarks—literary grace, political engagement, and a commitment to tackling broad questions (the roots of economic inequality, the sources of liberalism's strength as a dominant political philosophy, the origins of what appeared to some as a revolt against modernity itself in American political culture)—that intersected with and influenced larger currents of social and political thought. The Columbia school of political historians was also defined by an eschewal of explicit theory and an aversion to insular scholarly camps of the kind that would come to characterize much historical scholarship of the 1970s. Brinkley, along with Eric Foner and other Columbia historians, took up this mantle and extended this public-minded tradition at Columbia into the late twentieth and early twenty-first centuries; they not only produced seminal scholarship but also took up broad questions about slavery, freedom, liberalism, and conservatism that reached audiences beyond the academy and influenced debates about American politics and policy.[16]

New York City turned out to be the best place for Brinkley intellectually and professionally; it seemed to widen his horizons and bring out his best as a scholar, teacher, and public intellectual. It was in this setting that Brinkley would exercise his greatest influence.

In April 2016, Columbia political scientist Ira Katznelson delivered closing remarks at a conference in honor of Brinkley's life in history. Katznelson, one of Brinkley's closest colleagues on Columbia's faculty, summed up not only what Brinkley's strengths as a historian were but also how Brinkley's scholarship and ideas triggered the revival of political history as a field of study. Brinkley's signature contribution, Katznelson explained, was in "how he thought about the state."[17]

Brinkley was not interested in authoring studies that exclusively dealt with "high" politics, chronicling the world of elite and mostly white men on whose broad shoulders the national experiment rested. His approach was subtler and more intellectually powerful. Brinkley thought about the state "not as a hierarchal set of institutions and bureaucracies" but "in terms of ideas and policies." Katznelson spoke of the signal importance for him of Brinkley's 1989 essay "The New Deal and the Idea of the State," which "changed radically the way in which I and many, many others began to ask questions about the trajectory of the New Deal." The essay came "at just the moment . . . when American political development sought . . . to bring the state back in," and "this was precisely the moment when political history . . . was increasingly on the margin of the mainstream of work in the historical profession."

Brinkley's "approach to the state . . . combined traditional, institutional understandings with conceptions of power understood behaviorally," declared Katznelson, and "in that conjunction . . . the history of politics opened up to all the other energetic trends in . . . social and cultural history, and . . . provide[d] a conjunction between parts of the social sciences . . . and the reviving of political history, whose revival Alan Brinkley was already leading."

At the same time, Brinkley led this revival by incorporating and complicating the consensus scholars' views of liberalism as America's sole political tradition and the New Left scholars' withering denunciations of liberalism's foibles and failures. Brinkley's writings, Katznelson suggested, marked a maturation of the historiography on liberalism because Brinkley had seen in liberalism "a set of zones of transactions between the state . . . and the economy, capitalism, markets, and civil society, a zone of contestation about . . . what rules should link the state to the economy and civil society."

Brinkley's approach was further complicated by his interest in assessing "what works and what doesn't work" as well as his quest to gauge whether "just outcomes" had been produced. In other words, Brinkley's scholarship on liberalism was focused not just on the rules that governed the conduct of the state but also on whether liberalism had resulted in "a more decent politics and society." Flamm observes that these concerns were evident in *The End of the Reform*. At that book's conclusion, he notes, Brinkley analyzed not only "what was lost when liberalism moved away from a fundamental restructuring of capitalism" but also what was gained. "That in some ways is the essence of Alan."[18]

Another dimension evident in Brinkley's leadership of this revival was "a kind of persistent anxiety that sometimes things can get worse," Katznelson said. Brinkley considered the liberal tradition in terms of the "liberalism of fear, a liberalism that aims . . . at preventing cruelty." The nuance in Brinkley's scholarship on liberalism was at least partially responsible for his "monumental career in history . . . and in human understanding," as Katznelson called it.[19]

Other aspects of Brinkley's approach to history were also notable for how he reinvigorated the Beard-Hofstadter tradition at Columbia and embraced his role as a full-fledged public intellectual engaged in urgent debates about history, politics, and public affairs. Katznelson quoted from Richard Hofstadter, who had written in 1970 that historians were "'caught between their desire to count in the world and their desire to understand it.'" Brinkley, Katznelson argued, "profoundly refused that choice."[20] Whereas other historians of Brinkley's generation became public intellectuals, few of them spoke to the public so frequently and prominently—or, more important, brought the consistent intellectual power of their scholarship to bear on contemporary debates about politics and policy—as Brinkley did. He was among the historians who paved the way for future historians of modern U.S. politics to write for academic and lay audiences alike.

Beyond rethinking twentieth-century liberalism and the state's influence in American society, Brinkley's scholarship often married social and political history into a seamless whole; in doing so, he broke through the fragmented character pervading some of the historical scholarship of the 1980s. David Greenberg points out that "especially in *Voices of Protest* but also in later works, he found a way to integrate those ideas with political history, so he wasn't writing straight 'high' political history. His use of the letters to Long and Coughlin, the effort to understand the popular bases of their support, is typical."[21]

Brinkley's scholarship was broad-minded enough to encompass non- and antiliberal traditions as fundamental to the study of twentieth-century American politics. Thus did his concern with dissenting voices from the liberal tradition create room for historians to see protesters and mass politics as something other than either fascistic mobs or noble activists—to understand them as "powerful alternative political traditions," as Brinkley once wrote.[22]

When asked to define Brinkley's approach to political history, his colleagues and students came up with distinct definitions—but ones held together by a few important threads that can be found in much subsequent historical scholarship. Brinkley's "abiding concern" was "with the ways in which ideas influence political behavior," said Brian Balogh, Brinkley's onetime colleague at Harvard and now a professor of history at the University of Virginia.[23] University of New Hampshire historian Ellen Fitzpatrick argued that Brinkley's leitmotif amounted to "the use and abuse of power in a democratic society that's ever struggling to realize its loftiest ideals."[24] Other historians, such as Sharon Musher, who did her PhD with Brinkley at Columbia, finds Brinkley's work to be part of a conversation with "the forces that shape political behavior," or political culture.[25] Brinkley left his mark on political history by synthesizing the best in historians' methodological and historiographical approaches, by tapping the complexity of America's diverse intellectual traditions, and by paying heed to dominant strains in political history including liberalism, the New Left critiques of liberalism, and conservative ideas and institutions. In so doing, he forged a vision of political history that was more fluid and more interdisciplinary than what political history had been prior to his contributions. Brinkley's scholarship demonstrated what a more mature political history should become and what it ultimately did become. Brinkley's achievement, then, among his most enduring contributions to the reviving of political history, was to provide a model in his scholarship of connecting the political narrative to social, cultural, and intellectual histories and enlarging the search for thematic patterns that give twentieth-century America its meaning.

As a complement to his scholarship's impact, Brinkley's role as an adviser to PhD students, many of whom became major political historians in their own right and whose own work reflects Brinkley's core scholarly interests, is significant. As adviser, mentor, and counselor to his students and other junior historians who sought his counsel and wisdom, Brinkley not only helped to resurrect political history but also helped to recast it as a field. Brinkley's students went on in their careers to push "his core set of interests into the mainstream of American political history," Balogh said at the Columbia conference honoring Brinkley's career. Brinkley's "most enduring contribution was to create . . . a village of scholars dedicated to the study of political history," Balogh added.[26]

To answer the question of how Brinkley achieved this, it is worth stepping back for a moment to consider why his students decided to study with him in the first place. The brief answer is that particularly in the 1990s, Brinkley's first decade at Columbia, he was a bright beacon for the study of political history to graduate students facing what Greenberg recalls as "a pretty bleak landscape" in twentieth-century U.S. political history. Greenberg's thinking was typical. He remembered that when he was considering graduate school in political history in the mid-1990s, the nation's leading history departments for the most part lacked senior scholars in twentieth-century political history. "At Yale, John Blum had retired and Steve Gillon had not been tenured. Harvard, having failed to tenure Alan, had no one squarely in my field. Princeton had Sean Wilentz, but especially at that time he was known as a nineteenth-century historian, and Dan Rodgers, really an intellectual historian. Really, the only places I was urged to apply to were Princeton; Columbia, where Alan had landed; Stanford, with David Kennedy; and Brown, with James Patterson." Moreover, Greenberg was drawn to Brinkley's "public writing as much as anything. . . . I liked that he wrote book reviews and pieces for the *New Republic* and the *American Prospect*. It comported with my vision of what a scholar should be."[27]

Flamm, who came to Columbia in 1991, Brinkley's first year, was attracted to Brinkley's work on political economy. Brinkley had been Flamm's undergraduate thesis adviser at Harvard, and Flamm found Brinkley extremely thoughtful, accessible, and deeply incisive—an ideal thesis adviser. So when it came time for Flamm to apply to graduate school in history, the call for him was fairly easy: he wanted to work with Brinkley.[28]

University of Oklahoma historian Robert Lifset, who says Brinkley had taught him "to see historical scholarship as the act of extending empathy in all directions," recalls that "when I began thinking about graduate school it was difficult to find academic historians focused on political history." His undergraduate adviser at the University of Chicago, Barry Karl, who had written on the Progressive Era, was about to retire and had trouble persuading his own history department to list political history in the job description for Karl's replacement. Karl urged Lifset to go to Columbia to do his PhD with Brinkley.[29]

Musher, who teaches history and American studies at Stockton University in New Jersey, recalls how she wanted to study with Brinkley because she was "drawn to [his] understanding of political culture—the forces that shape political behavior." Brinkley, she wrote in an email, had the

> ability to listen empathically to his sources and to explain how they fit into broader social and political trends. Alan's Charles Edmondson Historical Lectures, "Culture and Politics in the Great Depression," especially helped me to understand the types of cultural ideas undergirding the 1930s and how certain artists and their cultural expressions illustrated them. When I was a graduate student in the late 1990s, most cultural historians were focused on social construction and problems of representation. Instead, I was drawn to Alan's synthetic approach. He and his work encouraged me to think about the range of cultural enthusiasts engaged with the New Deal's art projects and the products they created according to my own conceptualization of them: art as grandeur, enrichment, weapon, experience, and subversion.[30]

Brinkley's role as adviser was a factor in yielding a broad reconceptualization of the practice of political history. The village that Brinkley built and nurtured involved at least three distinct, interwoven bands of political historians that, taken holistically, represent a larger phenomenon: the maturation and resurrection of political history, a sign that it had entered the mainstream in ways anticipated by Brinkley in his *Daedalus* essay. The first camp is made up of Brinkley students who "picked up where [his] work on the ideas embedded in the New Deal left off," as Balogh put it. "These scholars," Balogh said, "have followed the implications of liberalism for the durable governing arrangements that put such ideas into action. . . . They've considered how they have played out in test-beds for the New Deal at the local level like New York City."[31]

A second camp consists of Brinkley students whose scholarship built on his interests in non- and antiliberal traditions on both the left and the right in contemporary American history, and especially the way these more radical political groups and movements interacted, and came into conflict, with the dominant liberal political order. Beverly Gage's first book, *The Day Wall Street Exploded: America in Its First Age of Terror*, illustrated that "far from being an era of placid reform, the turn of the century was a moment in which the entire structure of American institutions—from the government to the economy—seemed to be up for grabs, poised to be reshaped by new movements and ideas."[32] In a similar vein, Brinkley student Moshik Temkin's first book, *The Sacco-Vanzetti Affair: America on Trial*, uncovered the multilayered domestic and international reactions to the case, eliciting praise from one academic reviewer who wrote that "political history . . . still has something to offer."[33]

Perhaps most famously, Brinkley's 1994 essay on "The Problem of American Conservatism"—an essay Jefferson Decker considers in depth in chapter 6 of this volume—"triggered a mass migration of political historians to the undiscovered country of the American right," as his former student Nicole Hemmer, now a historian at the University of Virginia's Miller Center, points out.[34] Brinkley's essay inspired a generation of Americanists to see conservatism as a rich tradition rooted in intellectual and political contradictions that had thus far eluded historical analysis.

Brinkley's essay bore fruit in the field of political history that is continuing to ripen nearly twenty-five years after its publication. Brinkley (and Foner) student Lisa McGirr, who became a professor of history at Harvard, grafted the study of social history onto the field of political history in her first book, *Suburban Warriors: The Origins of the New American Right*. Her analysis of grassroots conservative activists in post–World War II Orange County achieved what Brinkley had urged historians to do in his seminal essay because it treated conservatives as "rational, stable, intelligent people with a world view radically different from their own."[35] Flamm's interest in law and order and the rise of conservatism was cultivated during his time studying with Brinkley at Columbia.[36]

Numerous non-Brinkley students also heeded Brinkley's call to study conservatism as a central force within the American political tradition. His essay provided at least some of the intellectual ballast that powered the publication of important studies on the American right by historians such as Kim Phillips-Fein, Jennifer Burns, Joseph Crespino, and Kevin Kruse, to name a few. These historians are now tenured at leading universities, a sign that Brinkley's essay may have helped conservative political traditions gain acceptance as a legitimate field of scholarship within the academy.

Third, Brinkley's students made their mark in what Balogh identified as the most understudied, significant field in twentieth-century America: "the relationship between the changing media landscape and politics." Balogh posited how Brinkley's "students, whether identifying messengers, tracing shadows, or parsing spin, have marked out a crucial component of political history" and that Brinkley deserves credit for advising his students "to consider how political ideas are transmitted to and influenced by the messengers that carry them, the shadows they cast, and the structure of the media."[37] Two instances of Brinkley's influence in this area are Greenberg's *Republic of Spin: An Inside History of the American Presidency*, which traces the rise of the "tools and techniques of image making and message craft" along with the intellectual movements that helped shape the White House message machine, and Hemmer's *Messengers of the Right: Conservative Media and the Transformation of American Politics*, which revealed how the first generation of conservative media activists spread ideological messages through a complex web of media outlets.[38]

Brinkley's village should not be seen in terms of his students alone, although their impact was sizable. Rather, it ought to be grasped in terms of a younger generation of political historians who were influenced by Brinkley's scholarship and through their interactions with Brinkley, who was unfailing in his generosity. Princeton University historian Julian Zelizer, who authored *Governing America: The Revival of Political History*, explained that when he was an undergraduate, Brinkley inspired him to pursue a career in political history and shaped his thinking on how to write political history.[39] In 1991, Zelizer's undergraduate professor encouraged him to have lunch with Brinkley, and twenty-five years later Zelizer recalled that it was an "amazing lunch." Brinkley dissected historiographical debates and offered his thoughts on current politics, and he helped spark in Zelizer a desire to "study political history and bring the field back." Zelizer also took hope from Brinkley's book *The End of Reform*, which to him illustrated how historical scholarship could engage both crucial historiographical issues and contemporary political debates. Brinkley, he summed up, "was really . . . inspirational to me."[40]

If Brinkley played a key role in reviving political history, the subsequent generation of scholars has taken the subject in new directions. Though the call to bring the state back in shaped Brinkley's work, historians like Balogh and Zelizer have integrated historical institutionalism more fully into the field of political history.[41] Other scholars, such as Thomas Sugrue, Kevin Kruse, Robert Self, and Matthew Lassiter, have moved race to the center of twentieth-century American political history, enriching our understanding of both liberalism and conservatism.[42] Brinkley's work, in contrast, has tended to focus on the transmission of ideas and how they shape political behavior, the role of individuals in shaping politics and policy (he has written three biographies), and the telling of big stories that illuminate larger themes rather than a tightly focused reporting on case studies or discrete policy issues.

Clearly, the field of political history needs all of the above, and more, if it is to maintain its health and vitality in the years ahead. Thus, Brinkley's body of scholarship stands as a motivation and a challenge to political historians of the future. Trump's surprise election as president has spurred historians to reconsider the most valuable approaches to studying political history, to understand how Trumpism came to be, and to define what political history should be. Brinkley's essay on conservatism speaks to important definitional questions about what modern conservatism stands for and how historians can account for what it has become. More broadly, Brinkley's work endures by prodding historians to understand how ideas have shaped political behavior and how the lives of individuals intersect with broad social and cultural processes to influence American politics. His scholarship continues to loom as a kind of call to historians to take up big questions that attempt to synthesize broad swaths of American history and explain this history to a public that, even in the age of social media, remains interested in knowing something about the American past and how it has shaped their world.

Hemmer has said that Brinkley is "one of the foremost political historians of our time."[43] This is true, at least in part, because of Brinkley's influence in the revival of political history within the profession. In contrast to those who insist that the field of political history remains lifeless, other historians have persuasively argued that the interdisciplinary character and diverse approaches to the study of political history indicate that it is waxing, not waning. Brinkley was not the sole twentieth-century Americanist to put the state back in and bring the field back, of course. But in any accounting of how political history became a robust field of study integral to the modern historical profession, Brinkley's contributions—as scholar, adviser, and public intellectual—ought to be recognized. Whether Americans realize it or not, they are now profiting from a landscape in political history that Alan Brinkley's lifework fundamentally altered.

8

Houdini, Hip-Hop, and Dystopian Literature

ALAN BRINKLEY'S PATTERNS OF CULTURE

SHARON ANN MUSHER

Alan Brinkley admits that cultural studies are not his forte. Known mainly as a political historian, he has gone so far as to disavow any professional expertise in matters of culture whatsoever. He explained in 2005 that when he decided to add a feature called "Patterns of Culture" to a textbook he was editing, it was "an area with which I didn't have any scholarly connection." But, he added, "there was a lot of interesting material," and "I had some wonderful graduate assistants at Columbia University who helped me gather material and think about how to present it."[1]

There is no doubt that Brinkley's reputation as a historian rests on his contributions to our understanding of American politics. Scholars credit him for reviving interest in various aspects of political history, including liberalism, conservatism, and political dissent. He has integrated the study of national politics and elite actors with that of social movements. "It's no hyperbole," Georgetown historian Michael Kazin attested in a profile written in 2003, "to say that most people would consider him the best, or at least the most influential, political historian of his generation."[2]

But Brinkley's contributions to cultural history should not be overlooked. Indeed, once one starts looking for culture in his work, it is rather hard to miss. His students recall him quoting from the *Wizard of Oz* to explicate the feelings of disenfranchised populists in the 1890s and devoting lectures to comparing the 1893 World Fair's White City to another Chicago experimental community intended to be a model industrial town: Pullman.[3] Audiences at his public talks are familiar with how he weaves together photographs, dystopian literature, and self-help manuals to convey ideas at the heart of various American movements or moments. Readers of his textbooks know how he has found meaning in the difference between the folk music revival of the 1960s, expressive of young people's striving for a "more democratic, more honest, and more natural" America, and the 1969 Altamont Festival, which turned deadly and illustrated rock's capacity for destruction and violence.[4] Scholars know well Brinkley's investigations of how ideas—especially about middle-class American cultural norms and news—have moved through radio, TV, and especially print culture. And members of the general public have enjoyed his moonlighting as a TV critic for the *Wall Street Journal*.

In short, as a teacher, scholar, and public intellectual, Alan Brinkley has drawn heavily on popular culture and the arts to capture and to communicate the ways in which a range of individuals and institutions created and responded to the values and habits of their day. If culture never supersedes politics as an object of Brinkley's study, it nonetheless permeates his work as an abiding concern.

What does being a cultural historian mean? For several decades now, historians have come to understand culture in a capacious sense, no longer limiting it to what the English poet and cultural critic Matthew Arnold, in the nineteenth century, famously called "the best that has been thought and said." Today, the idea of culture, as scholars use it, typically incorporates the lowbrow as well as the highbrow. Studying it includes investigating its production, dissemination, and reception and the institutions and frameworks through which it is conveyed. Influenced by cultural anthropologists from Franz Boas to Margaret Mead to Clifford Geertz, scholars interpret culture as part of daily life. It signifies the ways that people act and what they think and feel about their behavior. Culture can also represent a form of consciousness—a set of beliefs, customs, values, and rituals unifying people and creating meaning for them.[5] Under this broad and generally accepted definition, Brinkley's work is indeed cultural: it aims to understand the ideas motivating political behavior; how individuals, institutions, the state, and the media create and disseminate cultural ideas; and the competing ways in which diverse people respond to the customs of their day.

If Brinkley modestly purports to be simply an amateur in or a visitor to the world of American cultural history, he unquestionably shows a sophistication about the field. He does not flatten culture into a single zeitgeist. Unlike consensus historians of the 1950s such as Daniel Boorstin and David Potter, he does not seek to capture a monolithic national character that can explain political behavior, such as a dearth of conflict in U.S. history (as Boorstin suggested) or the importance of material abundance (as Potter hypothesized).[6] Nor does he, in the style of American studies "myth and symbol" scholars, such as Henry Nash Smith and Alan Trachtenberg, identify and analyze key images and stories to understand dominant ideas in different historical periods.[7] His work is fueled neither by activism nor by theory, both of which drive so much of today's cultural analysis. Instead, Brinkley draws on diverse cultural and artistic expressions—including film, dance, literature, and photography—to paint complex portraits of conflicting perspectives within society, and he does so in a way that is both comprehensible to the public and intellectually adventurous, paying attention to subversive currents, countercultures, and undertones. Although some cultural historians might consider his work to be naïve or undertheorized (or perhaps even irrelevant), his close readings and contextualized analyses supplement and deepen an accessible portrait of the past. They often connect culture to other elements of American history in ways that many specialists struggle to do.

A lecture that Brinkley delivered at Oxford University on the eve of the twenty-first century exemplifies his approach. In that talk, Brinkley analyzed predictions of late nineteenth-century writers, such as H. G. Wells, Jules Verne, and Edward Bellamy, calling them "a window into the hopes and fears" of contemporaries who were imagining the twentieth century. Brinkley used such writing to understand the cultural transformations seizing the United States and Europe in the face of rising class conflict and violence, as well as a growing fear of the future of industrial capitalism and the survival of democracy. He contended that a number of writers imagined science and technology would offer peaceful solutions, creating new class structures that would promote progress and equality. Thorsten Veblen, for example, envisaged engineers assuming a type of scientific leadership that would create new, more progressive political and class structures.[8] And historian Mary Beard imagined that better educated and more socially aware women would transform women's social and familial status. Brinkley used such predictions to distinguish the optimism at the end of the last century from more recent skepticism and anxiety, envying and admiring the hope of a generation looking to the future—rather than the past—for a Golden Age. Although neither of these predictions came to fruition, Brinkley found in them a way to consider how shortcomings in the last century's racial, ethnic, and gendered imagination contributed to ongoing inequality.[9]

In addition to using culture to capture the spirit—or a number of conflicting spirits—of the time, Brinkley endeavored to preserve, publish, and disseminate the building blocks of cultural expression: primary sources. In 1997, at the start of a project to digitize and put online more than five million primary sources, curators at the Library of Congress initially selected some five hundred images, published in a volume called *Eyes of the Nation*.[10] The Librarian of Congress, James H. Billington, said the collection illustrated "how Americans have viewed themselves, and have been viewed by others."[11] Brinkley wrote the text to accompany these images and then integrated a number of them—as well as sources from many other archives—into a *Primary Source Investigator* CD-ROM to accompany one of his textbooks. The disc contained artifacts, audio clips, cartoons, government documents, publications, images, maps, private papers, and videos; it also included guidelines for interpreting them as, in Brinkley's words, "a new interactive tool for historical research [that] allow[s] you [the student] to act as a historian yourself and draw conclusions not just from what you hear in my book or in class, but from your own analysis of the traces of the past."[12]

The prefaces, introductions, and commentaries Brinkley has written for this and other primary source collections reflect his commitment to using firsthand and eyewitness accounts to uncover a range of experiences. An abiding critic of the idea of consensus—that a single overriding tendency has governed American politics—Brinkley finds diversity, too, in his cultural explorations. For example, in a volume of illustrations by artists such as Winslow Homer and Thomas Nast sent to newspapers during the Civil War, Brinkley notes that they "add to our understanding not just of the battles and campaigns but also of how soldiers lived during the Civil War."[13] Whereas some documents may capture a predominant spirit of the time—or shape our understanding of it—others reveal alternative developments. In a volume of photographs from political campaigns that was published in early 2001, Brinkley contends that even though the carefully tailored images of politicians might lead people to feel distanced from the leaders they portray, viewers nevertheless continue to search for "personal connection" to the political process through these photographs.[14] He also wrote an introduction to *The Forgotten Fifties*, a book highlighting *Look* magazine's representations of that decade. In it, he emphasizes the postwar period's cultural tensions through his reading of images that *Look* published highlighting civil rights, feminism, and the counterculture currents—developments usually located in the 1960s that actually have roots stretching back into the previous decade and beyond.[15]

In this quest to capture and call attention to a variety of cultural impulses rather than a single, dominant one, Brinkley seems to draw, consciously or not, on the work of Berkeley historian, Lawrence Levine, who died in 2006. Levine encouraged scholars to empathize with and listen to their subjects and to take seriously popular, folk, and mass culture. In "The Folklore of Industrial Society", in 1992, Levine mounted a defense of studying everyday art forms—still at the time a controversial proposition. He argued that scholars should study culture that is widely disseminated and viewed in order to ascertain the thoughts, feelings, values, and worldviews of people whose attitudes would otherwise be lost to the historical record. Culture that resonates popularly, he maintained, reveals "what kinds of fictions, myths, [and] fantasies they require, not primarily to escape reality but to face it day after day after day."[16] Levine focused especially on ways that historians could recover the unmediated voices of the dispossessed, such as black slaves and members of the working class.

Though less self-consciously a historian of marginalized cultures than Levine, Brinkley has also directed attention to previously disregarded perspectives to illustrate the range of ways that people in the past have understood themselves and made sense of their world. In an essay supplementing an exhibit on Harry Houdini first displayed in New York's Jewish Museum in 2010, Brinkley set Houdini's experience as a migrant to the United States in the late nineteenth century within the context of the prevailing xenophobic and anti-immigrant sentiment. With such views emanating both from prominent figures, including social gospel reformers like Josiah Strong, and from more marginal individuals, such as the half a million members of the American Protective Association, broad swaths of American society worked to shut down what is commonly referred to as second-wave migration. Such efforts culminated in the passage of the 1924 National Origins Act, which set quotas on migrants from eastern and southern Europe. Brinkley positions Houdini and his amazing feats against the type of exclusion that migrants, and specifically Jewish migrants, faced. Because they found themselves "barred from hotels, restaurants, and many stores, . . . beaches, and parks; mostly excluded from private schools and universities; and barred from all but a few neighborhoods" throughout the United States, Jewish migrants saw in Houdini's magical maneuvers far more than entertainment.[17] Brinkley argues that for a generation of Jews and other minorities who "felt imprisoned by poverty, prejudice, alienation, and tradition," Houdini provided hope.[18] He represented "a symbol of escape from the figurative shackles that immigrants sought to shed," constraints that as much as intolerance included the repression embodied in prohibition, antievolution arguments, and censorship of books, drama, and film. Situating Houdini within the context of late nineteenth- and early twentieth-century discrimination and repression allows Brinkley to understand why such a broad public connected with and was inspired by Houdini's magic.[19]

Brinkley's work also contributes to cultural history by creatively weaving together a distinctive mix of sources to elucidate broader cultural trends. Two lecture series that Brinkley delivered more than a decade apart, the Charles Edmondson Historical Lectures presented at Baylor University in 1998 and the Leonard Hastings Schoff Memorial Lectures given at Columbia University in 2010, illustrate this approach. Both talks analyze how Americans reacted to the Great Depression. They consider what Brinkley referred to as "some of the variety of American dreams that competed with, and sometimes complemented, one another in the midst of the Great Depression," when the very idea of an American dream first emerged.[20]

In the first set of lectures, "Culture and Politics in the Great Depression," Brinkley outlines and names four different instincts that coexisted during the 1930s: rebellion, persistence, community, and empathy. According to Brinkley, rebellion could be seen among those Americans who responded to the crisis by committing themselves to revolutionary politics, turning to the Communist Party and the Soviet Union to find ways to reshape America in a more egalitarian manner. But many more Americans, like those captured in Robert and Helen Lynd's surveys of the pseudonymous Middletown, focused on persistence. These Americans blamed themselves and their own shortcomings for the trouble they faced rather than developing systemic critiques; they kept faith with an American dream based on industrial progress and technology, individualism, materialism, and conformity despite their difficulties. Still others spurned such aspirations, instead embracing romantic notions of community, family, and "the People," embodied in John Steinbeck's *The Grapes of Wrath* and Frank Capra's films, where basic decency and communitarian values prevailed. A fourth and final response can be seen among people who opposed an industrial future in favor of what Brinkley broadly termed "empathy"—upholding an idealized past built on folk culture and realistic depictions of working-class and small-town America that connected middle-class audiences with a rural world. These approaches redefined the idea of American progress, Brinkley argues, but none of them significantly dismantled it.[21]

In the Schoff lectures a dozen years later, Brinkley develops the ideas outlined in his Edmondson talks through a close look at the experiences of three photographers working during the 1930s—photographers who by turns conformed to and resisted these responses. The first talk, on Margaret Bourke-White, examines her life and career to illuminate Brinkley's idea of persistence. How did Bourke-White's actions and creations, he asked, illustrate "the culture of ambition, success, and expertise" that characterized the 1920s and "survived in the midst of the greatest economic crisis in the nation's history"?[22] He argues that unlike other well-known photographers of the time, such as Dorothea Lange, Bourke-White did not empathize with her subjects or focus on their humanity. Instead, she attained celebrity and fortune by concentrating on technology, which she represented aesthetically as beautiful tools for salvation. Through her lens, ordinary objects and technological products—"machines, factories, buildings, ships, airplanes, [and] dams"—became "some of the great monuments of her age."[23]

In the remaining Schoff lectures, Brinkley takes up Dorothea Lange and Walker Evans. These photographers' lives and work allow him to explore additional nuances in a culture that challenged the drive for personal advancement that Bourke-White embodied. In Brinkley's reading, Lange's childhood adversities—which included contracting polio, being abandoned by her father, and being tyrannized by an abusive and alcoholic grandmother—encouraged her to empathize with the dispossessed. Photography became a way to elicit her viewers' empathy and call them to action to support New Deal programs, such as those created by the Farm Security Administration.[24] In Brinkley's account, Lange personified the empathy instinct that he had previously postulated. She drew visual attention to the struggles faced by migrant workers and sharecroppers and used such portraits to provide "simple, affecting glimpses of the human costs of America's economic failures."[25]

Other than in a passing reference, Brinkley does not engage with the long-standing historiographical debate over how Lange represented—or misrepresented—the "Migrant Mother" of one of her famous photographs.[26] Florence Thompson, the photograph's subject, a Cherokee descendant born on an Oklahoma reservation, objected in the 1950s and again in the 1970s to an image of her taken during the 1930s that left her penniless while Lange became famous. She began to change her attitude toward the iconic photograph only when donors responded to pleas by her grown children for her support by sending $30,000 in contributions.[27] Whereas Brinkley focuses on the photograph as exemplifying a cultural impulse toward empathy—Lange's for her subject and her viewers' for the "Migrant Mother"—other cultural historians have used her work to consider problems that emerge when middle-class reformers try to document the dispossessed. Brinkley's lack of focus here on some of the problems surrounding representation may be one reason why cultural historians have not engaged more with these lectures. Yet significant value remains in Brinkley's attempts to comprehend the messages historical actors like Lange sought to convey and the ways in which at least some of their viewers understood them. Brinkley's efforts to uncover and contextualize such meanings offer a window into the inner life of contemporaries, albeit a window with an imperfect view.

Although Brinkley does not generally address the politics of representation, he does consider it directly in his third Schoff lecture, on Walker Evans. Evans's aesthetic approach calls for such reflection. Unlike his peers, Evans disdained both Bourke-White's emphasis on technology and personal success and Lange's concentration on empathic documentation in pursuit of social change. Instead, he sought to use his photographs to create art that would communicate respect for his subjects' inherent dignity and capture their way of life in ways that were open to multiple interpretations. Brinkley argues that although Evans derided a New Deal aesthetic intended to promote reform policies, his financial needs led him to take jobs first with *Fortune* magazine and then with the Resettlement Administration.

At *Fortune*, Evans met James Agee, who shared his disdain for using art as propaganda. The two began an important collaboration that took them to Hale County, Alabama, where they spent months as participant observers in a community of tenant farmers. They were determined to record and respect the lives of those they documented without pitying or exploiting them by turning them into a political cause. Evans and Agee used their photographs and writing to wrestle with the question of how to document the poor without manipulating them. Toward that end, they produced a stream-of-consciousness-style, 500-page book, *Let Us Now Praise Famous Men*. When first published in 1941, it sold just a few hundred copies. The length, style, and timing of the book's publication—coming as it did as the world was turning toward war—explain its poor circulation. But Evans's photos, as Brinkley explains, "became revered works of art long before *Let Us Now Praise Famous Men* was rediscovered" in the 1960s, when its countercultural and deconstructed message went mainstream.[28] Brinkley's explication of this work and Evans's photographic approach—including its disjuncture with its time—elucidates both prevailing cultural norms and countercurrents. Cumulatively, Brinkley's Schoff lectures complicate notions of a single aesthetic approach in New Deal–era photography and enrich our under-standing of attitudes toward poverty, social change, representation, and even the so-called American dream.

If Brinkley's book introductions and lectures see him practicing cul-tural history much more than has been realized, his synthetic narratives and textbooks provide him an opportunity to integrate social and cultural subjects into larger political frameworks. "In the highly politicized, inter-dependent world of the twentieth century," Brinkley argued in 1984, "social history is, almost by definition, also political history"—and he might have said the same of cultural history.[29] He had already begun to seek out this integrated history in *American History: A Survey*, the textbook he inherited from Frank Freidel and first published as his own in 1982.

In revising that textbook, which had previously told an overwhelm-ingly political and diplomatic narrative, and also in writing a shorter one, *The Unfinished Nation*, Brinkley purposefully incorporated African American, labor, women's, and social history.[30] With the tenth edition of *American History: A Survey*, published in 1999, he also began to include the special boxed feature called "Patterns of Culture" mentioned above. This feature describes trends and historical developments in popular arts that provide insight into how people entertained themselves. Some of the more illuminating passages explain how Americans in different eras roman-ticized their own pasts, whether through minstrel and Wild West shows or Frank Capra films. Brinkley's brief descriptions of such events include attention to performances of race, gender, and sexuality, reflecting his train-ing in a post-1960s milieu.

By the thirteenth edition of *American History* and the eighth edition of *Unfinished Nation*, Brinkley had integrated "Patterns of Culture" into both textbooks, alongside other, older sections, such as "Where Historians Disagree," "The American Environment," and "America in the World." He also expanded the cultural offerings incorporated in the feature to include the aspirations of late nineteenth-century middle-class men to rise from rags to riches like Horatio Alger's *Ragged Dick* and of young women like Louisa May Alcott to challenge the expectations of their day that they aspire to romance and submission. Brinkley examines the "wonder, excite-ment, and escape" that Coney Island offered to working-class immigrants in the years before radio and movies. Additional features focus on yellow journalism, religious revivalism, Orson Welles and *The War of the Worlds*, the *I Love Lucy* show, malls, dance halls, swing, and rap.[31]

In naming his new section, Brinkley adopted the title of Ruth Benedict's influential 1934 anthropological study, *Patterns of Culture*. But there was a difference in how the two scholars used this phrase. When Benedict developed it, she meant the set of characteristics and behaviors that shape a society's institutions, values, and ideologies. She investigated how people learned those norms and how they responded to them, whether conforming to or deviating from social expectations. Her approach helped readers to understand other cultures—even ones that were radically different from their own—rather than judging them.[32] For Brinkley, the cultural unfamiliarity to be overcome is historical. In his "Patterns of Culture" textbook feature, he tends to describe cultural trends from bygone eras to make them comprehensible to contemporary readers.[33] As the promotional material for *American History* explains, "Patterns of Culture" provides "commentary on the changing ways in which Americans entertained, educated, and amused themselves through the centuries."[34] This focus on illuminating cultural trends may fall short of Benedict's project of explicating how individuals adjust to or resist cultural norms. But Brinkley has insisted that we cannot fully grasp the contours of American history without appreciating the diversity of American cultural production and experience. For example, a feature on rap music highlights its musical lineage as well as the controversies that have emerged among the various styles of rap—from message rap to gangsta rap and from New York to West Coast. Although acknowledging that conservatives often denounce hip-hop culture and the music it sired as "subversive, excessively sexual, violent, and dangerous," Brinkley concludes that "it has become another of the arresting, innovative African-American musical traditions that have shaped American culture for more than a century."[35]

A final way in which Brinkley can be understood as an important cultural historian is through his integration of culture into politics. The British cultural historian Peter Burke has argued that political historians expand cultural research through their investigations of "'political culture' in the sense of the attitudes and values that underlie political action."[36]

Brinkley's writing explores what political activity and ideology mean to ordinary people as well as how various political ideas—cultures of dissent, liberalism, and conservatism—coexist, how they shape political activity and individual agency, and, as he explains in *The End of Reform*, how they interact with and adapt to "larger changes in the social, economic, and cultural landscape."[37] In that book, Brinkley includes an account of the role that social movements and culture played in the replacement of a political culture that stressed economic reform with one emphasizing rights-based liberalism. "Understanding liberal ideas and actions," Brinkley explains, "requires . . . not just consideration of political elites and their institutional milieu, but consideration as well of the often elusive connections between the elite world of politics and the state, and the larger world of which politicians and intellectuals are part and to which they, like everyone else, respond."[38]

Brinkley explores the connections between leadership and broader cultural ideas perhaps most adeptly in *The Publisher*, in which he examines how Henry Luce used his various publications, especially *Life* and *Time*, to promote "ideas that were already emerging among a broad segment of the American population." The carefully researched biography argues that the publisher's major contribution was that he created "new forms of information and communications at a moment in history when media were rapidly expanding." Such knowledge, Brinkley argues, helped "transform the way many people experience news and culture"; it forged a common, national, middle-class, standardized worldview; and it promoted an American (suburban) dream as well as calling for the internationalization of American values and the creation of a prominent American role in the world.[39] Brinkley's biography explicitly examines how Luce and the cultural works he produced helped to shape American society and popular understandings.

Given all these contributions to our understanding of American culture, why—apart from his primary focus on politics—is Brinkley so rarely thought of as a cultural historian? Perhaps it is because he has pursued neither of the two major impulses that University of Wisconsin cultural historian Nan Ensted describes as dominating cultural history in the United States from the 1970s through the 1990s. According to Ensted, the 1970s and early 1980s saw a "visionary cultural history of subalterns," in which scholars sought to uncover the histories of slaves, members of the working class, and other subordinate peoples; to draw inspiration from their activism; and to understand their identity and heritage.[40] Such history was hopeful. Scholars turned to the past to identify heroes and heroines, to find evidence that activism could make a difference, and to be moved by stories of people overcoming hardships to create beauty, art, community, and change.[41]

In contrast, during the 1980s and 1990s, a cultural history rooted in the deconstruction of categories and hierarchies came to the fore.[42] In this latter approach, scholars recognized that, in the interest of political expediency, the categories they had previously historicized—women, laborers, and African Americans—often ignored the conflicting identities of minorities within each group. In raising collective awareness and forging narratives of resistance, scholars might portray all women as white, all laborers and African Americans as men, and everyone as heterosexual. Instead, a new, largely discursive cultural history emerged that analyzed the construction of categories, particularly those based on whiteness, masculinity, sexuality, and empire. Scholars pursuing this approach assumed that individuals are not autonomous agents whose choices are dictated by free will but rather socialized beings whose lives are, at least in part, controlled by the ways that race, class, and gender work. Such researchers trace the ways that language, policies, and practices condition the imagined possibilities in which people understand themselves, their collective identities, and their capacity for creating change.[43]

Brinkley's forays into cultural history focus neither on uncovering the dispossessed for the purpose of empowering them nor on investigating the formation of such cultural assumptions. But if his work mostly avoids theoretical discussions and terminology, it still explores and illuminates how cultural assumptions limit and shape historical agency. He has disseminated and categorized rich collections of primary sources in order to outline the tensions between human action and cultural expectations, to excavate cultural trends within particular historical moments, and to explore how political activity and ideology draw from cultural understandings. In this regard, Brinkley's contributions to our understanding of American culture have been substantial.

His influence also fits into a cultural approach to history that emerged, appropriately, from the artistic projects of the New Deal. In 1939, the historian Caroline Ware organized the annual meeting of the American Historical Association and edited a volume called *The Cultural Approach to History*, which was sponsored by the association and published the following year. In the book's introduction, Ware urged historians to adapt Benedict's idea of "patterns of culture" and to try to uncover the basic values of the societies they study by investigating their structuring institutions and ideologies.[44] Other speakers at the conference that year included not just historians but also employees of the New Deal's art projects, including photographer Roy Stryker, folklorist Benjamin Botkin, and musicologist Charles Seeger. Some of them, in their remarks, encouraged scholars to use nontraditional historical sources such as photographs, landscapes, folklore, and music to uncover the experiences of the otherwise historically marginalized.[45]

Brinkley's contributions to American cultural history proceed in this vein. They draw on diverse cultural sources to explicate patterns of culture and explore how individuals have adapted to and resisted prevailing trends. And they do so in a manner that is accessible to a broad public. His cultural efforts point to important ways that scholars of cultural history today might consider writing and thinking about how culture works. They also challenge historians who do not generally integrate culture into their work to take it more seriously.

9

The View from the Classroom

MICHAEL W. FLAMM

Alan Brinkley could have followed a different career path after Harvard Law School admitted him in 1972. But he chose to study and teach history, in part because he wanted to impart the skills and knowledge that students needed to achieve success in any field and in part because he sought to mold informed and engaged citizens. "Education," Brinkley wrote in *The Chicago Handbook for Teachers*, "is a way of keeping alive the true basis of democracy: the ability of people to know enough and understand enough about the great issues of their time to help guide their society into the future." Teaching also offered Brinkley a personal benefit. "The wonder and excitement that we sometimes encounter in our students when we help them discover a new area of knowledge," he noted, may enable us to "recapture that same wonder and excitement, which is continually within our grasp if we do not lose the will to find it."[1]

For more than four decades in the classroom, Brinkley never lost his passion for teaching history or his belief that it mattered for individuals and society. As a Princeton undergraduate, the political and social tumult of the 1960s became a self-described "kind of prism" through which he viewed the world, although he has never been a radical.[2] Educators, Brinkley came to believe, had an obligation to make history accessible and relevant to a wider audience. But they also had to balance commitment with detachment and political engagement with historical rigor.[3]

Within the world of higher education, Brinkley has had an enormous impact on both students and scholars. By mastering the art and craft of lecturing, he has inspired thousands of Harvard and Columbia undergraduates, who have crowded into large auditoriums to hear him expound on modern U.S. history. He has also served as a direct or indirect mentor to dozens of graduate students, many of whom have written important works on liberalism, conservatism, and other topics in American history. And he has influenced and improved the professional publications of colleagues— in not just the United States but also Britain, France, Italy, and elsewhere— through the comments he offers on paper, by email, or in person at seminars, conferences, and one-on-one meetings.

Outside the university, Brinkley has played a vital role in promoting the understanding and teaching of modern U.S. history. The full extent of his readership is hard to measure. In high schools across the country, instructors assign his textbooks, *American History: A Survey* and *The Unfinished Nation: A Concise History of the American People*, which he has regularly updated. At summer seminars organized by the Gilder Lehrman Institute, Brinkley has taught hundreds of precollegiate teachers and public historians about the New Deal and the interwar period. These teachers, in turn, have conveyed his insights in their own classrooms and institutions. The Gilder Lehrman website, which features videos of Brinkley and essays he wrote, also attracts millions of visitors a year.[4]

Brinkley's hallmarks as a teacher are patience, generosity, and a gift for precise, constructive criticism. When meeting students or colleagues in his office, he does not glance at his watch, stare at the ceiling, read his mail, or hint that he has better things to do (though he may). Students typically feel that they are at the center of his attention, that their concerns are important him. If you leave him a voice mail or send him an email, he replies within a day or two, and sometimes faster, even when consumed with administrative affairs, as he was when he served as provost of Columbia. Despite his many obligations, he finds time to write letters of recommendation, offer advice, and provide critiques of all kinds of unfinished projects. In short, Brinkley is the kind of teacher and colleague, mentor and role model, that we hope to encounter as students and strive to emulate as educators.

It is not clear precisely how or when Brinkley developed his talents as a lecturer. Perhaps he inherited the gift of writing and delivering a script from his father. His analytical abilities may have come from his insightful and highly literate mother. He also might have learned by observing and imitating a few of his professors at Princeton and Harvard. In any event, his abilities were apparent while he was still in graduate school. In the fall of 1976, Frank Freidel, biographer of Franklin Roosevelt and Brinkley's adviser, made him the lead teaching assistant and a frequent guest lecturer for "American Political History Since 1877." By many accounts, the full-year course was rather unchallenging and sparsely attended when Freidel himself was at the lectern. But students filled the hall when Brinkley took Freidel's place on the stage. "Alan set the lecture room on fire," remembers Charles Curtis, a junior at the time and today a lawyer in Madison, Wisconsin. "Everybody loved him—the jocks, the scholars, and the nerds like me."[5]

By the time Brinkley received his PhD in 1979 and then took a position at MIT, his teaching had earned him a reputation at Harvard. Students loved how he wove analysis and anecdotes into a seamless narrative surrounding a core theme or argument. His lectures "were crystal clear, vivid, and elegant," recalls Elizabeth Blackmar, a graduate student in the American Civilization program at the time and later Brinkley's colleague at Columbia. They were "beautifully structured, precisely timed, and utterly articulate and absorbing. . . . No rambling or loose ends and with his audience clearly in mind. It is a lost art."[6]

Doubtless, few in the audience fully appreciated the hours of preparation that Brinkley put into his lectures. He would first review his materials and formulate his thoughts. Then he would compose the presentation word by word, digressions, jokes, and stories included. "Writing a lecture out is the only way to be entirely sure you have worked through exactly what you want to say and how you want to say it," he once remarked.[7] His meticulous approach enhanced his ability to explain complex issues.

"The clarity of his thought was extraordinary," remembers Yanek Mieczkowski, one of Brinkley's first graduate students at Columbia, who later became a professor at Dowling College and now teaches at the University of Central Florida. "He spoke in discrete paragraphs. You could always distill his lectures into an important central thesis."[8]

As a lecturer, Brinkley has consistently placed a premium on structure. "Your lectures can be flamboyant, idiosyncratic, speculative, or fanciful," he has written. "But whatever else they are, they should also be carefully and transparently organized."[9] At the start of class, he would typically write an outline on the blackboard. Then he would seemingly leave it behind as he delved into the subject at hand. But he always returned to the outline— and imparted an implicit lesson about historical method. "In form as well as content, he expressed . . . a sort of dance between the detail and the interpretation" of the event, recalls Michael Kramer, a Columbia undergraduate who now teaches history at Northwestern University. "Instead of declaring the past an unknowable jumble of details, he offered a model of how to keep your balance as a historical thinker, pivoting continually between analytic breakdown and synthetic cohesion to find a place of convincing narrative."[10]

Brinkley has made the past come alive in the classroom by blending revealing details, stirring anecdotes, and penetrating analysis. His lecture on Joseph McCarthy and the Red Scare of the 1950s, for example, combined colorful anecdotes from the Wisconsin senator's personal life with a dramatic recounting of the Army-McCarthy hearings. But embedded within the narrative was also a sobering assessment of why, in part, the Republican politician was so popular and powerful for a time. Although most elites knew how reckless McCarthy's charges were, their failure to challenge him in public both emboldened him and weakened support for his critics and victims.

Brinkley's lectures have a literary quality as well and often feature exemplary biographical vignettes. To illustrate the disillusionment of the Lost Generation of the 1920s, he drew on Malcolm Cowley's memoir, *Exile's Return*, to relate the tragic fate of Harry Crosby, a wealthy young Bostonian who drove an ambulance during World War I and narrowly escaped death. Afterward, Crosby graduated from Harvard, had a scandalous affair with a married woman, and moved to Paris, where he wrote poetry and founded a religion based on sun worship before committing suicide with his lover. To depict the antimaterialist culture of the 1970s, Brinkley similarly recounted the popular fable of Jonathan Livingston Seagull, a bird who tires of food gathering and seeks a higher existence. "When [Brinkley] reached full literary flight," recalls Mason B. Williams, a former Brinkley student and teaching assistant who is now a professor at Williams College, "it felt audacious, almost risky. It was thrilling."[11]

Nonetheless, Brinkley's presentations represent a certain triumph of substance over style. He is not a conventionally charismatic or dynamic speaker; the power of his ideas and intellect is what captivates listeners. But unlike many academics, he can deliver a prepared lecture without droning or boring the audience. He has a dry sense of humor, even if he might blush when relating a slightly risqué anecdote about Lyndon Johnson. And he has generally proven unflappable, although an MIT student did once manage to irritate him by sitting in the front row of the lecture hall and reading a newspaper during every class. "One day," remembers Ellen Fitzpatrick, who taught the course with him and is now a professor at the University of New Hampshire, "Alan paused mid-lecture and said, 'If you are going to read the newspaper at least have the courtesy to sit in the back row where I can't see you.'"[12]

Brinkley's lectures reflect who he is as a teacher and person. Although he included a childhood photo of his brothers and him self, together with their mother, as part of his lecture on "The Culture of Consensus in the 1950s," he almost never shared private stories in public settings. But the way he presented historical figures and issues was always rooted in his core values of decency, fairness, and empathy. "Perhaps more than any other kind of teaching," he wrote in a moment of self-reflection, "lecturing puts the personality and the intellect of the teacher on display. It is, in a sense, a very personal kind of teaching, because in most cases it is you, much more than the students, who determines the nature of the classroom experience."[13]

Brinkley's students have usually responded with enthusiasm. In the spring of 1987, after Harvard had denied him tenure, a thousand undergraduates filled Sanders Theater, the university's largest space, for his course called America Since 1945. At the end of his final lecture, the students gave him a standing ovation. For several minutes, they clapped and stomped while the giant screen slowly lowered to reveal a message: Goodbye and Thank You, Professor Brinkley! "I think his eyes were humid at the time," recalls François Weil, a teaching assistant and visiting graduate student from France, "and so were the eyes of many of us."[14]

The Harvard history department was not a particularly warm and welcoming place in the 1970s. The student takeover of University Hall in 1969—and the administration's decision to call in the police to clear the building—had embittered and divided the senior faculty, who remained suspicious of the younger generation of graduate students. Older professors gave little thought to teaching or mentoring, as they concentrated on their research. But Freidel was open to and supportive of the interests of his students. "He was for many years the person to whom people with unorthodox projects would go," Brinkley said later of his mentor and role model. "He sponsored *All God's Dangers*, an oral history of a black sharecropper, at a time when it was hard to imagine anyone at Harvard would accept it."[15] Brinkley's own students, colleagues, and peers describe him in similar terms.

From early in his career, Brinkley supported all kinds of student ideas. As a Harvard undergraduate, Cliff Sloan already had two advisers for his senior thesis when he met Brinkley, then a tutor in Eliot House, who offered to assume an informal role. "He could not have been more generous, more insightful, more encouraging," recalls Sloan, now a lawyer in Washington, DC. "Alan is very interested in what you are interested in— he is not someone who is overbearing or judgmental or pedantic in terms of telling you what to do." Matthew Dallek, who was a graduate student of Brinkley's at Columbia, had a similar experience. When Dallek expressed doubts about his approved dissertation topic, Brinkley was sympathetic. "Another adviser," observes Dallek (who eventually chose a different subject), "might easily have said that I had to stick to my topic."[16]

After a student settles on a subject and begins to write, Brinkley reads the work and offers close edits. At times, his single-spaced pages of comments, which crystallize ideas, highlight inconsistencies, and connect narrow topics to broader themes, seem more substantive than the paper that inspired them. He spends an equal effort on his conferences with advisees. At weekly meetings to discuss his honors thesis, recalls Curtis, "Alan taught me a great deal about the historian's craft, the use of primary materials, making judgments and qualifying them, drawing analogies, writing and editing, and much more."[17]

In making his comments, Brinkley has always seen the benefits of benevolence. Weil, a professor of U.S. history at the École des Hautes Études en Sciences Sociales in Paris, remembers how Brinkley "was a little worried that, with my educational background, I would be tempted to teach my section in an authoritarian, top-down manner, and he took me aside at the beginning of the semester to give me advice about teaching and grading." His words of wisdom: never express contempt for the work of students, and always balance constructive criticism with positive reinforcement. Dallek, a professor at George Washington University, saw how helpful that approach was when he received comments on his dissertation. They became "the Bible" for how to turn it into a book—and how a professor should act. "His feedback to me had a direct impact on how I give feedback to students now," he says. "It is easy to forget, after you have been teaching for a while, the position of power that you're in when you're reading a student's paper."[18]

Brinkley never forgot, which is why he displayed rare flashes of anger when he saw other professors abuse their positions. Although he had staunchly liberal political views, he was careful not to impose them on his students, whom he loyally supported. Thaddeus Russell, a radical scholar, wrote a Columbia dissertation that was, in his words, "a direct, scorched-earth, frontal assault on everything [Brinkley] believes in, intellectually and politically." Yet Brinkley, he recalls, "made it as good as it could be" and "never once stopped being 100 percent genuinely intellectually curious and open to every single thing that I said. And I can say that about no other academic." Thomas Woods, a graduate student with conservative views who is now a senior fellow at the Mises Institute, had a similar assessment. "[Brinkley] has strong opinions—there's no question about that—but he was capable of having good, productive discussions with all sorts of people," he recalls. "He was very much a model of the kind of society that I would like to live in today."[19]

In commenting on the work of peers, Brinkley's interventions typically display two key features. "First, they entered as sympathetically as possible into the logic of the author and offered a criticism from within that standpoint," says Ira Katznelson, who for many years cochaired the twentieth-century U.S. politics and society seminar at Columbia with Brinkley. Second, they situated the text under discussion within a larger context: "it could be historiographical, it could be historical, it could be present-day or policy-related, but there was always a punch line that made the connections offered better than the author himself or herself had made." Brinkley was showing senior colleagues "ways to make their work sing more tunefully," recalls Katznelson, who adds that "this is a great skill, and to do it in a gentlemanly manner without any sacrifice of tough-mindedness or rigor was a very particular kind of gift."[20]

When Freidel died in 1993, the *Harvard Crimson* asked Brinkley to reminisce about his mentor. "On a personal level, he was extremely warm and helpful to his students," he remembered. "[He] invited us to his home often."[21] In Cambridge and then New York, Brinkley adopted this practice, occasionally inviting students to baseball games, local restaurants, or holiday dinners, where they mingled with his wide circle of friends and acquaintances. After the 2001 attacks on the World Trade Center, he opened his home to Daniel Scroop, an Oxford University graduate student he had mentored, who was stranded in New York for two weeks. "It was a very tense time," recalls Scroop, now a senior lecturer at the University of Glasgow. "Yet [Alan and his wife Evangeline] were incredibly generous."[22]

In 2010, at the Advanced Placement Reading in Louisville, where the exams were graded, Brinkley was the keynote speaker. After his remarks on "The Idea of the American Century," high school history teachers came up to him, asking for selfies and expressing their appreciation of his prompt and polite responses to their students' emailed questions, no matter how obvious or obnoxious. Later Brinkley remarked that as a child his family was routinely approached in public by people who recognized his father. "Only at the AP Reading do I get a sliver of that kind of celebrity and fame," he noted wryly.[23]

The source of his fame among AP teachers and students was his textbook, *American History: A Survey*, which has sold more than a million copies. First published in the late 1950s by Frank Freidel, Richard Current, and T. Harry Williams, it originally offered a traditional political and diplomatic account of the American past. After Brinkley assumed responsibility for the textbook in the late 1970s, when he was still a graduate student, he broadened the coverage to include social and cultural history. By 1995, when the ninth edition appeared and he at last accepted sole public authorship, he had updated most of the chapters and added sections on historiography ("Where Historians Disagree"), transnational history ("America in the World"), and popular culture. But the narrative voice remained clear and consistent—authoritative yet accessible, critical yet balanced. It also never condescended to younger readers by avoiding historical controversies.

Most textbooks are the products of committees or teams of authors. But after 1980, *American History: A Survey*—which spawned condensed versions like *The Unfinished Nation*—was the work of a single historian with a distinctive style. Every other summer was devoted to preparing new editions. To incorporate the latest scholarship in fields beyond his expertise, Brinkley recruited bright research assistants. The final product, however, was his own. Russell, who worked for him in the 1990s and now teaches at Willamette University, recalls that he was asked to read widely and then write drafts of selected chapters. He assumed that Brinkley would take credit for his words "like so many other big-name historians." But when the new edition appeared, he was "awestruck" because Brinkley "had changed every single word. It was 100 percent his own . . . and I got the sense that he did it out of principle."[24]

The textbook resonated with AP students across the country. Some responded by making T-shirts of Brinkley and sending them to him; he has a large pile (never worn) stacked in his closet.[25] Others opted for social media and created a host of Facebook pages in his honor, including "The Alan Brinkley Appreciation Society," "My Heart (and Life) Belong to Alan Brinkley," and "Alan Brinkley Is My Hero" (whose moderator wrote that "Brinkley is our king. But for the sake of democracy, we should vote for him to be president of the U.S. Maybe a historian will actually LEARN from the mistakes of the past"). Of course, with the cult-like reverence came some less positive (though still humorous) assessments, such as "Alan Brinkley Ruined My Life." Brinkley took that in stride. "It goes with the job, I guess," he told the *Columbia Spectator*.[26]

Frequent visits to high schools were also part of the job. At an Organization of American Historians conference, Eric Rothschild, an AP teacher at Scarsdale High School, invited Brinkley to speak to his class. Within a month, Brinkley took the train to Westchester. At first, the students could not believe that the author of their textbook was standing in front of them. "But their stunned silence quickly gave way to an exciting dialogue," recalls Rothschild, "as Brinkley led the class and brought the New Deal to life."[27] When I was a high school history teacher in the late 1980s, Brinkley visited my classroom twice—in New Jersey and New York—and dazzled my students with his historical knowledge and gracious manner; some later applied to Columbia specifically so that they could take classes with him.

Brinkley was also a founding member of the Advisory Board for the Gilder Lehrman Institute of American History. In the mid-1990s, recalls current president James Basker, "there was no way to know that the GLI would amount to anything." But Brinkley believed in the mission of the institute—to improve history education—and was a pillar of credibility. "If a scholar of his accomplishment and integrity supported the GLI, then it meant that it was not unimportant," states Basker, who first met Brinkley when both were at Harvard in the 1980s. Today, the institute has 13,000 affiliate schools across the United States and in forty countries. It also maintains a popular website dedicated to American history and holds weeklong teacher seminars at top universities across the country.[28]

For ten years—from 2000 to 2011—Brinkley led his own Gilder Lehrman seminar at Columbia on the decades between World Wars I and II. Even when he was provost, he continued to teach it because, as he often told the participants, the seminar was the highlight of his day. Nearly three hundred history educators, who on average would reach a thousand precollegiate students over the course of their careers, had the opportunity to learn the latest about the New Deal and bring that knowledge into their classrooms. "I am a high school teacher who needs and thrives on new information to make the history experience [for my students] as interesting as possible, like a chef creating a new recipe," later wrote a grateful Stefan Cohen of Rochester,

New York. After Brinkley's presentations, "I completely reframed my lessons on [the interwar] period," states Jennifer Collins, chair of the social studies department at Bishop McGuinness Catholic High School in Oklahoma City. Outside the seminar, the participants mingled with Brinkley. "He seemed perfectly at ease hanging out in a bar full of sweaty and tired high school teachers," recalls Collins.[29]

Although he was the product of an elite education, Brinkley has never been an elitist. "Alan's exposure to the world of power and privilege made him a small 'p' populist," recalls Gary Gerstle, now a professor at Cambridge University. "He liked a great diversity of people and variety of experiences." Those qualities made him an ideal bridge between the different spheres of history teaching. "Privilege, status, hierarchy—they did not impress him," adds Gerstle. "Some who rise quickly are quick to abandon their peers and colleagues. That was not Alan's way."[30]

Brinkley has never viewed the lecture hall or seminar room as a burden. He facilitates conversations, which he sees as the essence of teaching. He also appreciates that, as his friend and Columbia colleague Eric Foner puts it, "good teaching makes you a better scholar, and being an active scholar makes you a better teacher." Or, as Brinkley often says, "When you do not understand it, teach it."[31]

Brinkley's early success as a teacher may have indirectly contributed to Harvard's decision in 1986 to deny him tenure. Although some members of the history department publicly criticized the decision, it seems likely that others may have resented Brinkley's popularity.[32] Or perhaps they viewed his receipt of Harvard's Jerome Levenson Teaching Prize as proof that he was not a serious scholar—a common hazard at research universities. Ultimately, Harvard's action was principally due to the history department's unrealistic standard that internal tenure candidates in American history must already rank among the leaders in their field. But the attention that Brinkley devoted to his students and textbooks may also have slowed progress on his second major book, *The End of Reform*, which was eventually published in 1995 to considerable acclaim.

Brinkley seemed to share that thought when he announced in 1987 that he was joining the history faculty at the CUNY Graduate Center. "As much as I enjoy teaching," he explained in an interview, "it took up so much of my time that I didn't have enough of an opportunity to do my own work. I will be doing less teaching than I did at Harvard and I suppose that is one of my reasons for going there."[33] Yet just three years later Brinkley moved to Columbia in large part because he wanted to resume teaching undergraduates. In due course, the disappointment of losing the tenure battle at Harvard faded while he built a rich and vibrant life and career at Columbia, where he received the Great Teacher Award, and in New York City, where he and his family thrived. "How long does it hurt?" asked Fitzpatrick, who met the same fate at Harvard in 1996. "As long as you let it," he memorably replied.[34]

But Brinkley never expressed regret for his dedication to his students; to the contrary, he always took pride in them and followed their accomplishments closely. It made no difference whether he had taught them as undergraduates or graduate students or whether they were bound for careers in history, journalism, the law, business, government, or entertainment. (Late-night star and comedian Conan O'Brien, who took Brinkley's classes as a Harvard undergraduate in the 1980s, credits Brinkley with instilling in him "a real desire to keep reading up on everything I could about American history."[35]) It made no difference whether they achieved great professional success. He treasured the friendships that he made as he advanced from Harvard tutor to Columbia provost (and even then he insisted on offering at least one class a year). Teaching, he wrote, made for "a life that gives us the opportunity to convey our own passion for what we know to others in the hope that some of them, at least, will come to share it."[36] On behalf of all of us who came to love history and teaching because of Alan Brinkley, I wish to express our gratitude.

10

A Historian and His Publics

NICHOLAS LEMANN

Alan Brinkley has been profoundly shaped by an experience most people don't get to have: being the child of a very famous person. It's hard to communicate today how big a deal it was to anchor a nightly news program on network television during David Brinkley's precable, preinternet heyday in the 1960s and 1970s. Twenty million Americans, about 10 percent of the population, watched NBC's *Huntley-Brinkley Report* most nights (and it was only the second-ranked news program), and David Brinkley was the only news anchor living in Washington. That gave him an especially exalted status there.

Alan's attitude toward his father's world is one of profound but, in the end, productive ambivalence. He grew up around journalists and politicians and has always been intensely fascinated by them as types and by the sensation of watching history unfold roughly at first hand. That obviously contributed to his decision as a historian to focus on twentieth-century political history. On the other hand, he has no patience for big-time journalism's self-congratulatory and self-important aspect. Although he was always very close to his father, he also grew up highly attuned to the superficiality, clubbiness, and pomposity that were features of the circle in which David Brinkley moved in Washington. Alan was drawn to academic life as a refuge from some of the unattractive qualities of journalistic life, at least as it was lived in the upper reaches of the Washington establishment. And, conversely, David Brinkley, who was self-conscious about not having a college degree, took a special pride in Alan's academic career.

So it wasn't an accident that Alan has wound up having, for a historian of his generation, an unusually public-facing career. It was his way of compromising between the milieu where he had grown up and the milieu he entered by joining his profession. Historians older than Alan, like his friend Arthur M. Schlesinger Jr., attracted professional and popular audiences with their major works; in Alan's cohort, history had become more specialized and technical and less attracted to exploring the careers of political leaders. The people whom the public would have identified as the country's leading historians, on the basis of their books and television appearances, usually weren't historians at all in the literal sense of holding doctorates and being members of history departments. But Alan has had a deep, lifelong commitment to bridging the gap between the profession and the public.

I met Alan more than forty years ago, when he was a graduate student at Harvard and I was an undergraduate. I don't remember exactly how we met, but I do remember that he was a magnet for undergraduates who were interested in journalism. Alan was unusual among academics for being encouraging about that sort of aspiration. He was close in his interests to the present, where journalists dwell, and he made us believe it was possible to practice journalism in a way that was historically aware. His standard advice to undergraduates in those days was not to become an academic historian (one of academe's periodic entry-level employment crises was under way). However, he often encouraged students who had already decided on academic careers, by enrolling in graduate school, to pursue their impulse to do the kind of history that was in range of journalism: accessible, contemporary, and political. It's a significant aspect of Alan's career as a public intellectual that so many of his students and protégés have become either public-oriented historians or history-oriented journalists.

Another primary commitment of Alan's is to teaching large undergraduate survey courses; over the years, first at Harvard and then at Columbia, thousands of students had him as their primary guide to American history.

He does this because he wants his work to touch the lives of more than just a limited coterie of specialists. An important reason to be a historian, to him, is the opportunity it offers to create citizens who are deeply connected to the country's past and who understand the strengths and weaknesses of American democracy. That is also what has motivated him as a textbook writer, the role that has given him his numerically largest public audience (which includes my own children).

It would be difficult to perform a complete census of Alan's activities as a public intellectual because there have been so many of them: books, articles in publications like the *New York Times* and the *New York Review of Books*, television appearances, lectures, conferences, advice to active politicians and government officials, and participation on boards and commissions and in conferences. I'll give a few specific examples here to convey some idea of the breadth and range. These are all cases where I happened to witness Alan in action; there must be many more that didn't come to my attention.

Back in the 1960s, William Whitworth, a young reporter for the *New Yorker*, wrote a profile of David Brinkley and his news-anchoring partner, Chet Huntley, for the magazine. He met the teenaged Alan Brinkley in the course of his research. In 1980, Whitworth became editor of the *Atlantic Monthly*, then headquartered in Boston, and he reestablished contact with Alan, who was then an assistant professor of history at Harvard. Alan functioned as an informal, uncredited adviser to Whitworth, especially in the early years of his nearly two-decade editorship of the magazine. Whitworth was an old hand at magazines but relatively new to the world of public policy, which he wanted to be the magazine's central concern; Alan served as a guide, both to the dramatis personae in the policy and academic realms and to the major issues of the day.

Also in Boston in the 1980s, the great documentary filmmaker Henry Hampton was creating his production company, Blackside, and beginning work on an astonishing run of films, including *Eyes on the Prize*, his chronicle of the civil rights movement; a series on the War on Poverty; and a series on the Great Depression. Hampton, himself a veteran of the civil rights movement's student wing, wanted to recreate the "schools" that the Student Nonviolent Coordinating Committee and other movement organizations used to convene. As a result, Blackside became home to a long series of meetings where a multiracial group of academics, journalists, activists, and filmmakers, among others, would discuss ideas, scripts, and rough cuts for its films. Alan was one of the most frequent and devoted participants—and always a voice of calm authority in the discussions. He got a modest credit in the films, but mostly it was a large time commitment on his part made in service to the cause of greater public understanding of the past.

Alan has been especially involved with two nonprofit organizations, both of whose boards he eventually chaired: the Century Foundation (formerly the Twentieth Century Fund) in New York and the National Humanities Center in North Carolina, his father's home state. These are quite different institutions, but both represent aspects of the public-facing part of Alan's career. The Century Foundation has a long history as the liberal think tank most closely associated with the core principles of the New Deal (its board chair for many years was Adolf Berle, one of Franklin Roosevelt's original brain trusters). Alan's work as a historian of that period made him ideally suited to the foundation; he was especially interested in keeping the best elements of the New Deal tradition politically viable in the present. The National Humanities Center has nothing to do with politics. Its mission is to nurture and sustain the humanistic concerns that reside mainly in universities and also to connect them to public life. That, too, is a central concern of Alan's.

When Alan became provost of Columbia University in 2003, one of his first major initiatives was to secure funding from the Mellon Foundation for a new kind of professorship in the humanities. The idea was to bring to the university people who could work productively in both academic and nonacademic environments, as Alan did and as great Columbia professors in the past, like Lionel Trilling, Richard Hofstadter, and Meyer Schapiro, had. I served on the search committee for the Mellon Professors, which was an education for me, as a new arrival at the university, in how difficult it has become to integrate the academic and the public spheres in the humanities (Columbia wound up appointing two Mellon Professors, Elizabeth Alexander and Mark Lilla). Alan already knew, of course, how difficult it would be, and his resolve to forge ahead was a sign of how committed he was to the cause.

During his time as provost, Alan accomplished what's nearly impossible for people who hold such positions: he finished his most recent book, *The Publisher*, his long-gestating biography of Henry Luce. This was an unusual project for a major historian to take on because it was not only a biography but also a biography of a leading businessman. That he took it on is another sign of his commitment to writing for the public (I'd say *The Publisher* is the most accessible of his books) and of his lifelong ambivalent fascination with the upper reaches of politics and journalism that Luce inhabited. I don't think a nonhistorian who took on this project would have been as diligent as Alan about slogging through all of Luce's, and his magazines', copious papers; I don't think a more standard-issue academic would have been able to resist as fully as Alan did the temptation to present Luce as an all-powerful media baron who had expertly moved public opinion to the right. Alan's Luce is closer to a tragic figure, denied happiness in his celebrated marriage and political fulfillment in the cause that mattered most to him, restoring Chiang Kai-shek to power in China. The book itself stands as a model for writers who are attracted to public-oriented historical writing to emulate.

"Complaints about the divorce between academia and the larger public are not without foundation," Alan wrote in an essay called "Historians and Their Publics" that appeared in the *Journal of American History* in December 1994. He addressed this issue without scoring any easy points: he knew that one of the main causes of the divorce was an admirable shift in historians' focus away from "the affirmative, nationalistic assumptions that once shaped historical writing." Still, he insisted, it was worth it, indeed essential, for historians to make the special effort it would take to communicate with the public. He ended his essay with this impassioned peroration: "The attempt to understand the past . . . is not an arcane academic activity. It is part of a society's struggles over policy and belief and present action. It is part of the effort to enable individuals to resist power, to make independent judgments, to evaluate for themselves the claims and counterclaims about the past that form the core of much public discourse."

Alan's calm, imperturbable demeanor makes him easy to misread. It takes a great deal of determination to move between two cultures, as he has done for decades—it's not where the currents naturally take you. For Alan, being a public intellectual has been a lifelong cause during a period when that type was thought to be disappearing. To say that this has been a hard-won accomplishment, though, implies a certain joylessness that doesn't accurately capture Alan. The world has been too intensely interesting to Alan for him to be able to stay away from it. He has always seemed to know everybody worth knowing and to be in on everything worth being in on. He has demonstrated that being a public intellectual is not just a duty, though it is that, but also a pleasure.

PART II

Reminiscences

11

The Lost Masterpiece

A. SCOTT BERG

In September 1967, Alan Brinkley entered Princeton University, where he roomed with three classmates from Landon School in Bethesda, Maryland. By the end of freshman year, the foursome had disbanded, except for Alan and Nicholas Hammond, who bunked together until graduation. By the end of freshman year, I had become friends with Nick, and that inevitably threw me into Alan's orbit; and by fall of sophomore year, we three were charting a summer tour of Europe.

That winter, word suddenly spread across the Princeton campus that a generous alumnus was about to renew his annual offer of a few dozen summer jobs to Princeton undergraduates. Gordon T. Beaham III, of the Class of 1953, headed his Kansas City family's business, the Faultless Starch Company. Innovative and entrepreneurial, he had successfully expanded this consumer products empire, and he would soon unleash the Garden Weasel upon America. Because he famously paid his summer workers well, potential hires had to pounce fast—especially this year, because one special position needed to be filled.

G3, as he was known, had a new product he hoped to merchandise, a waste-water filtration system called Sani-Cell, and he intended to send one Princetonian to Europe for the summer to research markets there.

Selling ourselves as a team—three of us working for the price of one—we landed the $5,000 job. To this day, I presume that was because one of Alan and Nick's dorm mates, a Kansas Citian, told G3 what everybody on campus was already saying about Alan—that he was "the Arthur Schlesinger of our generation." Figuring a week of concentrated work could subsidize the rest of our summer, we promptly purchased our tickets on the Princeton charter flight to Paris in early June and paid in full for the rental of a four-door Renault. As that left each of us with $1,000 to last 100 days, we began dog-earing Arthur Frommer's *Europe on $5 a Day*.

Alan's future wife, Evangeline Morphos, often inflated his résumé, bragging that her illustrious husband had sold septic tanks one summer. That boast is patently false. We were market researchers, not salesmen; and Sani-Cell was not a septic tank! "No, sir," we were instructed to say, "Sani-Cell is better than a septic tank." It was a revolutionary new means of purifying water with enzymes and filters that had solved that eternal problem of sludge with its unique blend of aerobic and anaerobic bacteria, thus creating an end product so clean that one could walk into a bar whose restrooms used the Sani-Cell system and confidently order a "Scotch and effluent."

Our simple duty was to gather enough data (restrictions, requirements, demographics, and any other anecdotal information) in England (and Switzerland) to enable G3 to decide whether or not he should promote Sani-Cell in Europe.

Before our departure, G3 added that he also wanted us to test the European waters regarding a comic strip that had sprung from a local arts project he underwrote, a crudely drawn series about inner-city kids called *Butter and Boop*. Charles Schulz's *Peanuts* was the obvious inspiration, with its sly wisdom, whimsical drawings, and gentle humor. Unfortunately, *Butter and Boop* lacked all those qualities. After reading several weeks of the strip, Nick and I found a few kind things to say about it; Alan read the same panels and offered his assessment: "These are awful."

Our adventure began in early June 1969. After ten days touring France, we crossed the Channel and buckled down to work in London. We made an appointment at the Thames Conservancy, which was responsible for the water of Greater London and beyond, both its supply and its waste. Nick, the son of an English actress, was our front man, a charmer who easily broke into the Queen's English, giving us immediate credibility; I carried a stenographer's pad and became our official interrogator, posing most of our questions; and Alan was our assiduous scribe, not only recording those essential details that would give substance to our report but also listening hard enough to follow up with vital questions. Formidable team though we were, the most beneficial moment of our meeting arrived when we departed and were handed an armful of pamphlets that answered all our questions in considerable detail.

We ventured west for a week in the Cotswolds, where villages' names alone suggested they were promising founts of research material—Stow-on-the-Wold, Moreton-in-Marsh, Bourton-on-the-Water. Spending one afternoon after another exploring these storybook towns convinced us that the time-tested ecosystems were too precious for us even to set up a meeting in the region.

We proceeded to Stratford-upon-Avon, which we quickly concluded was also too historic to risk spoiling. But as long as we were there . . . we caught the Royal Shakespeare Company's latest offering, *The Winter's Tale*, featuring a promising young actress we all concluded would have a great career—Judi Dench. It was the first of many productions that Alan would enjoy in that theatre.

Stratford put us just a few miles from Royal Leamington Spa, where—ever mindful of our mission—we interviewed a water commissioner, sounding much more informed than we had during our interview in London. As a result of Alan's questioning, we learned that the town had earned its "Royal" honorific in 1838 because of a visit from Queen Victoria herself; and Alan, of course, could not resist showering details of her reign upon this poor government worker who just wanted to get back to his sanitation duties.

Returning to London, we spent a day on Fleet Street when it was famously home to a dozen newspapers. In office after office, Nick and I shamelessly insisted that young people in America were gobbling up *Butter and Boop* like *Peanuts*; Alan just sat there in uncharacteristic silence and typical disdain. After quickly examining a half dozen of our samples, one editor after another wore a look of utter bewilderment before politely showing us the door.

Confident that we had gathered more than enough information on both the water services and the cartoon tastes of the United Kingdom, we returned to the Continent, heading for Switzerland—but not without a little more time in Paris and a leisurely tour of the chateaux of the Loire Valley. In Geneva, we met with an official from the World Health Organization who made it quite clear how strict Switzerland—and all of Europe, really—was about the purity of its water. And with that, we felt well versed enough in the European potential for Sani-Cell to enjoy what we all agreed was a well-earned holiday.

After exploring Salzburg and Vienna, we discussed the need to find some time to write our report, but we decided instead to find a beach. Yugoslavia, particularly Dubrovnik, had become the rage in the late sixties, and so we headed to the Dalmatian coast.

We reached the Adriatic at Rijeka, which, Alan informed us, had formerly been named Fiume; and I still recall bits of his discourse on its place in the peace talks that ended World War I. After one night in the bleak town, we decided to continue southward. A relentlessly hot drive through progressively desolate scenery got us only as far as Zadar by midafternoon, and we were still not even halfway to Dubrovnik.

Although Zadar was far from the swinging seaside we imagined lay ahead, we discovered an extremely inexpensive "resort" where we might remain, instead of risking hundreds of more miles over a crude highway to a town that was sure to disappoint. We checked into this cinder-block complex, and by three o'clock, we had made our way to the beach. With the sun still blazing, we stopped at the "gift shop" to buy a metal tin of suntan cream called *Solea*. Alan slathered an especially thick coat over his entire (very pale) body.

At dinner that night, Alan literally glowed; and by the time we awakened the next morning, it appeared that *Solea* might be Serbo-Croatian for "Crisco." Burned to a radioactive crisp, he was swollen from head to toe, running a fever, and in too much pain to get out of bed. Nick and I brought him food through the day, but he was too ill to eat. Even though turning the pages of a book was an effort, Alan read Faulkner's *Light in August* in its entirety by the time he fell asleep that night. The next day he was still unable to venture to the dining room; when we returned from the beach that afternoon, we discovered that Alan had made the most of his time by pulling from his bag all the notes and pamphlets from our market research, along with a tablet of ruled white paper and felt-tip pens. He began writing.

Nick and I offered to help him pull our report together; but Alan said he had formulated it all in his head and he thought he should continue alone—which he did in his perfect printing, as precise as a typewriter. After one more day in confinement, he had composed a magnificent thirty-page draft. Weaving apt quotations from our interviews and government pamphlets, he enumerated the many reasons why Faultless Starch should not squander another penny promoting Sani-Cell in Europe. *Butter and Boop*, he insisted, promised even less of a return.

Nick and I could hardly believe how brilliantly "we" had processed the wealth of our material. I remember venturing one small editorial comment: that Alan might consider removing the paragraph he had written about the Victorian era while describing the laws governing waste water in Royal Leamington Spa. I thought it felt like padding. Alan conceded as much but suggested it might distract from our obvious paucity of scientific facts. It remained. As Alan needed one more day in which to recuperate, he prepared the final report, which meant little more than copying his first draft.

We returned to the open road, circling back toward Italy, where we spent the next few weeks—Venice, Rome, Florence, and the Ligurian coast. Finally, after our exhausting travels, we took time to relax in Nice before our flight home from Paris. Alan insisted we could not entrust our precious report to the postal service of Yugoslavia—"and Italy's even worse," he said. So we mailed our packet from the South of France to G3 in Kansas City.

Shortly after our return to school for junior year, we learned that Gordon Beaham was thrilled with the report. He found it much more sophisticated than anything he had expected from college students, incisive and decisive. Over the years, we heard repeatedly that he characterized our trip as money very well spent.

The single copy of the report is apparently lost to the ages, perhaps to be discovered one day preserved in spray starch in some Midwestern storage vault. Until such time, you'll just have to take my word—and that of Nicholas Hammond, who shares my opinion—that it was dazzling. The following facts certainly remain unarguable:

While the lost masterpiece marked the end of Alan's promising career in market research, the Faultless/Bon Ami company flourishes to this day—mostly, we have convinced ourselves, because the report saved it from a potentially fatal investment in Europe. And shortly after our return, *Butter and Boop* wrapped its last fish.

More important, that missing document from our golden summer of 1969 bonded us market researchers for life, forging an indestructible friendship based on love, admiration, and laughs. I can't recall a single get-together in the last fifty years at which at least one of us three didn't make a point of ordering a "Scotch and effluent," which then reduced us all to fits of laughter.

Perhaps most important, "Sani-Cell European Market Report #1" bore all the hallmarks of Alan's later work—cogency, eloquence, and complete mastery of material, even when the subject was sewage.

Thus, Alan Brinkley entered the ranks of professional writers.

And the rest, as they say, is History.

12

The Skinny One with Glasses and Receding Hairline

NANCY WEISS MALKIEL

I first met Alan in the spring of 1970. He was a junior at Princeton, concentrating in the Woodrow Wilson School, which offered an undergraduate major in public policy. I was in my first year as an assistant professor of history. The venue was a precept in History 300, Arthur S. Link's storied course in twentieth-century American political history. I was teaching five precepts—not atypical for a new assistant professor. What was unusual was that they were far from precept size. The word had gotten out that it would likely be Link's last time offering the course; instead of the usual ten to twelve, there were twenty-five students in each precept. (Indeed, it was Link's last hurrah as an undergraduate lecturer; the deal was that I would give six of the lectures, and if I passed muster with him, I would henceforth inherit the course.)

"You may not remember me," Alan wrote later, tongue in cheek, in a letter asking me to recommend him for admission to history graduate school. "We were the ones who played basketball with a tennis ball and trash can before you arrived every week, and I was the skinny one with glasses and receding hairline who sat next to Mark Wine (the fat one with glasses and receding hairline). I'm sure that if you don't remember me specifically, you at least remember the collective wit and brilliance of our group."

How could I not remember him? He was easily the best student of the 125 I taught in precepts in that course. I was continually impressed by his knack for coming up with thoughtful, penetrating insights that would clarify and draw together disparate threads of discussion. His examination paper, like his oral contributions, was a model of clarity and good reasoning.

The next year I advised Alan's senior thesis on Huey Long. It was an unusual pleasure to work with him; he was an exceptionally gifted student, the kind who educates teachers while they are teaching him. He was amazingly well organized, and he had his entire thesis completed weeks before the due date. His rough draft read like a polished finished product. His research was exemplary; he exhausted relevant primary source materials and showed excellent judgment in assessing what he found. His presentation was particularly striking, for he wrote with a grace and flair unusual in an undergraduate. Even then, he had an uncanny feel for language—a sense of pace, style, composition, and felicitous phrasing all too rare among historians in general, let alone history students.

In terms of content, he posed an excellent analytical problem, framing Long's national political career in terms of the interaction between his personal drive for power and his commitment to wealth redistribution. He developed it into a beautifully organized, very well-supported argument. He asked the right questions, was sensitive to subtleties and ticklish points of interpretation, and invariably came up with good, sound, sensible answers. His success with the thesis was all the more noteworthy because of the recent publication of T. Harry Williams's major biography of Long. One might have thought at first glance that Williams would have preempted the scholarly field on Long for the time being, but Alan managed to frame and develop an important problem that really was not covered in the biography. The thesis, of course, later provided the jumping-off point for Alan's dissertation at Harvard and later his National Book Award–winning book.

Alan spent the two years after graduation thinking about where he wanted to go in his life. His abilities were such that he could have been a great success in law, journalism, or any of several other fields; in fact, he turned down an offer of admission to Harvard Law School the year before he applied for history graduate school. During that time, he advanced his career as a historian, albeit unexpectedly and by a peculiar route. The National Endowment for the Humanities had asked me to undertake a brief study of the life and career of William Bourke Cockran, the orator and Tammany Hall politician. (My senior thesis at Smith College, which became a published book, was about the last great boss of Tammany Hall, Charles Francis Murphy.) Although the project seemed intriguing, the reason for it was rather bizarre. President Richard Nixon had become interested in Cockran, and the endowment seemed to feel that the most politic response to his inquiries would be to commission a study. Because I already had other scholarly commitments of my own, I suggested that the endowment consider Alan instead. (He was at that time on the research staff of the U.S. senator from Maine, Edmund S. Muskie, who had run for vice president of the United States in 1968 on Hubert H. Humphrey's unsuccessful ticket and who was seeking—also without success—the Democratic nomination for president in 1972.)

The endowment agreed to have Alan do the study under my supervision (which turned out to be entirely nominal), and he spent the summer of 1972 doing research. Even though we were skeptical of the way in which the study was commissioned, we decided to construe it as a latter-day Federal Writers' Project. At the end of the summer, the endowment asked Alan to pull together a sixty- to seventy-page summary of his findings about Cockran on one week's notice because the White House had been asking for it. (Why Nixon was interested in Cockran we never found out.) In other words, Alan was being asked to write a mini–senior thesis in one week, a seemingly impossible task. But he pulled it off with incredible aplomb and style. The piece so impressed William R. Emerson, director of research at the endowment, that he offered Alan a year of support to expand it into a full-scale biography of Cockran, though Alan chose not to accept it.

Alan and I have built professional careers that have many parallels, but in every case, Alan is the one who achieved greater distinction. We were both PhD students of Frank Freidel at Harvard, but Alan became Frank's successor on the Harvard faculty, and he collaborated with Freidel on and later took over his twentieth-century American history textbook. We both taught twentieth-century American history, but Alan won university teaching prizes at Harvard and Columbia. We both published in the field, but Alan became the best American political historian of his generation—and one of the most influential scholars of any age writing in the field. We both became university administrators—I, dean of the college at Princeton; Alan, provost at Columbia.

No student I have ever taught has been more brilliant, more accomplished, or more humble about his achievements. The Alan I described in recommendations over the years is the Alan I have known as my treasured friend: patient, poised, steady, stable, calm, and disciplined, with a great sense of humor and a delightfully engaging personality. Alan and I—and later Evangeline and Burt—have shared so many wonderful experiences over the years: our respective weddings, countless dinners, lively conversations about politics and theater, stories about the exploits of our much-loved small dogs, and so much more. Burt and I were privileged to attend the dinner at Columbia celebrating Alan upon his retirement as provost in 2009; in 2011, Alan and Evangeline participated in the festivities marking the end of my deanship at Princeton. Most recently, in November 2016, Alan and Evangeline hosted a spectacular book party for me in New York.

I wish the conversations could go on forever.

13

Lord Root-of-the-Matter

JONATHAN ALTER

Harvard College can be a forbidding place. In the spring of 1977, nearly halfway through my time there, I had yet to establish any kind of relationship with a Harvard professor. Even the friendly ones—like David Herbert Donald of the history department—dwelled on Mount Olympus, from where they delivered brilliant lectures while letting their graduate students do the actual teaching in "sections" of fifteen or so and—for history majors like me—"tutorials" with a half dozen students.

I was a nineteen-year-old sophomore, using—often squandering—my free time at the *Harvard Crimson*, the campus daily. One day in the tattered newsroom, unchanged since the 1940s or earlier, I let it be known by the water fountain that I was an American history major. Tutorials began sophomore year, and I had a good one, but my tutor had been assigned to me. I had learned that I could get into a junior tutorial in a different "house," as the Harvard dormitories for all but freshmen are called.

"Brinkley!" the *Crimson* president said. "You gotta get Alan Brinkley!" The president—the editor in chief—that year was a frenetic Philadelphia kid named Jim Cramer. He was pushing Alan Brinkley on me the way he pushes stocks nowadays on CNBC's *Mad Money*. If this grad student Brinkley was good enough for Cramer and—a couple years earlier—another

Crimson president, Nick Lemann (later a *New Yorker* writer and, thanks partly to Alan, dean of the Columbia School of Journalism), then he was good enough for me.

Brinkley was the American history tutor in Eliot House, and I was in Lowell, but I figured maybe I could get him if I lobbied hard enough at Robinson Hall, where the history department had its offices. The history department was one of my beats at the *Crimson* (a clear conflict of interest), and I begged the administrators I was supposed to be covering to bend the rules and let me in. They wouldn't, but when I appealed directly to Alan, I learned, as so many students would over the years, that he was a soft touch for anyone who shared his thirst for American history and politics.

Alan's tutorial was one of those rare experiences in life that exceeds expectations. We read deeply in all eras of American history, but I was especially happy with how much we focused on the twentieth century. He assigned *The Power Broker*, by Robert Caro. The book's subject, Robert Moses, the "master builder" of modern New York City, was retired but still alive. Much of what Moses did took place in our lifetimes. I shared Alan's belief that recent history could still be history, though this surprisingly controversial view would come back to haunt him.

The long conversations that my four fellow tutees and I had with Alan every week in his spacious suite in Eliot House were easygoing and rigorous at once. Alan would gently pose a question and then watch placidly behind his rimless glasses as we struggled to answer. Finally, he would offer a fresh, jargon-free, and exceptionally penetrating insight into the historical or historiographical subject at hand.

Alan had high standards. I was a mediocre student except in history, where I usually received straight As. In Alan's tutorial, I never managed better than an A-minus on any paper but was always thrilled to get my papers back. Attached to the last page were 500–1,000 words of typed (!), single-spaced comments on what I had written—acute, practical, and full of the wise suggestions a generation of his own grad students would come to expect. Never before or since have I received such careful attention to my work.

Alan was twenty-eight and at work on his dissertation, which was eventually published in 1982 as *Voices of Protest*. I remember stacks of draft chapters all over the room and Alan wryly describing the challenge he would face preparing an academic work for publication as a trade book. He was also helping historians Richard N. Current, Frank Freidel, and T. Harry Williams with the 1979 revisions of *American History: A Survey*.

At the time, I didn't pay much attention to Alan's textbook work. But in taking over later editions of that and another textbook, he eventually became a rock star to my daughters and hundreds of thousands of other high school students. They found "Brinkley" less a textbook than a friendly and quirky relief from their other assignments that prepared them superbly well for the Advanced Placement test and college. Alan's narrative gifts, insights, and clarity of expression were so superior to what they read elsewhere that even years later he is remembered fondly by Americans who never took a college history course.

Before it was cool, Alan was a confirmed ironist, with a warm laugh that conveyed the absurdities of Harvard life and the world at large. In private, he had an acerbic wit, usually directed at conservatives, but he also showed me how to avoid letting skepticism descend into cynicism. Whenever I would sound off on someone or something, he would deepen my hot take with historical context and the wisdom of someone twice his age.

A year after I graduated, Alan gave me a job. Along with Charlie Curtis, Cliff Sloan, Mark Powden, and Peter Fitzsimmons, I worked part-time in 1980 as a research assistant on David Brinkley's book *Washington Goes to War*, a sprightly, informative social history of how World War II transformed the capital. David Brinkley was still famous for coanchoring *The Huntley-Brinkley Report* on NBC in the 1960s, but ratings for his later newsmagazine shows were disappointing, and the legendary anchorman was temporarily out to pasture. The following year, 1981, Roone Arledge resuscitated his career by hiring him at ABC News. This was good news for David, who anchored the *This Week* Sunday show for the next fifteen years, but less so for Alan, who was left to ghostwrite much of his father's book.

After teaching for a couple of years at MIT, Alan became an assistant professor at Harvard, where he would introduce himself to his lecture classes with the line "No, I am not related to Christie Brinkley. . . ." His 500-student classes on twentieth-century history became so popular in the early 1980s that entrance was determined by lottery. By some estimates, as many as one-third of Harvard undergraduates took a Brinkley course.

His scholarship was impeccable and compelling—*Voices of Protest* won the National Book Award (then called the American Book Award)—and he was widely considered one of the finest professors in the entire university. My wife, Emily Lazar, took his class on the Progressive Era and remembers that "his calm storytelling and accessible insights left you leaving the lecture hall feeling as if you'd had a one-on-one conversation with the professor."

But Harvard, just after announcing a plan to promote more junior faculty, denied Alan tenure in 1986. The history department had recommended Alan for tenure, but under the university's peculiar system, a tiny number of senior history professors were able to weigh in, and the dean of the faculty could reverse the decision. According to what trickled down to us, they seemed to believe as a matter of perverted principle that no one young and untenured could possibly be worthy of consideration and that nothing after 1945 should be considered "history," which made Alan some kind of outlier for wanting to teach a period that actually interested students. And rumor had it that his popularity—including occasional television appearances— rendered him suspiciously unrigorous in their jealous eyes.

I wasn't the only Brinkley backer left apoplectic by the decision. This wasn't just bad for Alan; it was also disastrous for Harvard's history department, whose American history professors had an average age of 61. Henry Kissinger is said to have quipped that "academic politics are so bitter because the stakes are so small," but in this case, the consequences for Harvard were large. Arthur M. Schlesinger Jr., himself a former Harvard history professor, snapped up Alan for CUNY, and not long after, he landed at Columbia, where he went on to a storied career. Many of the best young Americanists followed him, which helped Columbia's history department lap Harvard's for thirty years.

When my wife and I moved to New York, we became good friends with Alan and his wonderful wife, Evangeline, who was my freshman expository writing teacher. They hosted fun, eclectic dinner parties with historians, novelists, and media personalities—many of the most interesting people in the city. Any time I had a challenging column to write or faced an important personal decision, I could always count on Alan to be, as Winston Churchill dubbed Harry Hopkins, "Lord Root of the Matter." I will treasure the gift of his friendship for the rest of my life.

14

Careers in Counterpoint

LIZABETH COHEN

I hope it won't sound too presumptuous on my part to say that the distinguished American historian Alan Brinkley and I have led somewhat parallel lives, with periodic intersections. Those shared experiences, I think, give me a singular perspective on Alan's career. We both went to Princeton for our undergraduate degrees, two years apart, where we were inspired by an outstanding history faculty. We both moved to Boston upon our graduations, where we had in common a relationship with my partner and later husband, Herrick Chapman, who had been a classmate of Alan's at Princeton. Our three major books (my third not quite finished) followed similar intellectual pathways, and we both have authored U.S. history textbooks that compete in the college and Advanced Placement markets.[1] We both have spent time in the history department at Harvard, mine I dare say with a happier outcome than his. Nine years apart, we both had the privilege of serving as the Harmsworth Professor at Oxford University, with veteran Alan generously offering himself as a helpful guide when my turn came.

Our paths have crossed often over the last forty plus years: during the five I lived in New York City while teaching at New York University and he was at Columbia University; at many conferences; in Oxford when

Alan and his wife, Evangeline, made their annual pilgrimage during my Harmsworth year; and at periodic theater performances in New York and in Cambridge, where they were sometimes guests of our mutual friend Susan Ware. On every occasion, I was reminded that Alan is a colleague and friend who wears his own achievements lightly and demonstrates great warmth and caring toward others.

First, Princeton. In a remarkable piece Alan wrote for the class of 1971's fortieth reunion, "Our Generation: A Princeton Memoir," he turned his talent as a historian toward interpreting the experience of his college cohort. Displaying the conceptual skills that distinguish his historical writing, Alan argued that his classmates had lived through a unique time that began in the fall of 1967 as "the last semester of the F. Scott Fitzgerald Princeton" and ended four years later as a very different place—coeducational, more politically engaged, less elitist, and with the university's FitzRandolph Gate now permanently unlocked and open to the outside world. Still, Alan took pride in pointing out that "academic life at Princeton remained a remarkable thing"; a great university uniquely devoted to undergraduate education was continuing to make itself "a vibrant and intellectually challenging place to learn." In comments accompanying this reunion e-book, Alan's classmates enthusiastically endorsed his rendering. "You helped distill and clarify a poignant time, and bring it back intact," wrote one admiringly.[2] What strikes me in reading Alan's essay now is not only his mastery as a writer and analyst but also his ability to achieve the stance of an observer. Alan Brinkley the historian was both in this Princeton story and apart from it—both the participant and the witness. It signals for me a role that Alan has been comfortable fulfilling throughout his life: someone who modestly and empathetically seeks to see the world from many angles, not simply from his own.

It was working on his Princeton senior thesis on Huey Long, "The Gospel of Discontent: Huey Long and National Politics 1932–1935," that Alan later recounted as his exciting initiation into the pleasures of primary research. Of his first trip to the Roosevelt Library in Hyde Park, New York, he would write: "I'll never forget the feeling of opening, for the first time, a box of papers, and holding in my hand a letter that Franklin Roosevelt had written and signed, and the sense of being a part of the great tradition of historians who have built their work around this exposure to the imme-diate product of the minds of the great figures, and not so great figures, of our history."[3] By the time this work became his Harvard dissertation (which he finished in 1979), it would expand to include Father Charles Coughlin. Three years later it would appear as his acclaimed first book, *Voices of Protest*.[4]

Among several themes in the book, Alan paid particular attention to how Long and Coughlin used the radio to communicate with their ador-ing publics, challenging FDR's own masterful fireside chats on their own ground. This was the first place where my work and Alan's intersected. Whereas he was fascinated with how Long and Coughlin used the radio to mobilize their supporters, I, too, explored the impact of early radio in my dissertation and first book, *Making a New Deal: Industrial Workers in Chicago, 1919–1939*.[5] We had different perspectives—Alan, the political historian, focused on these ideologically motivated broadcasters, and I, the social historian, was more interested in audience reception—but we shared a conviction that the radio transformed politics in the 1930s. We both explored how ordinary Americans shifted their allegiance from local political authorities to national ones as they sought, in the midst of the Great Depression, to assert themselves more effectively. In the 1990s, as tensions emerged between practitioners of traditional political history and social historians like me who argued for a more expansive definition of politics and political history, Alan served as the profession's mediator, an open-minded emissary from the old world of political history who ecu-menically welcomed the new. Again, Alan was ever the fair-minded umpire who could see value in both sides of the debate.

His second book, *The End of Reform*, was the "big book" that secured his reputation as the éminence grise of twentieth-century U.S. political history.[6] Here he laid out the ideological contests and resulting evolution of a distinctive liberal economic and political way of thinking during the New Deal. Alan's subject was how different economic approaches vied for dominance in Roosevelt's administration until a Keynesian embrace of consumption as a means to bring about economic recovery won out by the late 1930s. By the war's end, the template was set for a postwar America in which mass consumer capitalism, even if monopolistic, would be accepted as the most viable route to widespread national prosperity. I, too, would probe the emergence of a consumer orientation to the economy and the polity in my second book, *A Consumers' Republic: The Politics of Mass Consumption in Postwar America.*[7] The triumph after World War II of what I called a "consumers' republic" opened the door somewhat to broader and more egalitarian participation in political life, such as when in the 1950s African Americans employed their power as consumers through boycotts and sit-ins to assert their equal rights as citizens. But in cases of unequal access to consumer goods, as when consumers were unable to purchase a suburban home in a community that offered good schools and other avenues to opportunity, the consumers' republic created new kinds of social inequality. In many ways, our second books were a bound set—paired in graduate seminars and explicitly sold that way on Amazon—Alan's book serving, in a way, as the prequel to mine. Once again, Alan's focus was on the policy makers and politicians, whereas mine was more often on ordinary Americans. But we both appreciated that an important form of modern behavior—mass consuming—had implications far beyond the purchase of goods.

Alan's third major book, *The Publisher*, was a labor of love that he somehow managed to write during his six years–from 2003 to 2009—as provost at Columbia.[8] (I have to admit that my similar stint in academic administration—at the time of writing, I am in my seventh year as dean of the Radcliffe Institute for Advanced Study at Harvard—has not yielded for me the same level of scholarly productivity.) Here Alan returned to his earlier fascination with the impact of the mass media on the American political environment. But he approached it differently than he had before, selecting the figure of Henry Luce—creator of *Time, Life, Fortune, Sports Illustrated*, and more—as a revealing biographical vehicle for exploring larger questions. His subject was as much of a household name as Alan's own father—but one who invented a mass-circulation instrument that aimed not only to deliver the news but also to shape the very way that middle-class American audiences understood the world. Luce, the media mogul, promoted an ideology of the American century that was internationalist in foreign policy and antistatist domestically. The thread that ran throughout Alan's work—that American political history was made as much by popular figures wielding cultural influence as by officeholders and policy makers—was fully developed in this magisterial rendering of Luce's life.

My own work has ironically taken a similar turn. I am now finishing a book, *Saving America's Cities: Ed Logue and the Struggle to Renew Urban America in the Suburban Age*, that focuses on urban redeveloper Logue to complicate understanding of postwar urban renewal and its evolution over time beyond a simplistic opposition of Robert Moses (bad) and Jane Jacobs (good).[9] As Alan did, I have undertaken the challenge of using a life story to probe an important aspect of twentieth-century U.S. history where agency is often elusive—in his case the rise of mass media, in mine the shifting strategies of urban redevelopment. This kind of biographically inflected history appealed to us both, I would suggest, because of its unique combination of interpretive power and narrative appeal to readers.

Along the way, Alan has also made many other contributions, but perhaps one of the most significant has been his devotion to teaching, both of undergraduates new to historical analysis and of graduate students for whom he has served as a committed adviser. At the Columbia conference that his former students organized in his honor in April 2016 and that set the stage for this volume, we heard story after story about Alan's talents as a mentor: wise but encouraging students to find their own way, demanding but compassionate. Most impressive and quite evident in the essays in this book is the fact that Alan's students have done many kinds of historical writing, ranging from institutional political history to diverse cultural and social analyses. This sweeping breadth of Alan's mentoring may make the strongest statement of all about his generosity of intellect and spirit. He has always sought not to replicate himself but to inspire originality in his students. Here Alan has put into real-life practice the conviction that guides his historical writing: that the actions taken by those in positions of influence make a tremendous difference for the lives of others.

15

History as a Humanizing Art

IRA KATZNELSON

I knew Alan Brinkley's incisive scholarship and reputation as a pellucid teacher well before we first met for an extended conversation at Sarabeth's on Amsterdam Avenue in the spring of 1992. But I had not yet personally experienced his probing intelligence, quiet but demanding persona, ironic wit, range of reading, exceptional curiosity and knowledge, or institutional commitments.

At the time, I was being recruited, primarily by the political science department, to come to Columbia University; Alan had joined the Department of History there not long before, in the fall of 1991. When we sat down to talk, I was inclined to accept an offer of a joint appointment in political science and history but was not yet sure. By the time we parted more than two hours later, I knew that I would. The prospect we discussed— of convening a workshop crossing disciplinary lines to explore twentieth-century American politics and society—especially appealed to me.

What I did not then know was that our work together would last two decades or how much it would influence the main currents of my writing and teaching. And I certainly could not have predicted that at the start of Alan's tenure as provost, in 2003, I would serve down the hall in Low

Library for a single academic year as acting vice president for arts and sciences, a post that would give me the chance to watch a guardian of the best values of the university work at the center of the university's administration.

But I did gain a sense of our potential intellectual connection as Alan talked about the book he was finishing, with the still tentative title of *The End of Reform*. Much of our discussion turned on his manuscript's engagement with the perspectives and cast of mind Richard Hofstadter had exhibited in *The Age of Reform*, which Alan had described in a beautifully realized 1985 assessment as "the most influential book ever published on the history of twentieth-century America."[1]

It was this essay, even more than Alan's many other inspiring writings, that had made me so anxious to meet Alan when I was trying to decide whether or not to move to Columbia. That reconsideration of Hofstadter's controversial treatment of populism, progressivism, and their legacies demonstrated Alan's wish to critically embrace that work's orientation to history, a position Hofstadter called "analytical history," at the intersection of the crafts of history and social science, which he first had announced in the mid-1950s.

I had first read Hofstadter's "History and the Social Sciences" essay as an undergraduate, when he shared it with me during one of our almost weekly sessions as he supervised my senior thesis. Ever since, the ambitions it named as analytical history have guided my choice of subjects and means of pursuing them. So it was a wonderful revelation to discover that Alan Brinkley broadly shared these bearings, if with his own original understanding and voice.

Writing in 1956, Hofstadter had sought to find means to remedy the concern that "authors of narrative histories rarely hesitate to retell a story that is already substantially known, adding perhaps some new information but seldom in systematic fashion or with a clear analytical purpose," whereas "many a monograph . . . leaves its readers, and perhaps even its author, with misgivings as to whether that part of it which is new is truly significant." Seeking an alternative, he counseled more attention to the insights and creative possibilities proffered by the social sciences, whose use "promises to the historian . . . a special kind of opportunity to join these two parts of his tradition in a more effective way."[2] Hofstadter thus appealed to his colleagues to renew history as a vocation by developing

> a somewhat new historical genre, which will be a mixture of tradi-
> tional history and the social sciences. It will differ from the narra-
> tive history of the past in that its primary purpose will be analytical.
> It will differ from the typical historical monograph of the past in that
> it will be more consciously designed as a literary form and will focus
> on types of problems that the monograph has all too often failed
> to raise. It will be informed by the insights of the social sciences
> and at some points will make use of methods they have originated.
> Without pretending to be scientific, it may well command more
> reciprocal interest and provide more stimulation for social scientists
> than a great deal of the history that is now being written.[3]

When Brinkley reviewed Hofstadter, he reflectively embraced this mode of doing history, all the while taking note of its complications, challenges, and, at times, oversimplifications. As I first read and later reread Alan's review essay, I was moved by its sympathetic critique, its wry sensibilities, its fair-minded capacity for appraisal, and its normative ambitions. I also was struck by his willingness to probe the American experience through fresh appraisals with an array of sometimes unexpected tools and literatures, all the while looking for a thread of interpretive logic geared to better understanding the language and substantive directions of American liberalism, to navigating the then-vibrant debate about conflict and consensus, and to finding a pathway between appreciation of the political order's achievements and disappointment at its shortcomings. Readers of *The End of Reform* soon were to see just how powerfully and persuasively these traits and themes could be deployed as they engaged with the book's identification of the late 1930s as a point of inflection in America's chances to focus impulses of improvement and change on fundamental conundrums of political economy.

Though Brinkley has never imitated Hofstadter—indeed, they differ in many aspects of historical appraisal and understanding—Alan's exceptional writing has worked with similar determinations, not least the wish to deploy rigorous history as an aspect of a larger public conversation about the meaning and prospects of the American experience. Both Hofstadter and Brinkley always refused to confine their attention or audiences to professional ones, even as they never compromised the standards of their discipline. Both declined to choose between, in Hofstadter's words, the "desire to count in the world and their desire to understand it."[4] I believe that this double ambition has directed Alan to his topics: not just his pioneering, influential work on the New Deal but also his considerations on liberalism more broadly as well as his wonderful biography of Henry Luce. It has also shaped Alan's profound commitment to history as a humanizing art.

When his review of Hofstadter appeared, I was first turning to the New Deal in my own research, with particular attention to the role of the South in national politics, especially Congress. To my great profit, the temporal arc of my work on this era overlapped the period from my first engagement with Alan's New Deal scholarship to the conclusion of our efforts together at Columbia. The latter included the twentieth-century workshop and the chance to work with some of the country's most talented graduate students in American history, especially political history.

I thus owe Alan significant debts. His persistent, informed, crucial commentary advanced how I thought about the 1930s and 1940s as he probed my questions and arguments, suggested pathways for analysis, encouraged a combination of assertiveness and modesty, and signaled themes and literatures that I needed to better apprehend. My *Fear Itself* would have been a much different book if not for Alan's guidance and intense support.[5]

In our workshop, his deeper knowledge of the range of work under way, especially among cohorts of younger historians, significantly broadened my understanding of the field, particularly the vulnerabilities and possibilities of political history inflected not only by the social sciences but also by social, cultural, and economic history. It became our joint ambition to advance both historical political science and analytical political history at just the time when political history was in trouble and the subfield of American political development was emerging in political science.

Alan never thought of himself as a political theorist. But he has been quite a profound student of the liberal political tradition, at the intersection of liberalism as a body of ideas based on norms of consent, law, rights, and representation and liberalism as a policy location within the spectrum of partisan views in the United States. This joining has made him sensitive to state theory, interested in social contract theory from Locke to Rawls, and concerned with understanding the entanglement of ideas and institutions that have shaped the course of conflict and agreement within the ambit of a manifestly liberal political regime.

His historical writings sometimes seem traditional in their literary and temporal qualities, their appealing insistence on complexity, and their skepticism about fashionable but often evanescent trends. Yet the Brinkley corpus is anything but ordinary. Though deeply worried about the direction of the country and concerned with comprehending and acting on various crises at home and abroad, Alan has avoided deriving politics and policy directly from history, refusing simplification or didactic approaches, and all the while teaching by example how it can be possible nonetheless to connect distinguished historical scholarship to public concerns of the highest importance.

16

Two Kids from Chevy Chase

FRANK RICH

I would like to believe I recognized all the qualities that I and so many others revere in Alan Brinkley at the moment I met him: his generosity, loyalty, wisdom, selflessness, wit, and modesty and, of course, his bottomless capacity for friendship and his brilliance as a teacher, writer, and historian. Given that we first met in the Washington hospital room where we were born on the same June day in 1949, such prescience was unlikely. But I choose to believe that much of Alan was present almost immediately thereafter, for I have nothing but sweet memories of him from earliest childhood, when we became best friends as soon as we were ambulatory.

We lived around the corner from each other in Somerset, a woodsy Chevy Chase neighborhood just across the District line in Maryland, and attended the same elementary school. We watched the first *Huntley-Brinkley Report* together from his living room couch in 1956. That fifteen-minute NBC network newscast would soon make Alan's father famous. I was lucky enough to also know Alan's mother, Ann Fischer Brinkley, whose virtually lifelong friendship with my mother was what had led to their hospital cohabitation on the occasion of the colliding births of their first children. Ann, like my mother, was a product of a very specific Washington enclave little known to official Washington, let alone tourists:

Jewish Washington, an insular set of families who were part of a transient city's permanent civic furniture. They tended to cluster in the same areas (Northwest Washington, Montgomery County), ran many of the city's small retail businesses (my father was in shoes), and, in the case of the Fischers, produced top-tier doctors and commercial real-estate developers.

Alan's mom was what we'd now call a pistol: tiny of stature, sharp, witty, outspoken. When she was driving us in a carpool at a tender age, I was shocked when she cheered a radio bulletin that some famous person had died. (When I asked my mother about this breach of decorum once home, she did her best to bring my five-year-old consciousness up to speed on Joe McCarthy.) How Ann ended up with David, a tall, laconic, gentile reporter from the South, is a story I wish I knew. But together they produced a son who was a fascinating amalgam of their qualities: Ann's intellectual curiosity and passion and David's dry humor, political acumen, and gift for spinning elegant sentences.

In the end, both of our parents would get divorced, a relatively rare occurrence in our middle-class world of that time. I would move out of Somerset at the end of second grade, just months after *Huntley-Brinkley* went on the air. Yet forever after, Alan and I would revisit our formative years there, remembering our own early friendship, from our joint birthday parties to our misadventures exploring the nearby forest to the idiosyncratic personalities of our other friends' parents. More than a few fathers were psychiatrists, occasionally with anger management issues. More than a few mothers, our own included, were captivated by Democratic politics in the Eisenhower era. I still have the "All the Way with Adlai" button I was awarded for canvassing Somerset with my mother in my last autumn there. Alan and I were not precocious enough to read newspapers or follow the news, but our parents, the neighborhood, and the looming presence of the nation's capital just past Wisconsin Circle all whetted our curiosity about politics. That our mothers were both big readers and, true to the Jewish cultural habits of the time, avid theatergoers had an impact on our development as well.

Once I had moved away, Alan and I drifted apart—he to the then-distant suburb of Potomac and a boys' school, Landon, and me to public schools in the city. We did not overlap at Harvard, where he entered graduate school the autumn after I graduated from Harvard College. But Ann remained friends with my mother, and they cooked up a reunion for their sons as we were turning thirty. Effortlessly, Alan and I picked up where we left off, bound together by our Somerset years, our nearly identical intellectual interests, our sardonic sensibilities, and our mutual contempt for the provincial company town we had both fled after high school, never to return. By then, Alan was teaching history at MIT, and I was starting my job as drama critic of the *New York Times*. When Alan visited New York, he'd often be my theater date—the best kind, with no expectations of actually seeing something good. We'd have dinner afterward so we could talk about everything, least of all the play. It turned out we had mutual adult friends, many of them in journalism, and our lives seemed to fold together much as they had when we were kindergarteners chasing the Good Humor truck in Somerset.

But there were setbacks for both of us after we reconnected at the dawn of the 1980s. I had a painful divorce from my first wife; Alan had a painful divorce from his teaching career at Harvard. He traveled to New York to console me and to help me settle into my single father's digs, and I went to Boston to try to do anything I could to bolster his spirits. The injustice of his treatment by the Harvard history department shocked me and still angers me. I shouldn't have been shocked: the three great historians who taught me as an undergraduate there—Peter Stansky, Neil Harris, and Kevin Starr—were all denied tenure by Harvard and, like Alan, went on to extraordinary careers elsewhere. That such injustice would be inflicted on Alan was doubly vexing because he is the soul of judiciousness. Not the least of his contributions to our understanding of American history has been his successful campaign to encourage young scholars (some of them his own students) to devote serious, nonpolemical attention to the alternately neglected and derided history of American conservatism. Alan's fair-mindedness was the antithesis of the hornet's nest of academia in Cambridge.

Soon Evangeline would enter Alan's life, and such was my enthusiasm for them as a couple that I trailed them (from a proper distance) on part of their European honeymoon; it's been a running joke among us ever since. Rarely have three people—soon to be joined by a fourth, my wife,

Alex—had so many passions in common: politics, theater, journalism, history, and, most of all, family. Once Alan settled on Columbia as his new academic home, we were living a few blocks away from each other on the Upper West Side, much as we had in Somerset. I could not have imagined a luckier and happier continuity in life.

Alan's mother died a cruel death from ALS, and Alan never left her side. His father had his own unraveling late in life, and Alan was present and patient at every tough juncture. Before that, Alan helped him research and write *Washington Goes to War*, a memoir of David's apprenticeship as a young reporter covering FDR and the capital as it bulked up to mobilize for a world war. There's no better portrait of Washington in any era, and in its piquant and touching narrative, you can find a father's and a son's droll voices collaborating to enchanting and insightful effect.

For years, I have heard secondhand about how enthralling Alan is a lecturer. Even though I never attended one of his lectures, I was his student. My own writing about politics and history was from the start influenced by Alan, who bounced around ideas with me, pointed me in fresh directions, and let me prevail upon him to read a draft of a piece in progress. His thoughts were always sparkling, but even they are secondary to the glow of his humane spirit, which suffuses his life as much as his lasting body of work.

Appendix

TRANSCRIPT OF C-SPAN'S *BOOKNOTES*:
AN INTERVIEW BETWEEN HOST BRIAN LAMB
AND ALAN BRINKLEY, AUGUST 31, 1993

BRIAN LAMB, HOST: Alan Brinkley, why did you call your history book
The Unfinished Nation?

ALAN BRINKLEY, AUTHOR, THE UNFINISHED NATION: Well, there's
several reasons, I think, that have to do both with the character of
the United States and the character of historical writing. America is a
nation of almost unparalleled diversity, I think. And as we certainly
are aware today, with our present battles on multiculturalism, the task
of melding a single nation out of all of the component parts of the
American people is a very difficult one and, I would argue, an unfinished one.

America's also a nation that is constantly changing, regardless of
diversity. It's growing; it's expanding; it's transforming itself constantly, and so it's an ever-unfinished society in that sense as well.
And then the title was also a reference to the way historians view the
past and the way in which historians are constantly redefining their
own view of the past. The past, of course, doesn't change, but the way
we look at the past changes and so the writing of history is also an

Transcribed from the C-SPAN *Booknotes* program with Alan Brinkley on 8/31/1993. Copyright by C-SPAN.

unfinished process, and the title was meant to refer to all of those things.

LAMB: Do you have a favorite character in history?

BRINKLEY: Well, I'm not sure I do. I mean, I have people I admire greatly in history, and like most historians and like most Americans I admire Lincoln. I admire Jefferson. I admire—maybe this is not quite so universal— I admire Franklin Roosevelt and many people who are less prominent in history. I can't say that I have any single favorite historical figure.

LAMB: Do you have a period of American history that you like to mess around with the most?

BRINKLEY: Well, my own period—the period in which I do my own research and writing is primarily the 1930s to the 1940s. And I've written a book about political dissenters in the 1930s. I'm just finishing a book now about New Deal liberalism in the late '30s and World War II. So the sort of middle third of the twentieth century is the period that I've focused my own research on, primarily.

LAMB: Do you teach?

BRINKLEY: I teach at Columbia. I teach twentieth-century American history.

LAMB: To what year students?

BRINKLEY: To all levels, from freshmen to graduate students. And it's a real challenge to find a way of teaching history that reaches so many different levels of students.

LAMB: How do you do it?

BRINKLEY: Well, I try to make history as accessible as possible by linking it to—particularly for undergraduates—by linking it to a series of stories that they can understand and by combining the storytelling quality of history with some effort at interpretation and analysis. I think also it's important in teaching to be very organized in your thinking and in the way you convey ideas. I mean, much of what you do in teaching at the university level is lecturing, which may be an unhappy quality of the university system, but that's the way it is. And students need to be able to take notes. They need to be able to organize what you say in their own minds. And so I think being precise and organized is very important in teaching as well, particularly in the lecture format.

LAMB: I heard a story about you—and I know I'm going to step on a line or two, so I'll just try to get it out and see what your reaction to it is—and this is from one of your former students. And I was talking to some folks one day and asked them if they could, you know, what they remembered from their days in school. And this particular individual said he remembered when you were teaching at Harvard—and I don't know the circumstances—that you were not going to stay at Harvard or whatever, and you had a limit to the number of students who were allowed in a classroom. And the moment that he'll remember was the day that—say that there were 600 kids allowed in this class—that you said you didn't care how many took your course and that something like 1,200 were there waiting for you when you arrived. Is that a true story?

BRINKLEY: Well, something like that. I had been teaching a course on America since World War II at Harvard for some years—a course, I now teach at Columbia. And I had always placed a limit of 500 students on it—roughly 500 students. And the demand was much higher than that, but the capacity of the room was not. My last year at Harvard I was placed not in the lecture hall that I had normally been in, but in Sanders Theater, which was the large—essentially it was a concert hall, the Harvard concert hall, which seats over 1,000 people. And so I didn't see any point in turning people away. And so I—that's absolutely right. For the first time, I said that anyone who wanted to take the course could take it. And, in fact, exactly 1,000 people signed up for it in the end.

LAMB: Were you surprised when you showed up at the class?

BRINKLEY: A bit. I mean, I had been very surprised, when I first began teaching the course, at the size of the crowds. By the time this happened I had been having big crowds for some years and so I was a lot less surprised, but I've always been a little puzzled by why the course attracted such vast numbers of people.

LAMB: Did you ever ask the students why so many came?

BRINKLEY: Well, it's hard—you know, it hard to ask 500 or 1,000 people and get an answer that would apply to more than a few of them. I think it was, in large part, that students are very curious about the recent past. And I know people at Harvard sometimes tried to make it sound as though it was simply me and my popularity that drew all these students, but I don't think that's really the case. I think people are very curious about the recent past. They tend not to know as much about it as they feel they should, partly because in high school courses teachers tend to run out of time sometime around World War II or even earlier. And also because these are events that are constantly referred to in public discourse today. And when people hear talk about the Vietnam War or the civil rights movement or the Korean War or the Great Society, Malcolm X, they want to know something about it and there are not very many easy methods of learning that in our culture.

LAMB: In your history book that we're looking at here, you have periodically what you call American voices and they're just one—usually one page. And I'm going to hold one up because you just mentioned one of them. And this particular one here is some copy that was originally written or spoken by Malcolm X. Explain this technique in the book and why did you use this?

BRINKLEY: Well, I wanted to convey something of what made Malcolm X seem so menacing to so many white people and even some black people when he was alive, and also why he seems now so prophetic, in that the rage he expressed, the anger he expressed, the critique of American society he expressed is now a much more mainstream position, certainly, among African Americans and even among many liberal and left-wing white Americans. So I think that's what I tried to do with almost all of these pieces of testimony from figures in American history that run through this book, is try to convey something, both of what made them seem important in their own time, if, in fact, they were important. And many of the people quoted here were very ordinary people who were not known at all in their own time, but Malcolm X obviously was—is—different and also why they seem important to us today.

LAMB: Where did you grow up?

BRINKLEY: Here, in Washington.

LAMB: Where did you go to school?

BRINKLEY: I went to the Landon School which is in Bethesda, a private boys' school. And then I went to Princeton—I did my undergraduate degree at Princeton and I did my graduate work at Harvard.

LAMB: Do you remember when you first got interested in history?

BRINKLEY: Well, I think it's hard to grow up in Washington and not be interested in history. I mean, I think my interest in history grew up sort of alongside my interest in politics. And both of them, I think, were a result of growing up in Washington and growing up in a family that was very interested in public events. And I had good teachers in high school and in college who made history seem exciting to me and important to me. Actually, one of the things that most interested me in history as a possible career was taking a course in Princeton with the new head of the National Endowment for the Humanities, Sheldon Hackney, who was then a professor in the history department at Princeton and who taught courses in southern history. And reading southern history and southern literature—even though I'm not myself a historian of the South, primarily—really gave me a sense of how powerful history can be and how important historical writing can be.

LAMB: What did your parents do for a living?

BRINKLEY: My father's a journalist and my mother was a journalist before she got married.

LAMB: Your father, David Brinkley.

BRINKLEY: Right.

LAMB: I asked that of Doug Brinkley, who was here doing a history book and he . . .

BRINKLEY: No, we're . . .

LAMB: . . . said, "No, it's the other guy."

BRINKLEY: . . . we're not related.

LAMB: What impact did living around your father's profession have on you?

BRINKLEY: Well, I think it gave me an interest in writing. And there were— it was a house full of books. And it certainly gave me an interest in politics and political people and I grew up around other journalists and political figures. It didn't make me a journalist, obviously, but it perhaps moved me into a field of history that is—as its critics often point out—is perhaps closer to journalism than other fields. I'm not a medievalist, for example. Both my brothers are journalists. So I think growing up in my family, obviously, had an effect on the way I think and what interested me.

LAMB: We have a lot of journalists sit in that seat and a lot of academics, and there's always that dispute between history when academics write it and when journalists write it. Can you explain the kind of techniques that you have to use in a book vs. what a journalist does on history?

BRINKLEY: Well, I don't think it's a rigid distinction. And there are journalists who write very good history, and there are historians who write journalism from time to time, including me. I think the difference between journalism and history—and I want to make a distinction between journalism and history and journalists and historians, because that's the distinction that's much fuzzier—is a level of analysis, that in journalism the effort is to explain events in the context of today. And many journalists even writing history attempt to use history as a way of illuminating some very particular contemporary issue. There's also a tendency in journalism to emphasize story. And that's, I think, one of the reasons why so much popular history, the history that ordinary Americans and the general readership reads, is written not by scholars, but by journalists, because they have a real sense of narrative and story that among academic historians has been, I think, in many ways, sadly in decline for some years.

On the other hand, academic history, it seems to me, strives, at least, to reach a little deeper into stories than journalism does. And to link up the particular historical stories that we're telling with larger theoretical and analytical arguments that are going on within the profession and sometimes also within the society as well. I'm sounding very vague here and it's because there isn't any very easy way to explain the distinction. And it's not in any way a rigid distinction. As I say, some of the very best history, particularly of relatively recent events, is written by people coming out of journalism, rather than out of the academy.

LAMB: In the back of your book—and, first of all, let me see if we can get a good close-up here, Craig—real close on this. But where did this come from—the cover?

BRINKLEY: That's a painting in the National Gallery of Art of New York City in the late nineteenth century by Sloan, an American artist. And...

LAMB: Was it your idea?

BRINKLEY: No. It was found by the designer. I think it's a very handsome painting.

LAMB: The book was written—it's a Knopf book—written for what audience?

BRINKLEY: Well, it was written for two audiences. It's the trade edition, which you're holding in your hand, is published by Knopf and that's obviously aimed at a general readership. It's sold in bookstores and the idea is to tap into an audience of readers who are interested in a general history of the United States and don't find very many of them now. There's also another edition—it's the exact same book, but another published by McGraw-Hill, which is meant for the college textbook market. And...

LAMB: How does that work, by the way? I mean, McGraw—who owns Knopf?

BRINKLEY: Knopf and McGraw-Hill are completely separate.

LAMB: Both selling the same book?

BRINKLEY: Yes. And it was a deal between the two publishers. McGraw-Hill is the principal publisher of this book and Knopf reached an agreement with—my others are nontextbook books with Knopf so that, perhaps, was one reason why Knopf was eager to do this. But there was an agreement between the college division of McGraw-Hill and the trade division of Knopf that McGraw-Hill would publish a college edition and Knopf would publish a trade edition.

LAMB: Is it hard to sell a book for 40 bucks?

BRINKLEY: Well, I haven't seen the sales figures, but I suspect it is. But it's a big book and heavily illustrated.

LAMB: What's McGraw-Hill charge for it?

BRINKLEY: Well, it's hard to say because their pricing system for textbook marketing is very arcane and I don't really even know what—it varies from place to place, depending on how many copies are being sold and . . .

LAMB: In the back you have, as a matter of fact, some statistics that could probably solve a lot of arguments that we have right here at this immediate area when we do call-in shows and that, about numbers of people that vote and the number of people that, you know, breakdown of the population and the different kinds of people that live in this country. At least let me ask you why you put these in. First of all, you put the Declaration of Independence and the Constitution in the back of the book. Any other reason than the obvious for publishing them?

BRINKLEY: Well, I assume it's obvious. I think those are documents to which readers of American history and students of American history need and—or want constantly to refer—the Constitution, in particular. And I don't know of any general history in the United States that doesn't include those at some point.

LAMB: Then you have the presidential elections and the thing I found interesting was the list of those that ran for the presidency—the different years—but the percentage of the voter turnout.

BRINKLEY: Yeah.

LAMB: And as a matter of fact, you go back—I think the first one you've got listed here is John Quincy Adams, where it shows that only 26.9 percent voter participation. That's far and away the lowest?

BRINKLEY: Well, it is. And the reason that is that in the early nineteenth century there were so many restrictions on voting that great numbers of people—I mean, there were obvious categories of people who could not vote and, in fact, weren't even counted. Women are not even counted in those figures because women couldn't vote until— couldn't vote universally until 1920. But there were also property requirements and other restrictions on the franchise. And one of the reasons for putting those figures in there is to show the dramatic changes in the levels of turnout from the 1820s onward, as some of these property requirements were removed and white men, at least, were permitted to vote, largely without restriction.

LAMB: Then...

BRINKLEY: And then in the twentieth century, of course, the issue of voter turnout is one that still concerns us and I think it's interesting and important to know how the voter turnout has fluctuated since the end of the nineteenth century.

LAMB: The voter turnout in 1860 for the Abraham Lincoln year was 81.2; earlier than that, the William Henry Harrison was 80.2. And then you come forward, you know—in the 1900s you had as high as 65 percent with William Howard Taft and I think that's about the highest on that page, there; you dip down—though, Warren Harding was only 49 percent turnout; Coolidge was 48 percent turnout. And then you come into a period where it's in the 60s all through.

BRINKLEY: Well, that's an interesting story.

LAMB: What—explain all that.

BRINKLEY: First of all, there was a big change in the level of voter participation starting around the turn of the century. And the reasons for that are debated among historians and probably more complicated than I should try to explain here, but they involve the declining importance of parties in American life in the early twentieth century. One of the things that made the early twentieth century such an age of reform, as it's often called, was a sense that the political parties had acquired too much power in American life. And so there were assaults on parties from all sides and in many different forms. And many of the features of political life today that we sometimes find useful or troubling, the referenda questions on state ballots, the non-partisan elections in some cities for mayor, even such little things as moving some local elections to off years—mayoral elections in New York, for example.

Right now we're beginning a mayoral campaign which was deliberately moved to a year that was not a presidential year to limit the power of parties because the assumption was that parties wouldn't be able to turn out the vote as effectively for a—simply for a local election as they could for a national election.

So a whole range of reforms and also a different political style emerged in the twentieth century, which made parties less important, and once parties became less important, voting became less important. People didn't vote in such large numbers in the late nineteenth century because they were more politically aware and knowledgeable than they are now; it was because they had a sort of emotional bond with their political parties. It was comparable to the bonds that people often have with their families, with their churches or their communities. And that bond was weakened in the early twentieth century, and that resulted in this slide in the total number of people voting, that began early in the century and has continued in fluctuating ways since then.

Now the other point you note is the declining voter turnout in the 1920s and then it rebounded in the '30s and for a while, beyond that. And that, although I'm not sure that this is the only explanation, but I think the primary explanation is that in 1920 women got the vote for the first time and so they're included in these figures. And for the first few elections women were not accustomed to voting, not yet registered to vote in large numbers and so many potential voters—female voters—just didn't vote for the first few national elections. And then, by the time women became absorbed into the electorate about the same level as men, you find the voter turnout returning to, more or less, the same level that it had been in the period just before women's suffrage. You can make the same case, actually, about voter turnout—declining voter turnout since the early 1970s. That's when 18-year-olds began to vote. And voter turnout rates dropped precipitously as soon as 18-year-olds were enfranchised. And they've remained low because 18-year-olds still don't vote in high numbers.

LAMB: The other thing on the list that you notice sticks right out—first of all, the only person in history to get more than 50 million votes—and I may be—correct me if I'm wrong—is Ronald Reagan. And that right beside it is—you know, electoral vote—he got 525. Only 13 for the other side. He just seems to stick out there as a tremendous vote-getter. Well, how . . .

BRINKLEY: Well, obviously . . .

LAMB: . . . how do you read that?

BRINKLEY: . . . he was. Now the absolute number of votes—that he was the only person to get 50 million votes says more about the fact that the population was growing and he got a much smaller percentage of the vote—or at least a significantly smaller percentage of the vote—than Richard Nixon did in 1972 and that Franklin Delano Roosevelt did in 1936, Lyndon Johnson in 1964. But given our contemporary political malaise as I think it might rightly be called and the difficulties that almost every president since Lyndon Johnson has had in getting and sustaining popularity, Ronald Reagan does stand out as a striking anomaly. Now he had his problems, of course, in his second term. But he's really the first president since Dwight Eisenhower, I think, who managed to leave office with a reasonable level of popularity. And of course, he's the first president since Eisenhower to serve two full terms.

LAMB: You know, we always see from time to time the listing, by academics, of the best presidents in history. How do they do that?

BRINKLEY: There's a poll that some historians launched—I forget when, I think in the early '60s—that's sent around to members of the—I think it's through the Organization of American Historians, which is the largest professional organization for historians who write about the United States, as opposed to, you know, Americans who write about France and Germany and other places. And these polls have been published in the *Journal of American History* and elsewhere from time to time over the last 30 years or so. I've always been somewhat skeptical of them. I'm not sure that historians are in any better position to judge who was a good or a bad president than anyone else. I mean, their judgments are just as political as any other person's judgment would be. But they're interesting, nevertheless. And what's particularly interesting is to see how the reputations of presidents rise and fall in polls.

LAMB: Would you list, in order, I mean—and not all, obviously, all 42—or all 41 individuals—but who are your top five?

BRINKLEY: Who are my top five? Well, I've never been asked, actually, to do this. It's been a while since any of these polls have been conducted and I don't remember ever having been polled on this subject. I think, like most historians and like all the polls that have been conducted, the top four or five—and not necessarily in this order—for me, as I say, for most scholars, it would probably be Lincoln, Washington, Jefferson, Franklin Roosevelt. Beyond that it gets harder. And it's a question of balancing different elements of presidencies against one another. Woodrow Wilson, I think, was a very great president in many ways and a terrible failure in other ways. Harry Truman, I admire in many ways, and but also strongly disagree with many things he did.

LAMB: What about the four or five worst in history, in your opinion?

BRINKLEY: Well, I would have to say—and I'll leave out the very recent presidents because I don't think I would be judging them by anything more than my own polemical standards, but I think probably you'd have to say that the worst few presidents were the ones immediately preceding the Civil War, James Buchanan, Franklin Pierce—now granted, it was a terrible time to be president and in crises that were extraordinarily difficult to solve. But they were—Buchanan, particularly—were strikingly ineffective presidents in the face of extraordinary problems.

And I think there have been probably worse and less competent men who have been president than James Buchanan: For example, Warren Harding probably was the least capable man to be president, but he didn't do as much damage. He didn't face the same level of challenges. And that, I think, has to be part of your evaluation, just as it does when you're trying to find great presidents. Theodore Roosevelt always complained that he would not be remembered as a great president because he didn't live in times that cried out for greatness. Now some might disagree and some do argue that he was a great president. But certainly Franklin Roosevelt seems to have a greater claim to greatness, not necessarily because he was a better man than Theodore Roosevelt, or a smarter man or a more capable man, but because he lived in times that rewarded leadership to a greater degree than his cousin, Theodore, did.

LAMB: Another thing that you do throughout the book—and I want to get back to some of those numbers because they're interesting things to ask you about—is you have, periodically, two pages called "Debating the Past." And I'll hold this up here. This particular one is about the Civil War. What's the point of this?

BRINKLEY: The point is to help readers to understand that while—in reading this book, they're reading a narrative and they're reading a fairly straightforward story told by me and presenting history as if it is a fixed set of events and facts and interpretations—that, in fact, the ideas that they're reading in this book are challenged by historians.

Now I try to give some sense of—even in the text itself—that not everything is cut and dried in history, and that there are disagreements about most issues. But I don't think anything can do that as effectively as simply showing the ways in which historians disagree with one another and have always disagreed, and the way in which historical interpretations tend to reflect the time in which they are written, the backgrounds of the people who are writing them. And that's what these little essays debating the past are trying to demonstrate.

LAMB: On the Civil War, you say there are revisionists today that disagree with the original theory that it was accidental, unnecessary—"the work of interested or fanatical agitators." That was one theory. And the other one, "irresponsible conflict between opposing and enduring forces."

BRINKLEY: Well, the revisionists, just in the lingo of the profession, have tended to be the people who see the Civil War as a great and avoidable accident, a product of what one historian called "a blundering generation." And the more traditional view has been that it was an irreconcilable conflict born of irreconcilable differences between the North and the South, particularly on the issue of slavery.

This is not an issue, frankly, that historians debate very much right now—the causes of the Civil War. Historical controversies sort of rise and fall and the issue of the causes of the Civil War just doesn't seem to interest historians very much anymore, but it probably does interest the American people a lot more than it interests us. And I thought it would be interesting to readers to see the way in which historians, over time, have disagreed on this issue and still, to some degree, disagree about it when they choose to argue about it.

LAMB: What techniques do you use to keep students interested? Or do you care about whether they're interested or not?

BRINKLEY: Of course, I care about whether they're interested. If they're not interested, they're not learning. Do you mean in my teaching or in writing this book?

LAMB: No. When you teach. I mean, how big are your classes at Columbia now?

BRINKLEY: Well, Columbia's a much smaller college than Harvard and my classes there are much smaller. I've had, I don't know—150, 200 people in—I've only been at Columbia two years so I don't have any vast pile of data to draw from. But the course I taught most recently, which was last spring, had about 200 students.

LAMB: And what techniques do you use? I mean, how many times do you meet them? How long are your classes?

BRINKLEY: Well, these large courses are lecture courses and they meet twice a week at Columbia for an hour and a quarter. Most places it's 50 minutes. So that's an additional challenge, is trying to keep people in their seats for over an hour. One thing I try to do, given this longer class period that I have now, is to spend some of the time in each class responding to questions and trying to provoke discussion. It's not easy to do that in a large group, but I think it creates a somewhat more relaxed atmosphere and it also breaks down the sense that students often have in a lecture course, that there's this sort of barrier between them and the instructor. The instructor's a kind of performer standing up at the front of the room and is completely unapproachable.

LAMB: How long were you at Harvard?

BRINKLEY: I was at Harvard—well, in various capacities, I was at Harvard for about 13, 14 years, first as a graduate student and then as a member of the faculty.

LAMB: Have you taught anywhere besides Harvard and Columbia?

BRINKLEY: I taught at MIT for a few years right after I got out of graduate school and before going back to Harvard, and then I taught at the City University of New York graduate school for several years, just before I came to Columbia.

LAMB: Do you notice a change in the students over these last 15 years?

BRINKLEY: Well, I do and it's hard to know how much of it is a change that reflects the different universities I've been teaching in and how much of it is a change that reflects the different times in which I've taught, but yes, I do. When I first started teaching—when I was a graduate student in the mid-'70s and began teaching—there was still, I think, among college students—at least at Harvard—a very visible residue of the '60s left, and a kind of skepticism and a questioning. Students were certainly much less radicalized than they had been when I was in college in the late '60s. But the questions that they asked tended to have been shaped by the controversies of the '60s—the Vietnam War, which, of course, continued until, in one form or another, until 1975.

By the early '80s, that element in the undergraduate student body seemed to me to be shrinking and students asked different kinds of questions. And it's not that they were less skeptical, but they were skeptical about different things. And it would be too simplistic, I think, to say that students became more conservative in the 1980s, although I think that happened. But they became less interested in ideology, I think, and less attracted to ideologies than students in the '70s had been. And I don't know whether that's changing again now or not. You know, our political climate seems to be changing, although in what direction is hard to say, and students will change along with it. But I'm not sure at this point how to characterize any change in the '90s.

LAMB: Have you ever been involved in government or politics?

BRINKLEY: No, no.

LAMB: Any interest in doing that?

BRINKLEY: Well, I'm certainly interested in government and politics. I don't have any particular interest in holding government office nor has anyone asked me to do so. But my field is primarily political history and so, obviously, I'm very interested not just in the history of politics and government, but in what's going on in politics and government today.

LAMB: Do you have a family?

BRINKLEY: I do. I have a wife and a two-year-old daughter.

LAMB: One of the things I didn't see in this book is a dedication. Is a book like this—I mean, do most of your books have dedications to them?

BRINKLEY: Yes. I think because this book was aimed at in part, at a sort of college textbook market, for which dedications are not normally included, I didn't think to include one. I wish, in a way, I had put one in, but I didn't think of it.

LAMB: You point out in the beginning that this is a—you did a much longer series of writings about history with some of your colleagues, Richard Current, Frank Freidel, and Harry Williams.

BRINKLEY: Right. This book emerged out of a much longer book that I have been the principal author of for, oh, about 12, 13 years now, which is a more conventional college textbook called *American History: A Survey*, a rather prosaic title for which I'm not responsible, which I inherited, in effect, from the three historians you mentioned—Frank Freidel, who was my adviser at Harvard and who passed away earlier this year; T. Harry Williams, who's a famous Civil War historian and also biographer of Huey Long at LSU, who died in the '70s; and Richard Current, who's a Lincoln scholar and—among other things, who is still very much alive, and still writing and publishing. But I took the book over from them in, I guess, 1980, and I've been the only author of that book since then—the only active author. And that's not a book that I think a general readership would tend to read because it's, first of all, much longer than this. It's almost twice as long as this book. And it has much more of the apparatus of a textbook threaded through it.

This book came about for two reasons. It came about out of a sense among the college textbook publishing people with whom I work that there was a growing market among students and faculty for shorter and more readable histories, that the big textbooks that are so much a feature of academic life are now coming to be too big for many students, partly because a lot of professors like to assign collateral reading and they don't have time for people to read so much of a textbook. And for other reasons as well.

Then the other motive behind this book was the sense that there might be a market among a general readership, too, for a relatively succinct—this is not a short book by any means, but compared to college textbooks, it's a relatively succinct history of all of American history. Historians—academic scholars—don't write these kinds of syntheses anymore for any purpose other than textbooks. Textbooks are really the only kind of synthetic writing—broad synthetic writing—that historians do anymore. And since most textbooks have multiple authors and most textbooks are market-driven, rather than driven by the interests and interpretations of the authors, they tend to have a kind of fragmented quality that doesn't make them particularly interesting to general readers.

I wanted, in this book, to take the kernel of a textbook, this act of synthesis that historians engage in, and turn it into something that would be more readable and more accessible, both to students and to general readers. And how well I've succeeded, the readers will have to decide, but that was the idea.

LAMB: And . . .

BRINKLEY: And so I stripped out a lot of the detail that instructors expect in big textbooks and I tried to make the narrative flow more smoothly. And I tried to make it a little more interpretive then textbooks generally are.

LAMB: In the back, you list under every chapter—in a bibliography—all the books that were suggested that you can go get more detail on. Unfair question, possibly, but have you read all those books?

BRINKLEY: Oh, of course not. I mean, there are thousands of them, hundreds, at least, and perhaps thousands of books back there. No, that's really—those are not footnotes. Those are not sources I have used. I have read many of them, but not anywhere close to all of them, probably not even a majority of them. But it's an effort to give students an idea of what books are available to them if they want to learn more about the areas in which they're reading in such concise form in this book.

LAMB: In the back, as we talk again—I mean, we talked earlier—there are charts. And another chart that you have back here is—I lost my place—is population of the United States. And because of the way it's configured, it's hard for the audience to see it on the screen, but the thing you can easily report here is that—of course—every year the population—every 10 years has gone up. The percentage of increase this last time, around 1990, is one of the smallest in history.

I mean, over the years—it was up in the 30s in the early years, and it was only 9.9 percent increase in 1990. Next to that is the population per square mile. That's gone from 4.5 in the early days, up to 70.3 population per square mile. Percent of urban vs. rural, that keeps going up. In the early days it was 5.1; it goes all the way up to the highest it's ever been, to 77.5 percent of urban to rural. Percentage of white and nonwhite: that started out at 80.7 percent white in the United States, back in 1790, and it went all the way up to—where at one point—back in the '50s, it was 89 percent; back now down to 80.3, where it was in the beginning. One more here and I'll let you get your response to all this.

The median age—the earliest year recorded was back in 1820. It was 16.7. That was the median age. And it has gone all the way up now to the highest point in history, to 32.9. What does all that tell you about what's happening in the country?

BRINKLEY: Well, it tells us many things, I think, and maybe the best way to answer that is just to explain why the figures like that seem to me to be useful in a book like this.

I think when we tend to focus in our discussion of contemporary public events—and to some degree, also in our discussion of historical events on people, on events, on things that are easily visible. And it's easy to forget that, underlying what is happening to us today and what's happened to America throughout history, is a series of profoundly important demographic changes in the size of the population, the structure of the population, the geographical and spatial distribution of the population. And while it's very hard to draw direct connections between those changes and the specific events that we tend to focus on when we're writing history, it seems to me—and to many other historians—very clear that these large structural and demographic changes have at least as much to do and probably much more to do with the way our history evolves than what presidents have done at any particular time, or what any particular leader or group has done or institution has done.

And, obviously, putting numbers like that in a chart in the back of a book doesn't do very much to explain their significance. But I've tried, in the text of the book as well, to make reference to these demographic changes and I wanted to make it possible for readers to get a sense of how dramatic some of these changes were.

LAMB: The next page is—I think there may be an opportunity for you to comment on why. It's employment from the year 1870 to 1990. And in 1870 there were 12.5 million people employed in the United States, and it's gone up steadily to 124.8 million people. Next to it, though, its male-female employment ratio, back in 1970, was 85 percent male; 15 percent female, all the way now to where it's the closest it's ever been. It's 54 percent male; 46 percent female. And then in the next column—and I'll hold it up so the audience can see—is the number of people in unions, the percentage of people in the United States in unions. It keeps going down, and you can see in 1990 it's gone down to as low as 16 percent of the workers that are part of unions, there in that column.

What do you read into those numbers?

BRINKLEY: Well, I think the division between male and female employment speaks for itself, and that's been one of the most stunning social changes in our recent history. And I suspect that number will continue to narrow. I don't know that it will ever reach parity, although it might. But it speaks, I think, to the enormous impact that feminism and other social forces that have driven women into the workplace have had in the last 50 years or so. The percentage of people in unions, I guess that also, more or less, speaks for itself. I mean, you say it continues to go down and that's true in the last 30 years or so, but there's also a period in the twentieth century when it went steadily up and reached a peak shortly after World War II.

LAMB: The highest percentage here was in 1940, when 20 percent of the population were members of unions.

BRINKLEY: And I think that speaks both about the early institutional successes that unions have had and the institutional problems they've
had since then. And maybe more to the point, it speaks to the relative
importance of the industrial sector of our economy in recent years,
and one of the reasons that unions have declined so dramatically in
recent years is that industrial jobs, where unions are most likely to be
effective, have declined as well.

LAMB: Early in the book, you quote—I don't know if I can find it—
Gladstone, the famous Brit, as saying—it's either about our Con-
stitution or about this country as being the greatest ever created.
Can you remember that?

BRINKLEY: The Constitution, I think, is what Gladstone was referring to
and I actually don't remember the precise quote that you're referring
to, but there is an important theme in American history and we see
this certainly today in debates about what the Supreme Court should
be doing and what the Constitution means. One of the things that
made the United States so different from England, politically, after the
American Revolution, was that we chose to write down our Constitution. The English constitution, which is much venerated in England,
is an unwritten document. It's simply an understanding of the way
things work. And the first generation of citizens of the United States,
the revolutionaries, and their successors who wrote the Constitution,
believed that one of the things that had created the difficulties between
the United States and England and that had corrupted English society
in a way that made the Revolution necessary was precisely the fact that
the constitution was unwritten and, therefore, could be corrupted and
perverted by venal and self-interested leaders, as they believed the king
and some of his ministers had been.

So creating a written Constitution for the United States was one
of the crucial things that separated the United States from England.
Having done that, Americans tended to give to this document a
kind of veneration that, in many ways, survives to this day, although
perhaps not as strongly as it once did. And the Constitution was
described as sacred, the framers of the Constitution were remembered as the "Founding Fathers"—that's a phrase that really didn't

come into currency until the 1920s—but were treated almost as demigods by later generations.

During much of the nineteenth century, when the federal government was very weak and American society was very provincial and fragmented, the veneration of the Constitution was one of the few things that gave Americans a sense of themselves as being part of a single nation. In the twentieth century that veneration has survived in many ways, but it has also started to be challenged, and we now see, on the one hand, people insisting on using the Constitution as a bulwark against social changes, social and cultural changes, insisting on interpreting it through the idea of original intent; and others who argue that the Constitution is a very flexible document that was meant to respond to changes in the times. And then there are others now who say that the Constitution itself is archaic, that it's saddled us with a government that may have worked very well in the nineteenth century but is not working well in the twentieth century.

LAMB: I found the quote. William Gladstone says, page 147, "The U.S. Constitution—the most wonderful work ever struck off at a given time by the brain and purpose of man."

BRINKLEY: Well, that was a view widely shared by Americans and perhaps still is. It's hard to argue with the idea that—I mean, I'm not sure I'd use quite the superlatives that Gladstone uses, but it's hard to argue that the American Constitution has [not] been an extraordinarily successful experiment. I mean, a government that was created at a particular moment by a group of men that has survived now for almost 200—well, a little over 200 years. And for all the problems that our government has today, it's still a remarkably stable political system. And one has to be impressed. Now there were flaws in the Constitution, some of which we have corrected over time through amendments and some of which remain uncorrected. But it's hard to think of another moment of state building, of Constitution building in the history of human civilization that has created so successful a political system and so enduring a one.

LAMB: You said earlier that your father is a journalist and your two brothers are journalists. Where do they work?

BRINKLEY: My brother Joel works for the *New York Times*. He's an editor in the Washington bureau and prior to that was the *Times* correspondent in Israel. And my brother John is the Washington correspondent for the *Rocky Mountain News*, which is a Scripps-Howard paper.

LAMB: Now when you all get together, you're the only historian in the family. Do you find that you look at the world differently?

BRINKLEY: Not particularly. I think many people like to believe that when one becomes a historian, one has a perspective on the world that is different and, therefore, of particular value to everyone else. And I make no effort to disabuse them of that, but I think to some degree it's a myth. I don't think that my view of contemporary events is any more knowledgeable or perceptive than that of my brothers, maybe less so. I think I know more about history than they do, but they probably know more about today than I do.

LAMB: You said earlier that one of the things you find when you teach students about the twentieth century is that there's a lot that they don't know. What are the things that you can remember that most surprise your students about the early twentieth century or even later, in the '40s and '50s?

BRINKLEY: Well, it's hard to say. I mean, I don't have a pipeline into my students' mind in what does and does not surprise them. I think back to my own experience as a college student studying history and I think what surprises people most often are things they learn that contradict sort of popular conventional wisdom.

I mean, history is referred to constantly in our public conversations, not always very reflectively, but it's, you know, today we refer constantly to the legacy of Vietnam, to the legacy of the '60s, or a Munich analogy. And I think what surprises students is how much more complicated and contested these legacies are than the glib way in which they're used in contemporary politics would have led them to believe.

I think what also surprises students is that people who are remembered popularly in black and white as the heroes of recent history or the goats and villains of recent history are also more complicated and interesting, usually, than they would tend to believe. People are very surprised when I talk about Franklin Roosevelt and surprised to find out, first of all, how much of the New Deal didn't work, how much of it was abandoned even before Roosevelt died; how complicated Franklin Roosevelt was and how complicated his ideology was. And that's just one example.

People are surprised when I talk about Richard Nixon, who is not a figure whom I admire. But nevertheless, I think there are many extraordinarily impressive things about Nixon's career and about his presidency. And people are very surprised to discover, for example, that it was Richard Nixon, not a Democrat, who proposed the only really profound reform of the welfare system since 1935, the family assistance plan, which was never passed, but it was presumably a conservative Republican who's the only president ever to have proposed a guaranteed income as the basis of our welfare system.

LAMB: When you lecture, do you speak extemporaneously or do you speak from notes? Do you have audiovisual aids or . . .

BRINKLEY: I don't have audiovisual aids. I do have notes and I speak from the notes sometimes, and I speak extemporaneously at other times. But I do like to work out pretty carefully what I'm going to say before I stand up to say it.

LAMB: When you test a student, what system do you use?

BRINKLEY: Well, I tend to ask people to write essays and I tend to give them fairly broad, sort of interpretive statements to respond to, and ask them to find examples and illustrations to support their argument. So I don't ask specific questions very often. I don't think history is a process of memorizing names and dates and it should not be, although—of course—it's important to know some names and dates. I think understanding history means learning how to think about history and how to marshal the so-called facts that you know behind an argument, an interpretation. And that's what I encourage students to try to do.

LAMB: Do you have a favorite or favorite historians that you look to— people that you either have modeled your own writing after or people you would go pick up off the shelf and read if you had time?

BRINKLEY: Oh, well, there are many historians whom I admire and whom I always read when their books come out or—some of them, of course, are no longer living or no longer writing. I mean, I hate to make a list because I—at the risk of offending the people I leave off it, but one historian whom I've always deeply admired is Richard Hofstadter, whom I never knew, who died in the early '70s, but who taught at Columbia, as I do. And even though his books now seem, in many ways, very dated and present interpretations that most historians, including me, largely disagree with now, he I found to be an extraordinarily inventive and creative historian, a historian who was willing to take chances and, using interdisciplinary methods, a historian who wrote beautifully, who tried to make his writing important not just to scholars, but also to other readers. I can't say I've modeled my career on Richard Hofstadter and, you know, I mean, I should be so lucky as to be as great a historian as he was, but he certainly has had an influence in the way I've thought.

I'm a great admirer of C. Vann Woodward, who is, of course, still very much alive, still writing and is a friend of mine and whose—reading his work in college—his work on southern history had a big impact on me and on the way I thought about history. And I think I'll stop there. I mean, there are many others whom I admire, but I . . .

LAMB: What's next?

BRINKLEY: Well, I'm finishing, I hope in the next month or so, a book that I've been working on—that I worked on alongside this one for more years than I'd like to admit, about the way in which liberals—New Dealers—in the late '30s and the 1940s redefined what they thought the government should do. And it's a book about what came after the war to be known as "New Deal liberalism" took the form it did, which in many ways is very different from the form it had in the early and mid-'30s, when the New Deal itself was most active. So that's what I'm working on at the moment. And then I'm also just starting a biography of Henry Luce, the founder and publisher of *Time* and *Life* and *Fortune*.

LAMB: Why Henry Luce?

BRINKLEY: Well, I think—I mean, there are lots of reasons why I'm doing it, but what I think makes him interesting to me is that it's an opportunity to look in a very precise way at some of the intersections between politics and culture. I think the magazines that Luce created and that he guided so directly through most of his life had an enormous impact on American culture and also were enormously reflective of at least some strains of American culture. Luce was also very active in and, at times, influential in politics. And the combination of those two things made him interesting to me. I think politics and culture have tended to be treated as very separate areas and I think anyone watching our politics today has to be aware that they're not separate at all; they're inextricable. And so I hope, in this book, to be able to explore that connection.

LAMB: Our guest has been the author of this book called *The Unfinished Nation: A Concise History of the American People*. Professor Alan Brinkley is at Columbia University and we thank you very much for joining us.

BRINKLEY: My pleasure.

Notes

2. THE "DISSIDENT IDEOLOGY" REVISITED

1. Frank Freidel, *Franklin D. Roosevelt* (Boston: Little Brown, 1952).
2. Alan Brinkley, "Comparative Biography as Political History: Huey Long and Father Coughlin," *History Teacher* 18, no. 1 (November 1984): 9–16.
3. See, e.g., N. D. B. Connolly and Keisha Blain, "Trump Syllabus 2.0: An Introduction to the Currents of American Culture That Led to 'Trumpism,'" Public Books, June 28, 2016, http://www.publicbooks.org/trump-syllabus-2-0/; and "Trump 101," *Chronicle of Higher Education*, June 19, 2016, https://www.chronicle.com/article/Trump-Syllabus /236824. It is suggestive of *Voices of Protest*'s significance that it made it into the original "Trump 101" syllabus offered in the *Chronicle* and, after that syllabus was criticized for not including the perspectives of scholars of color or addressing racial issues, Connolly and Blain also included the book in "Trump Syllabus 2.0."
4. Richard Hofstadter, *The Age of Reform: From Bryan to FDR* (New York: Vintage, 1955); C. Vann Woodward, *Origins of the New South, 1877–1913* (Baton Rouge: Louisiana State University Press, 1951).
5. Alan Brinkley, *Voices of Protest: Huey Long, Father Coughlin, and the Great Depression* (New York: Knopf, 1982).
6. Anders Stephanson, "Panel: The Scholarship of Alan Brinkley," at Protest, Politics, and Ideas in the American Century: A Conference in Honor of Alan Brinkley, Columbia University, New York, Facebook video, April 16, 2016, https://www.facebook.com /columbiahistory/videos/1680208195565278/.
7. For a brief but insightful analysis of Woodward's book by a former Brinkley student, see Keith Orejel, "What Does Woodward's *Origins of the New South* Have to Say to

the Twenty-First Century Reader?" Tropics of Meta, September 8, 2014, https://
tropicsofmeta.wordpress.com/2014/09/08/what-does-woodwards-origins-of-the
-new-south-have-to-say-to-the-twenty-first-century-reader-2/#_ftn1. See also, e.g., the
essays in John Boles and Bethany L. Johnson, eds., *Origins of the New South, Fifty Years
Later: The Continuing Influence of a Historical Classic* (Baton Rouge: Louisiana State
University Press, 2003). On American populism, see, e.g., Michael Kazin, *The Populist
Persuasion: An American History* (New York: Basic Books, 1995). Kazin sees popu-
lism primarily as a political language, used by different sorts of political figures and
groups over time. For a study of the actual "populists," see, e.g., Lawrence Goodwyn,
The Populist Moment: A Short History of the Agrarian Revolt in America (New York:
Oxford University Press, 1978). For American populism in the present day and pos-
sible connections to the past, see John B. Judis, *The Populist Explosion: How the Great
Recession Transformed American and European Politics* (New York: Columbia Global
Reports, 2016).

8. For Lippmann's output, see especially his *Public Opinion* (New York: Harcourt, Brace,
1922) and *The Phantom Public* (New York: Harcourt, Brace, 1925). In these works, he
drew on earlier European thinkers worried about the masses and politics: e.g., Gustave
Le Bon, *The Crowd: A Study of the Popular Mind* (London: Unwin, 1897). Brinkley cites
some of the more prominent Cold War literature on authoritarianism and mass politics,
all of which contain criticism of Long and/or Coughlin along those lines, including
Daniel Bell, ed., *The Radical Right: The New American Right, Expanded and Updated*
(Garden City, NY: Doubleday, 1963); Theodore Adorno, Else Frenkel-Brunswik,
Daniel J. Levinson, and R. Nevitt Sanford, *The Authoritarian Personality* (New York:
Harper & Brothers, 1950); Seymour Martin Lipset and Earl Raab, *The Politics of Unrea-
son* (Chicago: University of Chicago Press, 1970); Edward Shils, *The Torment of Secrecy*
(New York: Free Press, 1956); and Arthur M. Schlesinger Jr., *The Politics of Upheaval:
The Age of Roosevelt*, vol. 3 (Boston: Houghton Mifflin, 1960).

9. Brinkley, *Voices of Protest*, xi.

10. Brinkley, xi; T. Harry Williams, "The Gentleman from Louisiana: Demagogue or
Democrat?" *Journal of Southern History* 26 (1960): 21, which was the 1959 presidential
address of the Southern Historical Association; Jacques Maritain, *Man and the State*
(Washington, DC: Catholic University of America Press, 1951), 141. See also Williams's
Huey Long (New York: Knopf, 1969).

11. Hofstadter, *Age of Reform*, 21.

12. Brinkley, *Voices of Protest*, xi.

13. Brinkley, 143.

14. For one vivid example of Long speaking in December 1934, see "Huey Long: Share
Our Wealth," video, 3:48, accessed January 8, 2018, https://www.youtube.com/watch?v
=hphgHi6FD8k.

15. Robert Penn Warren, *All the King's Men* (New York: Harcourt, Brace, 1946); *All the
King's Men*, directed by Robert Rossen (Culver City, CA: Columbia Pictures, 1949).

16. Brinkley, *Voices of Protest*, 156–57.

17. C. Vann Woodward, "Pennies from Heaven," *New York Review of Books*, September 23,
1982, http://www.nybooks.com/articles/1982/09/23/pennies-from-heaven/.

18. Robert Sherrill, "American Demagogues," *New York Times*, July 11, 1982, http://www
.nytimes.com/1982/07/11/books/american-demagogues.

19. Alan Brinkley, "Huey Long, the Share Our Wealth Movement, and the Limits of
Depression Dissidence," *Louisiana History: The Journal of the Louisiana Historical
Association* 22, no. 2 (Spring 1981): 117–34.

20. Williams, "Gentleman from Louisiana," 18–21.

21. Brinkley, *Voices of Protest*, 23.

22. Brinkley, 269–83.

23. American conservatism may have seen an explosion of scholarly attention in the wake
of Brinkley's 1994 essay on the topic (see chapter 6 in this volume by Jefferson Decker),
but the far right, especially in its 1930s iteration, remains an understudied topic. An
important work that appeared at the same time as *Voices of Protest* is Leo Ribuffo, *The
Old Christian Right: The Protestant Far Right from the Great Depression to the Cold War*
(Philadelphia: Temple University Press, 1983), which looked at many of the figures who
claimed Long's mantle (such as Gerald L. K. Smith) and later moved to the far right.
Ribuffo's book has not enjoyed the longevity of *Voices of Protest* and is out of print.

24. Robert O. Paxton, *The Anatomy of Fascism* (New York: Vintage, 2005), 197–207.
Other historians have looked at the earlier decade of the 1920s—a period of relative
prosperity—as the moment when fascism could be found in America, notably in the
form of nativist groups such as the Ku Klux Klan and the American Legion. See, e.g.,
Nancy MacLean, *Behind the Mask of Chivalry: The Making of the Second Ku Klux Klan*
(New York: Oxford University Press, 1995). See also Linda Gordon, *The Second Com-
ing of the KKK: The Ku Klux Klan of the 1920s and the American Political Tradition*
(New York: Norton, 2017). For a recent study, see Richard Steigmann-Gall, "Star-
Spangled Fascism: American Interwar Political Extremism in Comparative Perspec-
tive," *Journal of Social History* 42, no. 1 (January 2017): 94–119.

25. In the 1940s and 1950s, the term *totalitarianism* (born in the 1920s in the wake of
the fascist seizure of power in Italy) came into vogue and soon dominated academic
and intellectual discourse about fascism and communism, with specific linkage to
Nazism and Stalinism. One inspiration for this was George Orwell's dystopian novel
1984, published in 1949; another was Hannah Arendt's masterwork *The Origins of
Totalitarianism*, published in 1951. For overviews, see Enzo Traverso, "Totalitarianism
Between History and Theory," *History and Theory* 56, no. 4 (January 2017): 97–118;
Michael Geyer and Sheila Fitzpatrick, eds., *Beyond Totalitarianism: Stalinism and
Nazism Compared* (New York: Cambridge University Press, 2008); and Abbot Glea-
son, *Totalitarianism: An Inner History of the Cold War* (New York: Oxford University
Press, 1997).

3. THE END OF REFORM

1. Alan Brinkley, *Franklin Delano Roosevelt* (New York: Oxford University Press, 2010),
ix–x.

2. Alan Brinkley, *The End of Reform: New Deal Liberalism in Recession and War* (New
York: Knopf, 1995). A recent overview refers to *The End of Reform* as "the most

important interpretation of the New Deal published since Leuchtenburg's *FDR and the New Deal*": see Jason Scott Smith, *A Concise History of the New Deal* (New York: Cambridge University Press, 2014), 190.

3.   Brinkley, *The End of Reform*, quote at 116.

4.   Arthur M. Schlesinger Jr., *The Age of Roosevelt*, 3 vols. (Boston: Houghton Mifflin, 1957–60); Richard Hofstadter, *The Age of Reform: From Bryan to FDR* (New York: Knopf, 1955). See also Eric Goldman, *Rendezvous with Destiny: A History of Modern American Reform* (New York: Knopf, 1952).

5.   E.g., Barton J. Bernstein, "The New Deal: The Conservative Achievements of Liberal Reform," in *Towards a New Past: Dissenting Essays in American History*, ed. Barton J. Bernstein (New York: Pantheon, 1968), 263–88; Ronald Radosh, "The Myth of the New Deal," in *A New History of Leviathan: Essays on the Rise of the American Corporate State*, ed. Ronald Radosh and Murray N. Rothbard (New York: Dutton, 1972), 146–86; and Howard Zinn, "The Limits of the New Deal," in *The Politics of History*, 2nd ed. (Urbana: University of Illinois Press, 1990), chap. 7.

6.   Steve Fraser and Gary Gerstle, introduction to *The Rise and Fall of the New Deal Order, 1930–1980*, ed. Steve Fraser and Gary Gerstle (Princeton, NJ: Princeton University Press, 1989), x.

7.   Brinkley, *The End of Reform*, 14.

8.   Brinkley, 271.

9.   The landmark account of the New Deal's business policies is Ellis Hawley, *The New Deal and the Problem of Monopoly: A Study in Economic Ambivalence* (Princeton, NJ: Princeton University Press, 1966). Though the two books differ in their findings and particularly in the economic and political contexts in which they were written, both recognize the diversity of New Deal economic thinking, and both see the late New Deal as a pivotal moment in American political economy.

10.   Arthur M. Schlesinger Jr., *The Age of Roosevelt: The Politics of Upheaval, 1935–1936* (Boston: Houghton Mifflin, 1960), esp. 284–408 (quote at 397).

11.   Arthur M. Schlesinger Jr., "Memorial Day Service in Memory of Franklin D. Roosevelt, Hyde Park, New York, May 26, 1975," box 1, Roosevelt Small Collections: Franklin D. Roosevelt—Addresses Relating to, 1945–1980, Franklin D. Roosevelt Library, Hyde Park, New York. Among revisionist accounts of the NRA, Ira Katznelson's is perhaps the most striking. See Ira Katznelson, *Fear Itself: The New Deal and the Origins of Our Time* (New York: Liveright, 2013), chap. 7.

12.   Brinkley, *The End of Reform*, 11.

13.   Brinkley, 13.

14.   Alan Brinkley, "The New Deal and the Idea of the State," in Fraser and Gerstle, *The Rise and Fall of the New Deal Order*, 85–121.

15.   For overviews of this literature, see Lawrence Glickman, ed., *Consumer Society in American History: A Reader* (Ithaca, NY: Cornell University Press, 1999); and "Exchange: American Consumerism," *Journal of American History* 93, no. 2 (September 2006): 385–413. Among the seminal works Brinkley cites are Roland Marchand, *Advertising the American Dream, 1920–1940* (Berkeley: University of California Press, 1985); T. J.

Jackson Lears and Richard Wightman Fox, eds., *The Culture of Consumption: Critical Essays in American History, 1880–1980* (New York: Pantheon, 1983); and Lizabeth Cohen, *Making a New Deal: Industrial Workers in Chicago, 1919–1939* (New York: Cambridge University Press, 1990).

16. Robert H. Wiebe, *The Search for Order, 1877–1920* (New York: Hill and Wang, 1967), quoted at xiii. See also Brinkley's discussion of the organizational synthesis in Alan Brinkley, "Writing the History of Contemporary America: Dilemmas and Challenges," *Daedalus* 113, no. 3 (Summer 1984): 132–34.

17. See, e.g., Nelson Lichtenstein, "From Corporatism to Collective Bargaining: Organized Labor and the Eclipse of Social Democracy in the Postwar Era," and Ira Katznelson, "Was the Great Society a Lost Opportunity?" in Fraser and Gerstle, *The Rise and Fall of the New Deal Order*, chaps. 5 and 7; and David Plotke, *Building a Democratic Order: Reshaping American Liberalism in the 1930s and 1940s* (New York: Cambridge University Press, 1996). Subsequent histories, asking similar questions, have emphasized the conservative nature of the New Deal itself (e.g., David M. Kennedy, *Freedom from Fear: The American People in Depression and War, 1929–1945* [New York: Oxford University Press, 1999]) and the atypical character of American culture during the mid-twentieth century (Jefferson Cowie, *The Great Exception: The New Deal and the Limits of American Politics* [Princeton, NJ: Princeton University Press, 2016]). Though much of the earlier work focused on what Brinkley called the New Deal's "active phase," some seminal works did treat Roosevelt's second and third terms as pivotal. See, among others, James MacGregor Burns, *Roosevelt: The Lion and the Fox* (New York: Harcourt, Brace, 1956); James T. Patterson, *Congressional Conservatism and the New Deal: The Growth of the Conservative Coalition in Congress* (Lexington: University of Kentucky Press, 1967); and Richard Polenberg, *War and Society, 1941–1945* (Philadelphia: Lippincott, 1972).

18. Brinkley, *The End of Reform*, 268.

19. Brinkley, 269.

20. Brinkley, 3.

21. Brinkley, 268.

22. Franklin Roosevelt, "January 20, 1937: Second Inaugural Address," University of Virginia, Miller Center, accessed January 14, 2018, https://millercenter.org/the-presidency/presidential-speeches/january-20-1937-second-inaugural-address.

23. Franklin Roosevelt, "Address at Madison Square Garden, New York City, October 31, 1936," University of California at Santa Barbara, American Presidency Project, accessed January 14, 2018, http://www.presidency.ucsb.edu/ws/?pid=15219.

24. Roosevelt, "January 20, 1937: Second Inaugural Address."

25. Max Lerner, quoted in Brinkley, *The End of Reform*, 16.

26. Harold Ickes and Henry Wallace, quoted in Brinkley, *The End of Reform*, 30.

27. Brinkley, 139.

28. Brinkley, 139.

29. Brinkley, 224.

30. Brinkley, 271.

31. See, e.g., David M. Kennedy, "Hey, Big Spenders," *New York Times*, March 12, 1995.
32. "Forum: Alan Brinkley's *The End of Reform*," *Studies in American Political Development* 10, no. 2 (Fall 1996): 405–25. On the relationship of political history to American political development at the time of *The End of Reform*'s publication, see Julian Zelizer, "History and Political Science: Together Again?" in *Governing America: The Revival of Political History* (Princeton, NJ: Princeton University Press, 2012), chap. 3.
33. See esp. Kenneth Finegold, "Ideology and Institutions in *The End of Reform*," *Studies in American Political Development* 10, no. 2 (Fall 1996): 410–14.
34. Alan Brinkley, "The Transformation of New Deal Liberalism: A Response to Michael Brown, Kenneth Finegold, and David Plotke," *Studies in American Political Development* 10, no. 2 (Fall 1996): 424.
35. Brinkley, "The New Deal and the Idea of the State," 86.
36. Sean Farhang and Ira Katznelson, "The Southern Imposition: Congress and Labor in the New Deal and Fair Deal," *Studies in American Political Development* 19 (Spring 2005): 1–30; Katznelson, *Fear Itself*. See also Margaret Weir, *Politics and Jobs: The Boundaries of Employment Policy in the United States* (Princeton, NJ: Princeton University Press, 1992).
37. Brinkley, *The End of Reform*, 9–10.
38. On the relation of social group identities to distributive political claims in the New Deal era, see Gary Gerstle, *Working-Class Americanism: The Politics of Labor in a Textile City, 1914–1960* (New York: Cambridge University Press, 1989); Lizabeth Cohen, *Making a New Deal: Industrial Workers in Chicago, 1919–1939* (New York: Cambridge University Press, 1990); and James T. Sparrow, *Warfare State: World War II Americans and the Age of Big Government* (New York: Oxford University Press, 2011).
39. For an overview, see Robin D. G. Kelley, "Identity Politics and Class Struggle," *New Politics* 6, no. 2 (Winter 1997): 84–96. See also Sarah E. Igo, "American Liberalism and the Cultural Imagination" (paper presented at the Institute for Advanced Studies in Culture, University of Virginia, 2013; in the author's possession).
40. Among many others, Ira Katznelson, *When Affirmative Action Was White: An Untold History of Racial Inequality in Twentieth-Century America* (New York: Norton, 2005); and Richard Rothstein, *The Color of Law: How Our Government Segregated America* (New York: Liveright, 2017).
41. Meg Jacobs, *Pocketbook Politics: Economic Citizenship in Twentieth-Century America* (Princeton, NJ: Princeton University Press, 2005).
42. Jordan Schwarz, *The New Dealers: Power Politics in the Age of Roosevelt* (New York: Knopf, 1993); Jason Scott Smith, *Building New Deal Liberalism* (New York: Cambridge University Press, 2006); Sarah Phillips, *This Land, This Nation: Conservation, Rural America, and the New Deal* (New York: Cambridge University Press, 2007); Brent Cebul, *Illusions of Progress: Business, Poverty, and Development in the American Century* (Philadelphia: University of Pennsylvania Press, forthcoming).
43. Brinkley, *The End of Reform*, 264. As Brinkley notes, most of the legislative fight over the Full Employment Bill occurred after Roosevelt's death in April, 1945.

44. Cf. Robert M. Collins, *More: The Politics of Growth in Postwar America* (New York: Oxford University Press, 2000); and Andrew Yarrow, *Measuring America: How Economic Growth Came to Define American Greatness in the Late Twentieth Century* (Amherst: University of Massachusetts Press, 2010).

45. Timothy Shenk, "Inventing the American Economy" (PhD diss., Columbia University, 2016).

46. See, e.g., Thomas Piketty, *Capital in the Twenty-First Century*, trans. Arthur Goldhammer (Cambridge, MA: Belknap Press, 2014). See also Samuel Moyn, "Thomas Piketty and the Future of Legal Scholarship," *Harvard Law Review* 128, no. 2 (December 2014): 49–55.

47. Nelson Lichtenstein, introduction to the new edition to *Labor's War at Home: The CIO in World War II*, 2nd ed. (Philadelphia: Temple University Press, 2003), xii.

48. For three early efforts, see Cowie, *The Great Exception*; Eric Rauchway, *The Money Makers: How Roosevelt and Keynes Ended the Depression, Defeated Fascism, and Secured a Prosperous Peace* (New York: Basic Books, 2015); and Jacob Hacker and Paul Pierson, *American Amnesia: How the War on Government Led Us to Forget What Made America Prosper* (New York: Simon and Schuster, 2016).

4. AFTER REFORM

1. Alan Brinkley, *Liberalism and Its Discontents* (Cambridge, MA: Harvard University Press, 1998).

2. A brief list of other important historical (as opposed to philosophical) works on postwar liberalism would include Godfrey Hodgson, *America in Our Time: From World War II to Nixon—What Happened and Why* (Garden City, NY: Doubleday, 1976); Robert Booth Fowler, *Enduring Liberalism: American Political Thought Since the 1960s* (Lawrence: University Press of Kansas, 1999); Neil Jumonville and Kevin Mattson, eds., *Liberalism for a New Century* (Berkeley: University of California Press, 2007); Paul Starr, *Freedom's Power: The True Force of Liberalism* (New York: Basic Books, 2007); and Eric Alterman and Kevin Mattson, *The Cause: The Fight for American Liberalism from Franklin Roosevelt to Barack Obama* (New York: Viking Press, 2012).

3. Richard Hofstadter, preface to *The American Political Tradition: And the Men Who Made It* (1948; New York: Vintage Books, 1967), xxvii.

4. Brinkley, *Liberalism*, xi, ix, x.

5. Alonzo L. Hamby, *Liberalism and Its Challengers: From F.D.R. to Bush*, 2nd ed. (New York: Oxford University Press, 1992); Michael Sandel, ed., *Liberalism and Its Critics* (New York: New York University Press, 1984).

6. Michael J. Sandel, *Democracy's Discontent: America in Search of a Public Philosophy* (Cambridge, MA: Harvard University Press, 1998); Robert D. Putnam, *Bowling Alone: The Collapse and Revival of American Community* (New York: Simon and Schuster, 2000); Robert Wiebe, *Self-Rule: A Cultural History of American Democracy* (Chicago: University of Chicago Press, 1995).

7. Alan Brinkley, "Liberalism and Belief," in *Liberalism for a New Century*, ed. Jumonville and Mattson, 77.

8. On October 26, 1988, fifty-eight eminent liberal intellectuals signed an ad in the *New York Times* titled "A Reaffirmation of Principle," defending the term *liberalism* and the values for which it stood because they believed that Michael S. Dukakis, the Democratic presidential nominee, had, along with other politicians, been insufficiently willing to do so. *New York Times*, October 26, 1988.

9. The term *progressive* has a venerable lineage, referring to the early twentieth-century reform movements and legislation embodied by, among many others, Theodore Roosevelt and Woodrow Wilson. But the term was always somewhat muddy, and when Henry Wallace and the fellow-traveling Left used it in the 1940s, its meaning only became more ambiguous. Since the 1980s, *progressive* has been used in two different ways. When used to name think tanks like the Progressive Policy Institute, which provided ideas to Bill Clinton's 1992 campaign, it was mainly a prettified synonym for the term *liberal*. In other cases, however, it has become a euphemism for leftist, radical, or even Marxist politics—not a synonym but rather a term that seeks to differentiate itself from liberalism. In public discourse, commentators rarely specify how they're using the term, contributing to intellectual imprecision and confusion. On the current-day vacuity of *progressive*, see Geoffrey Nunberg, "Progressive to a Fault," in *The Years of Talking Dangerously* (New York: Public Affairs, 2009), 76–80; and on some of the important differences in meaning, see Sean Wilentz, "Fighting Words," *Democracy*, no. 48 (Spring 2018).

10. Jodi Wilgoren with David Rosenbaum, "Defying Labels Left or Right, Dean's '04 Run Is Making Gains," *New York Times*, July 30, 2003.

11. Paul Starr, "Center-Left Liberalism," in *The Oxford Companion to American Politics*, ed. David Coates (Oxford, UK: Oxford University Press, 2012), 68.

12. Rex Tugwell, quoted in Michael Janeway, *The Fall of the House of Roosevelt: Brokers of Ideas and Power from FDR to LBJ* (New York: Columbia University Press, 2004), 4.

13. Arthur M. Schlesinger Jr., *The Vital Center: The Politics of Freedom* (Boston: Houghton Mifflin, 1949), xvii–xviii.

14. Lionel Trilling, *The Liberal Imagination: Essays on Literature and Society* (Garden City, NY: Doubleday, 1950), vii.

15. Brinkley, *Liberalism*, 282.

16. John Lukacs, *Democracy and Populism: Fear and Hatred* (New Haven, CT: Yale University Press, 2006), 28n.

17. For a recent statement, see Jacob S. Hacker and Paul Pierson, *American Amnesia: How the War on Government Led Us to Forget What Made America Prosper* (New York: Simon and Schuster, 2016).

18. In chapter 3 of this volume, Mason B. Williams takes up an analysis of *The End of Reform*. Though he does not fully endorse Brinkley's reading of how liberalism changed in these years, there is no mistaking the general contours of the shift.

19. Alvin Hansen, quoted in Brinkley, *Liberalism*, 50.

20. The classic text is Sidney Hook, *The Hero in History: A Study in Limitation and Possibility* (1943; Boston: Beacon Press, 1955).

21. Brinkley, *Liberalism*, 1.

22. Roosevelt identified as a liberal and not a socialist, radical, or progressive. See Wilentz, "Fighting Words."

23. Brinkley, *Liberalism*, 17, 37.

24. Brinkley, 86, 53.

25. Brinkley, 89.

26. Brinkley, 188.

27. Brinkley, 176, 209.

28. Brinkley, 211, 220.

29. Brinkley, 221.

30. Brinkley, 238, 247.

31. Brinkley, 159.

32. Brinkley, 236.

33. Brinkley, 295.

5. OBJECTIVITY AND ITS DISCONTENTS

1. Alan Brinkley, *Voices of Protest: Huey Long, Father Coughlin, and the Great Depression* (New York: Knopf, 1982), and *The Publisher: Henry Luce and His American Century* (New York: Knopf, 2010).

2. Robert E. Herzstein, *Henry R. Luce, Time, and the American Crusade in Asia* (Cambridge: Cambridge University Press, 2005), 1.

3. Herzstein, *Henry R. Luce*, 1.

4. Andrew Porwancher, "Objectivity's Prophet: Adolph S. Ochs and the *New York Times*, 1896–1935," *Journalism History* 36, no. 4 (Winter 2011): 186–95.

5. In making this argument, I am conceptualizing media as a site of epistemological production and reproduction. On objectivity, see Richard L. Kaplan, *Politics and the American Press: The Rise of Objectivity, 1865–1920* (New York: Cambridge University Press, 2002); Michael Schudson, *Discovering the News: A Social History of American Newspapers* (New York: Basic Books, 1978); and David T. Z. Mindich, *Just the Facts: How Objectivity Came to Define American Journalism* (New York: New York University Press, 1998).

6. Daniel Bell, *The End of Ideology: On the Exhaustion of Political Ideas in the Fifties* (Glencoe, IL: Free Press, 1960); Thomas Nagel, *The View from Nowhere* (New York: Oxford University Press, 1986); Jay Rosen, "The View from Nowhere: Questions and Answers," PressThink, November 10, 2010, http://pressthink.org/2010/11/the-view-from-nowhere-questions-and-answers/.

7. Brinkley, *The Publisher*, 90.

8. Brinkley, 129.

9. Brinkley, 243.

10. Brinkley, 252–73.

11. Richard Polenberg, "The National Committee to Uphold Constitutional Government, 1937–1941," *Journal of American History* 52, no. 3 (December 1965): 582–98.

12. Richard Norton Smith, *The Colonel: The Life and Legend of Robert R. McCormick, 1880–1955* (New York: Houghton Mifflin, 1997).

13. "How Accurate Is America's News?" *Facts Forum News*, April 1955, 28–29, 41, box 93, folder 13, Herbert A. Philbrick Papers, Library of Congress, Washington, DC.

14. Brinkley, *The Publisher*, 300.

15. Brinkley, xiii.

16. Daniel Bell, *The End of Ideology: On the Exhaustion of Political Ideas in the Fifties* (Glencoe, IL: Free Press, 1960); "Text of President Kennedy's Commencement Address to Yale's Graduating Class," *New York Times*, June 12, 1962.

17. Arthur M. Schlesinger Jr., *The Vital Center: The Politics of Freedom* (Boston: Houghton Mifflin, 1949).

18. Henry Luce, "The American Century," *Life*, February 17, 1941, 61–65.

19. Brinkley, *The Publisher*, 230.

20. Brinkley, 213, 393.

6. THE LIBERAL'S IMAGINATION

1. Alan Brinkley, "The Problem of American Conservatism," *American Historical Review* 99, no. 2 (April 1994): 409–29. The essay was reprinted in Alan Brinkley, *Liberalism and Its Discontents* (Cambridge, MA: Harvard University Press, 1998), 277–97. The citations that follow are from the latter version.

2. Matthew Dallek, *The Right Moment: Ronald Reagan's First Victory and the Decisive Turning Point in American Politics* (New York: Free Press, 2000); David Greenberg, *Nixon's Shadow: A History of an Image* (New York: Norton, 2003), esp. 1–35; Neil J. Young, *We Gather Together: The Religious Right and the Problem of Interfaith Politics* (New York: Oxford University Press, 2016); Jefferson Decker, *The Other Rights Revolution: Conservative Lawyers and the Remaking of American Government* (New York: Oxford University Press, 2016); and Nicole Hemmer, *Messengers of the Right: Conservative Media and the Transformation of American Politics* (Philadelphia: University of Pennsylvania Press, 2016), all began as dissertations under Brinkley. Lisa McGirr, who wrote *Suburban Warriors: The Origins of the New American Right* (Princeton, NJ: Princeton University Press, 2001), and Kim Phillips-Fein, author of *Invisible Hands: The Making of the Conservative Movement from the New Deal to Reagan* (New York: Norton, 2009), were also Brinkley students, although both of them worked with a different primary dissertation adviser.

3. By 2011, Kim Phillips-Fein could note that "historians might be forgiven for asking whether there is anything left to study in the history of the Right." Kim Phillips-Fein, "Conservatism: A State of the Field," *Journal of American History* 98, no. 3 (December 2011): 723.

4. Brinkley, "Problem of American Conservatism," 296.

5. Brinkley, 278.

6. Leo P. Ribuffo, "Why Is There So Much Conservatism in the United States and Why Do Historians Know So Little About It?" *American Historical Review* 99, no. 2 (April 1994): 438.

7. Brinkley, "Problem of American Conservatism," 279.

8. Brinkley, 281.
9. Brinkley, 279–81.
10. George Nash, *The Conservative Intellectual Movement in America, Since 1945* (New York: Basic Books, 1976).
11. Brinkley, "Problem of American Conservatism," 286.
12. Brinkley, 286.
13. Brinkley, 289.
14. Brinkley, 288.
15. Leo Strauss, *What Is Political Philosophy? and Other Studies* (Chicago: University of Chicago Press, 1988), 9–55. For the potential application of Straussian approaches outside of the academy, see Kenneth L. Deutsch and John A. Murley, eds., *Leo Strauss, the Straussians, and the American Regime* (Lanham, MD: Rowman and Littlefield, 1999).
16. Brinkley, "Problem of American Conservatism," 292.
17. Brinkley, 296.
18. There are too many examples for me to list in a single footnote, but for starters, check out the massive reading list in the footnotes to Phillips-Fein, "Conservatism," 723–43.
19. As a starting point, see John Baskin, "The Academic Home of Trumpism," *Chronicle of Higher Education*, March 17, 2017, http://www.chronicle.com/article/The-Academic-Home-of-Trumpism/239495, which offers a quick sketch of major schisms that have emerged over time between different kinds of Straussians (especially between the Chicago and West Coast wings of the subfield).
20. Race has been front and center in a number of histories that see struggles over school desegregation and related civil rights battles as the crucial events that forged the modern right. See, e.g., Kevin M. Kruse, *White Flight: Atlanta and the Making of Modern Conservatism* (Princeton, NJ: Princeton University Press, 2005); Matthew D. Lassiter, *The Silent Majority: Suburban Politics in the Sunbelt South* (Princeton, NJ: Princeton University Press, 2006); and Joseph Crespino, *In Search of Another Country: Mississippi and the Conservative Counter-Revolution* (Princeton, NJ: Princeton University Press, 2007).
21. See, e.g., Robert Lieberman, *Shifting the Color Line: Race and the American Welfare State* (Cambridge, MA: Harvard University Press, 1998); and Ira Katznelson, *When Affirmative Action Was White: The Untold History of Racial Inequality in Twentieth-Century America* (New York: Norton, 2005).
22. See, e.g., Michelle Alexander, *The New Jim Crow: Mass Incarceration in the Age of Colorblindness* (New York: New Press, 2010), esp. 6–7.
23. In cultural studies, this is sometimes framed as white America's "possessive investment" in illegitimate economic and political advantage, even when opposing "race conscious" policies, overt discrimination, or notions of racial inferiority. That particular language comes, in part, from George Lipsitz, *The Possessive Investment in Whiteness: How White People Benefit from Identity Politics* (Philadelphia: Temple University Press, 1998).
24. Even the "Powell Memorandum," the 1971 missive from future Supreme Court justice Lewis F. Powell to a friend at the U.S. Chamber of Commerce that helped inspire much

of the conservative institution building of the 1970s, was less a case for a completely free and unfettered marketplace than a lament over the declining cultural authority of American business. Lewis F. Powell to Eugene B. Sydnor Jr., August 23, 1971, Lewis Powell Jr. Papers, Washington and Lee University School of Law, Lexington, VA, http://law2.wlu.edu/powellarchives.

25. Nancy MacLean, *Democracy in Chains: The Deep History of the Radical Right's Stealth Plan for America* (New York: Viking, 2017), xxx.

26. This is not the place to sort out the extensive (and deeply polarizing) critical reaction to *Democracy in Chains*, but it is possible that some of the faults attributed to the book by its less partisan critics—especially MacLean's "tin ear for how libertarians and public choice economists actually think and argue"—result from her determination to reveal stealth agendas instead of performing acts of sympathetic imagination for the (admittedly often unsympathetic) historical figures at the center of her story. Quote from Henry Farrell and Steven M. Teles, "When Politics Drives Scholarship," *Boston Review*, August 30, 2017, http://bostonreview.net/class-inequality /henry-farrell-steven-m-teles-when-politics-drives-scholarship.

27. See Decker, *Other Rights Revolution*, esp. 197–210, 220–27.

28. Consider the 2011 exchange between Wilfred McClay and Kim Phillips-Fein in the *Journal of American History*. McClay asserted that historians need "more symmetry" in their approaches to the histories of the left and the right—without really explaining why that symmetry was justified. See Wilfred M. McClay, "Less Boilerplate, More Symmetry," *Journal of American History* 98, no. 3 (December 2011): 744–47. Phillips-Fein had asked historians to pay attention to the sometimes "bizarre" and "unsettling" aspects of conservatism without fully exploring what aspects of conservatism left her unsettled. See Phillips-Fein, "Conservatism," 736. In the end, the two scholars seemed to be talking past one another.

29. Early in 2016, *National Review*, which had long served as a gatekeeper of mainstream American conservatism, published anti-Trump essays from nearly two dozen conservative luminaries in hopes of slowing or shutting down his march to the GOP nomination. See Glenn Beck, David Boaz, et al., "Conservatives Against Trump," *National Review* 68, no. 2, February 15, 2016, 27–38.

30. Adam Smith imagined a small village in Scotland where a butcher, baker, and brewer realize they are better off specializing in one craft and trading with one another instead of becoming jacks-of-all-trades. That exchange would not have worked for long if each of the craftsmen felt the need to "win" every transaction and humiliate the other party in the process, which seems to be the essence of Trump's concept of deal making. See Adam Smith, *The Wealth of Nations* (New York: Barnes and Noble, 2004), 28.

31. Russ Buettner and Charles V. Bagli, "How Donald Trump Bankrupted His Atlantic City Casinos, but Still Earned Millions," *New York Times*, June 12, 2016, A1.

32. Rick Perlstein, "The Corrections," *New York Times Magazine*, April 16, 2017, 36–42. Perlstein offers a historiography of the racist and nativist right as a counterpoint to histories, including his own first book, that focused on the "conservative

movement," its politicians, and its institutions. See also David Greenberg, "An Intellectual History of Trumpism," *Politico*, December 11, 2016, http://www.politico.com /magazine/story/2016/12/trumpism-intellectual-history-populism-paleoconservatives -214518, which focuses on intellectual connections between Trump and so-called paleoconservatives.

33. As Mae Ngai has documented, some racial and ethnic minorities have found themselves in the contradictory category of "alien citizen" as a *legal* category—let alone a cultural one—at various points in the American past. Mae Ngai, *Impossible Subjects: Illegal Immigrants and the Making of Modern America* (Princeton, NJ: Princeton University Press, 2004), esp. 167–201. Rogers Smith has argued that exclusive or "ascriptive" Americanism is a long-standing American political tradition. Rogers M. Smith, "Beyond Tocqueville, Myrdal, and Hartz: The Multiple Traditions in America," *American Political Science Review* 87, no. 3 (September 1993): 549–66.

34. N. D. B. Connolly and Keisha N. Blain, "Trump Syllabus 2.0: An Introduction to the Currents of American Culture That Led to 'Trumpism,' " Public Books, June 28, 2016, http://www.publicbooks.org/trump-syllabus-2-0/.

35. Brinkley's account of the political ideas of Long and Coughlin also seems especially timely: they were "often muddled or simplistic, at times nearly incoherent"; "neither had much patience with complexities or ambiguities"; "some observers dismissed it all as meaningless and, as such, ominous: a demagogic attempt to delude the public with empty, impractical promises"; those critics "were not entirely incorrect." Alan Brinkley, *Voices of Protest: Huey Long, Father Coughlin, and the Great Depression* (New York: Knopf, 1982), 143–44.

36. This may be too strong a conclusion to draw from a single mock syllabus, especially one that was conceived, in part, as a corrective to a syllabus put together by the *Chronicle of Higher Education* that, in a glaring oversight, omitted any works by black scholars. (See Connelly and Blain, "Trump Syllabus 2.0" for details.) But if we are going to take seriously the notion that a historiographical essay by an Ivy League historian could have had sociological consequences in 1994, a reading list that went viral on social media has the potential to become a certification narrative today.

37. Leo Ribuffo, quoted in Perlstein, "The Corrections," 37.

38. Alan Brinkley, "Response to the Comments of Leo Ribuffo and Susan Yohn," *American Historical Review* 99, no. 2 (April 1994): 451.

39. Especially Alan Brinkley, *The End of Reform: New Deal Liberalism in Recession and War* (New York: Random House, 1995).

40. Less extensive but still very much there; see Hemmer, *Messengers of the Right*, for details.

7. ALAN BRINKLEY AND THE REVIVAL OF POLITICAL HISTORY

1. Tony Judt, "A Clown in Regal Purple: Social History and the Historians," *History Workshop Journal* 7, no. 1 (March 1979): 71, 73.

2. Peter H. Smith, quoted in William E. Leuchtenburg, "The Pertinence of Political History: Reflections on the Significance of the State in America," *Journal of American History* 73, no. 3 (December 1986): 585.

3. Julian Zelizer, "The Interdisciplinarity of Political History," *Perspectives on History*, May 2011, https://www.historians.org/publications-and-directories/perspectives-on-history/may-2011/political-history-today/the-interdisciplinarity-of-political-history.

4. Alan Brinkley, *Liberalism and Its Discontents* (Cambridge, MA: Harvard University Press, 1998), ix.

5. Michael Flamm, telephone interview with the author, July 28, 2017.

6. Lizabeth Cohen, *Making a New Deal: Industrial Workers in Chicago, 1919–1939* (Cambridge: University of Cambridge Press, 1990), 2.

7. Alan Brinkley, *Voices of Protest: Huey Long, Father Coughlin, and the Great Depression* (New York: Vintage Books, 1983).

8. Steve Fraser and Gary Gerstle, eds., *The Rise and Fall of the New Deal Order, 1930–1980* (Princeton, NJ: Princeton University Press, 1989).

9. See Theda Skocpol, Peter Evans, and Dietrich Rueschemeyer, eds., *Bringing the State Back In* (Cambridge: Cambridge University Press, 1985).

10. Alan Brinkley, *The End of Reform: New Deal Liberalism in Recession and War* (New York: Vintage Books, 1995), 12–13.

11. Alan Brinkley, "Writing the History of Contemporary America: Dilemmas and Challenges," *Daedalus* 113, No. 3 (Summer, 1984): 121–141.

12. Brinkley, 123–25, 138.

13. Eric Foner, quoted in Leuchtenburg, "Pertinence of Political History," 586–87.

14. Leuchtenburg, "Pertinence of Political History," 590.

15. Fox Butterfield, "Scholar's Tenure Denial Stirs Harvard Debate," *New York Times*, October 5, 1986.

16. For more on the history of the Columbia tradition as a home to leading political historians, see Eric Foner's foreword to this volume.

17. Quotations in this and the next three paragraphs are from Ira Katznelson, "Closing Remarks," at Protest, Politics, and Ideas in the American Century: A Conference in Honor of Alan Brinkley, Columbia University, New York, Facebook video, April 16, 2016, https://www.facebook.com/columbiahistory/videos/1680245098894921/.

18. Flamm, interview, July 28, 2017.

19. Katznelson, "Closing Remarks." Also see Katznelson's own landmark account of liberalism and the politics of fear, *Fear Itself: The New Deal and the Origins of Our Time* (New York: Liveright, 2013).

20. Katznelson, "Closing Remarks." For Hofstadter quote, see Richard Hofstadter, *The Progressive Historians: Turner, Beard, Parrington* (New York: Knopf, 1968), 463–466

21. David Greenberg, email interview with the author, July 26, 2017.

22. Brinkley, *Liberalism and Its Discontents*, xi.

23. Brian Balogh, "Comment," at Protest, Politics, and Ideas in the American Century: A Conference in Honor of Alan Brinkley, Columbia University, New York, Facebook video, April 16, 2016, https://www.facebook.com/columbiahistory/videos/1679906485595449/.

24. Ellen Fitzpatrick, "Public Panel: Alan Brinkley as Public Intellectual," at Protest, Politics, and Ideas in the American Century: A Conference in Honor of Alan Brinkley, Columbia University, New York, Facebook video, April 15, 2016, https://www.facebook.com/columbiahistory/videos/1679906485595449/.

25. Sharon Musher, email interview with the author, August 11, 2017.

26. Balogh, "Comment."

27. Greenberg, interview, July 26, 2017.

28. Flamm, interview, July 28, 2017.

29. Robert Lifset, email interview with the author, August 3, 2017.

30. Musher, interview, August 11, 2017.

31. Balogh, "Comment." See Mason B. Williams, *City of Ambition: FDR, La Guardia, and the Making of Modern New York* (New York: Norton, 2013).

32. Beverly Gage, quoted in Kevin Baker, "Blood on the Street," review of *The Day Wall Street Exploded*, by Beverly Gage, *New York Times*, February 19, 2009. Gage, *The Day Wall Street Exploded: A Story of America In Its First Age of Terror* (New York: Oxford University Press, 2009).

33. Stephen J. Whitfield, review of *The Sacco-Vanzetti Affair*, by Moshik Temkin, *Journal of Interdisciplinary History* 41, no. 3, (Winter 2011): 477–78. See Temkin, *The Sacco-Vanzetti Affair: America on Trial* (New Haven, CT: Yale University Press, 2011).

34. Nicole Hemmer, "The Publisher," at Protest, Politics, and Ideas in the American Century: A Conference in Honor of Alan Brinkley, Columbia University, New York, Facebook video, April 16, 2016, https://www.facebook.com/columbiahistory/videos/1680229412229823/.

35. Lisa McGirr, *Suburban Warriors: The Origins of the New American Right* (Princeton, NJ: Princeton University Press, 2001). Brinkley, "The Problem of American Conservatism," in *Liberalism and Its Discontents*, 296.

36. Flamm, interview, July 28, 2017.

37. Balogh, "Comment."

38. David Greenberg, *Republic of Spin: An Inside History of the American Presidency* (New York: Norton, 2016), "Overview"; Nicole Hemmer, *Messengers of the Right: Conservative Media and the Transformation of American Politics* (Philadelphia: University of Pennsylvania Press, 2016).

39. Julian E. Zelizer, *Governing America: The Revival of Political History* (Princeton, NJ: Princeton University Press, 2012)

40. Julian Zelizer, audience comment, "Public Panel: Alan Brinkley as Public Intellectual," at Protest, Politics, and Ideas in the American Century: A Conference in Honor of Alan Brinkley, Columbia University, New York, Facebook video, April 15, 2016, https://www.facebook.com/columbiahistory/videos/1679906485595449/.

41. See, for example, Brian Balogh, *The Associational State: American Governance in the Twentieth Century* (Philadelphia: University of Pennsylvania Press, 2015), and *A Government out of Sight: The Mystery of National Authority in Nineteenth-Century America* (New York: Cambridge University Press, 2009); and Julian Zelizer, *Taxing America: Wilbur D. Mills, Congress and the State, 1945–1975* (New York: Cambridge

University Press, 1998), and *Arsenal of Democracy: The Politics of National Security—From World War II to the War on Terrorism* (New York: Basic Books, 2010).

42. See, for example, Thomas Sugrue, *The Origins of the Urban Crisis: Race and Inequality in Postwar Detroit* (Princeton, NJ: Princeton University Press, 1996); Kevin Kruse, *White Flight: Atlanta and the Making of Modern Conservatism* (Princeton, NJ: Princeton University Press, 2005); Robert Self, *American Babylon: Race and the Struggle for Postwar Oakland* (Princeton, NJ: Princeton University Press, 2003); and Matthew Lassiter, *The Silent Majority: Suburban Politics in the Sunbelt South* (Princeton, NJ: Princeton University Press, 2006).

43. Hemmer, "The Publisher."

8. HOUDINI, HIP-HOP, AND DYSTOPIAN LITERATURE

1. Alan Brinkley, Gary J. Kornblith, and Carol Lasser, "The Challenges and Rewards of Textbook Writing: An Interview with Alan Brinkley," *Journal of American History* 91, no. 4 (2005): 1397.

2. Michael Kazin, quoted in Shira J. Boss-Bicak, "Alan Brinkley: Scholar, Teacher, Author-Provost," *Columbia College Today*, January 2004, http://www.college.columbia .edu/cct_archive/jan04/cover.php.

3. Over the years, historians have debated whether this classic tale is a populist allegory. For a recent overview (arguing that it isn't), see Bradley A. Hansen, "The Fable of the Allegory: The Wizard of Oz in Economics," *Journal of Economic Education* 33, no. 3 (2002): 254–64. For an argument as to the pedagogical merits of teaching the parable regardless of Baum's intentions, see Ranjit S. Dighe, "The Fable of the Allegory: The Wizard of Oz in Economics: Comment," *Journal of Economic Education* 38, no. 3 (2007): 318–24.

4. Alan Brinkley, *American History: A Survey*, vol. 2, 13th ed. (New York: McGraw-Hill, 2009), 832–33, 844–45.

5. For an excellent set of definitions of culture, see James W. Cook and Lawrence B. Glickman, "Twelve Propositions for a History of U.S. Cultural History," in *The Cultural Turn in U.S. History: Past, Present, and Future*, ed. James W. Cook, Lawrence B. Glickman, and Michael O'Malley (Chicago: University of Chicago Press, 2008), 6–12.

6. Cook and Glickman, 8. See, for example, Daniel Boorstin, *The Genius of American Politics* (Chicago: University of Chicago Press, 1958); and David Potter, *People of Plenty: Economic Abundance and the American Character* (Chicago: University of Chicago Press, 1954).

7. Henry Nash Smith coined the phrase "myth and symbol" in his *Virgin Land: The American West as Symbol and Myth* (Cambridge, MA: Harvard University Press, 1950). It refers to an interdisciplinary approach combining history, literature, and sociology that dominated the field of American studies for two decades. It reflected both American exceptionalism and consensus history in the midst of the Cold War by suggesting that American culture was unique and monolithic and could be expressed through a series of myths that shaped national behavior and attitudes. The approach came under sharp criticism in the 1970s, and American studies scholars

today tend to look down on it. Nevertheless, it saw a resurgence in the 1990s, when scholars analyzed the myths produced through a range of sources, including photographs, ads, literary texts, and physical spaces, to explore the complicated feelings and values shaping a range of cultural myths, including those about race, class, and gender. For additional information, see Daryl Umberger, "Myth and Symbol," in *Encyclopedia of American Studies*, ed. Simon Bronner (Baltimore: Johns Hopkins University Press, 2016).

8. Alan Brinkley, *Imagining the Twentieth Century: American Perspectives from Two Fins de Siècle: An Inaugural Lecture Delivered Before the University of Oxford on May 18, 1999* (Oxford, UK: Oxford University Press, 1999), 5–9.

9. Brinkley, 4, 5, 9, 19.

10. Vincent Virga, *Eyes of the Nation: A Visual History of the United States*, with historical commentary by Alan Brinkley (New York: Knopf, 1997).

11. James H. Billington, preface to *Eyes of the Nation*, by Virga, i.

12. *Primary Source Investigator* (Brief, Interactive Version), accompaniment to *The Unfinished Nation: A Concise History of the American People* (New York: McGraw-Hill, 2005).

13. Alan Brinkley, preface to *Civil War Sketch Book: Drawings from the Battlefront*, by Harry L. Katz and Vincent Virga (New York: Norton, 2012), xi.

14. Alan Brinkley, introduction to *Campaigns: A Century of Presidential Races from the Photo Archives of the New York Times*, by Ted Widmer (New York: DK Publishing, 2001), 17, 25.

15. Alan Brinkley, introduction to *The Forgotten Fifties: America's Decade from the Archives of Look Magazine*, by James A. Conaway (New York: Skira Rizzoli, 2014), 16–29.

16. Lawrence Levine, "The Folklore of Industrial Society: Popular Culture and Its Audiences," *American Historical Review* 97, no. 5 (December 1992): 1375.

17. Alan Brinkley, "The Immigrant World of Harry Houdini," in *Houdini: Art and Magic*, by Brooke Kamin Rapaport (New Haven, CT: Yale University Press, 2010), 59.

18. Brinkley, 63.

19. Brinkley, 65.

20. Alan Brinkley, "Seeing the Great Depression: Margaret Bourke-White" (unpublished manuscript, Leonard Hastings Schoff Memorial Lectures, Columbia University, New York, November 8, 2010, in the author's possession), 1.

21. Alan Brinkley, *Culture and Politics in the Great Depression: The Twentieth Charles Edmondson Historical Lectures* (Waco, TX: Baylor University, 1998).

22. Brinkley, "Seeing the Great Depression: Margaret Bourke-White," 1.

23. Brinkley, 19.

24. Alan Brinkley, "Seeing the Great Depression: Dorothea Lange" (unpublished manuscript, Leonard Hastings Schoff Memorial Lectures, Columbia University, New York, November 15, 2010, in the author's possession), 14.

25. Brinkley, 14.

26. James Curtis, *Mind's Eye, Mind's Truth: FSA Photography Reconsidered* (Philadelphia: Temple University Press, 1989); Charles Shindo, *Dust Bowl Migrants in the American*

Imagination (Lawrence: University Press of Kansas, 1997); Paula Rabinowitz, *They Must Be Represented: The Politics of Documentary* (New York: Verso, 1994).

27. Sharon Ann Musher, "Art and the New Deal," in *The New Deal and the Great Depression*, ed. Aaron D. Purcell (Kent, OH: Kent State University Press, 2014), 119.

28. Alan Brinkley, "Seeing the Great Depression: Walker Evans" (unpublished manuscript, Leonard Hastings Schoff Memorial Lectures, Columbia University, New York, November 22, 2010, in the author's possession), 1, 17.

29. Alan Brinkley, "Writing the History of Contemporary America: Dilemmas and Challenges," *Daedalus* 113, no. 3 (Summer 1984): 124.

30. Brinkley, "Challenges and Rewards," 1392.

31. Brinkley, *American History*, vol. 2, 13th ed., 426, 482–83, 516, 538, 552, 644, 674, 696, 718, 794, 876, 908.

32. Ruth Benedict, *Patterns of Culture* (Boston: Houghton Mifflin, 1934), 46; Margaret Mead, introduction to *Patterns of Culture*, by Benedict, xi.

33. Alan Brinkley, *American History: A Survey*, vol. 2, 10th ed. (New York: McGraw-Hill, 1998).

34. Alan Brinkley, "About the Book," *American History*, 10th ed., http://www.mhhe.com /socscience/history/usa/brink/over.htm.

35. Brinkley, *American History*, 13th ed., 908–9.

36. Peter Burke, "Cultural History and Its Neighbours," *Culture and History Digital Journal* 1, no. 1 (May 15, 2012): 6.

37. Alan Brinkley, *The End of Reform: New Deal Liberalism in Recession and War* (New York: Vintage Books, 1996), 4.

38. Brinkley, 13.

39. Alan Brinkley, *The Publisher: Henry Luce and His American Century* (New York: Knopf, 2010), 459–60.

40. Nan Ensted, "On Grief and Complicity," in *The Cultural Turn in U.S. History: Past Present and Future*, ed. James W. Cook, Lawrence B. Glickman, and Michael O'Malley (Chicago: University of Chicago Press, 2008), 321.

41. Ensted, 335.

42. Michael O'Malley, "Practicing Cultural History" in Cook, Glickman, and O'Malley, *The Cultural Turn*, 59.

43. Ensted, "On Grief," 322–25.

44. Caroline F. Ware, introductory note to *The Cultural Approach to History*, ed. Caroline F. Ware (New York: Columbia University Press, 1940), 10–12.

45. Ware, 308–30.

9. THE VIEW FROM THE CLASSROOM

1. Alan Brinkley et al., *The Chicago Handbook for Teachers: A Practical Guide to the College Classroom*, 2nd ed. (Chicago: University of Chicago Press, 2011), 168–69.

2. Cliff Sloan, interview with the author, July 12, 2017; "Brinkley Speaks on Why He Teaches," *Harvard Crimson*, October 23, 1985.

3. Gary Gerstle, interview with the author, July 13, 2017; Ellen Fitzpatrick, "Public Panel: Alan Brinkley as Public Intellectual," at Protest, Politics, and Ideas in the American Century: A Conference in Honor of Alan Brinkley, Columbia University, New York, Facebook video, April 15, 2016, https://www.facebook.com/columbiahistory/videos/1679906485595449/.

4. James G. Basker, interview with the author, July 10, 2017.

5. Charles Curtis, interview with the author, July 5, 2017.

6. Elizabeth Blackmar, interview with the author, June 29, 2017.

7. Brinkley et al., *Chicago Handbook*, 41.

8. Yanek Mieczkowski, interview with the author, June 16, 2017.

9. Brinkley et al., *Chicago Handbook*, 39, 41.

10. Michael Kramer, correspondence to the author, June 27, 2017.

11. Mason B. Williams, correspondence to the author, November 13, 2017.

12. Ellen Fitzpatrick, correspondence to the author, June 19, 2017.

13. Brinkley et al., *Chicago Handbook*, 38.

14. François Weil, correspondence to the author, July 14, 2017.

15. Alan Brinkley, quoted in "Freidel, Roosevelt Scholar, Dies at 76," *Harvard Crimson*, January 29, 1993.

16. Sloan, interview, July 12, 2017; Matthew Dallek, interview with the author, July 28, 2017.

17. Curtis, interview, July 5, 2017.

18. Weil, correspondence, July 14, 2017; Dallek, interview, July 28, 2017.

19. Thaddeus Russell, interview with the author, July 28, 2017; Thomas Woods, interview with the author, July 31, 2017.

20. Ira Katznelson, interview with the author, June 15, 2017.

21. Brinkley, quoted in "Freidel, Roosevelt Scholar, Dies at 76."

22. Daniel Scroop, interview with the author, June 15, 2017.

23. Mieczkowski, interview, June 16, 2017.

24. Russell, interview, July 28, 2017.

25. Evangeline Morphos, conversation with the author, May 4, 2017.

26. Shane Ferro, "Brinkley Fans Bring Their Love to Facebook," *Columbia Spectator*, August 23, 2013.

27. Eric Rothschild, correspondence to the author, June 20, 2017.

28. James G. Basker, interview with the author, July 10, 2017.

29. Stefan Cohen, correspondence to the author, June 1, 2017; Jennifer Collins, correspondence to the author, June 7, 2017.

30. Gerstle, interview, July 13, 2017.

31. Eric Foner, interview with the author, July 3, 2017.

32. Fox Butterfield, "Scholar's Tenure Denial Stirs Harvard Dispute," *New York Times*, October 5, 1986.

33. Jeffrey S. Nordhaus, "Brinkley Decides to Take Tenured Post at CUNY," *Harvard Crimson*, November 2, 1987.

34. Fitzpatrick, correspondence, June 19, 2017.

35. Conan O'Brien, video recording of remarks shown at Protest, Politics, and Ideas in the American Century: A Conference in Honor of Alan Brinkley, Columbia University, New York, Facebook video, clip at 51:30 mark, April 16, 2016, https://www.facebook.com/columbiahistory/videos/1680229412229823/.
36. Brinkley et al., *Chicago Handbook*, 168.

14. CAREERS IN COUNTERPOINT

1. Alan Brinkley, *American History: Connecting with the Past* (New York: McGraw-Hill, 2015); David M. Kennedy and Lizabeth Cohen, *The American Pageant* (Boston: Cengage, 2016).
2. Alan Brinkley, "Our Generation: A Princeton Memoir," in *Princeton University Class of 1971 eBook*, 2011. Author's copy.
3. Alan Brinkley, quoted in "Becoming Part of a Great Tradition: Historians Discuss Use of Manuscript Materials," *Library of Congress Information Bulletin* 55, no. 20 (November 18, 1996): 428, http://www.loc.gov/lcib/9620/manuscript.html.
4. Alan Brinkley, *Voices of Protest: Huey Long, Father Coughlin, and the Great Depression* (New York: Knopf, 1982).
5. Lizabeth Cohen, *Making a New Deal: Industrial Workers in Chicago, 1919–1939* (New York: Cambridge University Press, 1990).
6. Alan Brinkley, *The End of Reform: New Deal Liberalism in Recession and War* (New York: Knopf, 1995).
7. Lizabeth Cohen, *A Consumers' Republic: The Politics of Mass Consumption in Postwar America* (New York: Knopf, 2003).
8. Alan Brinkley, *The Publisher: Henry Luce and His American Century* (New York: Knopf, 2010).
9. Lizabeth Cohen, *Saving America's Cities: Ed Logue and the Struggle to Renew Urban America in the Suburban Age* (New York: Farrar, Straus and Giroux, forthcoming 2019).

15. HISTORY AS A HUMANIZING ART

1. Alan Brinkley, "Richard Hofstadter's *The Age of Reform: A Reconsideration*," *Reviews in American History* 13 (September 1985): 462.
2. Richard Hofstadter, "History and the Social Sciences," in *The Varieties of History*, ed. Fritz Stern (Cleveland, OH: World, 1956), 359, 362, 364. Reciprocally, he thought history could guide the social sciences to transcend transhistorical generalization.
3. Hofstadter, 363.
4. Richard Hofstadter, *The Progressive Historians: Turner, Beard, Parrington* (New York: Knopf, 1968), 464.
5. Ira Katznelson, *Fear Itself: The New Deal and the Origins of Our Time* (New York: Liveright, 2013).

Contributors

Jonathan Alter is a journalist and author specializing in the American presidency. His books include *The Defining Moment: FDR's Hundred Days and the Triumph of Hope* (Simon and Schuster, 2006); *The Promise: President Obama, Year One* (Simon and Schuster, 2010); and *The Center Holds: Obama and His Enemies* (Simon and Schuster, 2013).

A. Scott Berg is the author of five best-selling biographies, including *Max Perkins: Editor of Genius* (Dutton, 1978), winner of the National Book Award; *Lindbergh* (Putnam, 1998), winner of the Pulitzer Prize; and, most recently, *Wilson* (Putnam, 2013).

Elly Brinkley is the development coordinator for PEN America. Brinkley graduated with a joint concentration in philosophy and studies of women, gender, and sexuality from Harvard College.

Lizabeth Cohen is the Howard Mumford Jones Professor of American Studies at Harvard University. She is the author of *Making a New Deal: Industrial Workers in Chicago, 1919–1939* (Cambridge University Press, 1990) and *A Consumers' Republic: The Politics of Mass Consumption in Postwar America* (Vintage, 2003).

Matthew Dallek is a professor at George Washington University's Graduate School of Political Management. He is the author or coauthor of three books, including *Defenseless Under the Night: The Roosevelt Years and the Origins of Homeland Security* (Oxford University Press, 2016).

Jefferson Decker is associate professor of American studies and political science at Rutgers University. He is the author of *The Other Rights Revolution: Conservative Lawyers and the Remaking of American Government* (Oxford University Press, 2016).

Michael W. Flamm is associate professor of history at Ohio Wesleyan University. He is the author of several books, mostly recently *In the Heat of the Summer: The New York Riots of 1964 and the War on Crime* (University of Pennsylvania Press, 2017).

Eric Foner is DeWitt Clinton Professor of History Emeritus at Columbia University. He is the author of *Gateway to Freedom: The Hidden History of the Underground Railroad* (Norton, 2016), *The Fiery Trial: Abraham Lincoln and American Slavery* (Norton, 2011), and many other books.

David Greenberg is a professor of history and of journalism and media studies at Rutgers University. His books include *Nixon's Shadow: The History of an Image* (Norton, 2003) and, most recently, *Republic of Spin: An Inside History of the American Presidency* (Norton, 2016).

Nicole Hemmer is assistant professor at the Miller Center of Public Affairs at the University of Virginia. She is the author of *Messengers of the Right: Conservative Media and the Transformation of American Politics* (University of Pennsylvania Press, 2016).

Ira Katznelson is the Ruggles Professor of Political Science and History at Columbia University. He is the author of many books, including *Fear Itself: The New Deal and the Origins of Our Time* (Liveright, 2013) and *When Affirmative Action Was White: An Untold History of Racial Inequality in Twentieth-Century America* (Norton, 2005).

Nicholas Lemann is the Joseph Pulitzer II and Edith Pulitzer Moore Professor of Journalism at Columbia University. He is the author of many books, including *The Promised Land: The Great Black Migration and How It Changed America* (Vintage, 1992) and *Redemption: The Last Battle of the Civil War* (Farrar, Straus, and Giroux, 2007).

Nancy Weiss Malkiel is professor of history emeritus at Princeton University. She is the author of many books—most recently, *"Keep the Damned Women Out": The Struggle for Coeducation* (Princeton University Press, 2016).

Sharon Ann Musher is associate professor of history at Stockton University. She is the author of *Democratic Art: The New Deal's Influence on American Culture* (University of Chicago Press, 2015).

Frank Rich is writer at large for *New York* magazine and an executive producer of the HBO series *Veep*. His books include *The Greatest Story Ever Sold: The Decline and Fall of Truth from 9/11 to Katrina* (Penguin Press, 2006) and *Ghost Light: A Memoir* (Random House, 2001).

Moshik Temkin is associate professor of history and public policy at Harvard University's Kennedy School of Government and the author of *The Sacco-Vanzetti Affair: America on Trial* (Yale University Press, 2011).

Mason B. Williams is assistant professor of leadership studies and political science at Williams College and the author of *City of Ambition: FDR, La Guardia, and the Making of Modern New York* (Norton, 2013).

Index